COOKING WITH
David Burke

COOKING WITH

David Burke

AND CARMEL BERMAN REINGOLD

ALFRED A. KNOPF *New York* 1995

THIS IS A BORZOI BOOK
PUBLISHED BY ALFRED A. KNOPF, INC.

Library of Congress Cataloging-in-Publication Data
Burke, David.
    Cooking with David Burke / by David Burke and Carmel
Berman Reingold.
        p. cm.
Includes index.
ISBN 0-394-58343-4
1. Cookery, American. I. Reingold, Carmel Berman. II. Title.
TX715.B953 1994
641.5—DC20   93-48909
                                                        CIP

Manufactured in the United States of America
First Edition

For my sons, Connor and Dillon

Contents

A color photo insert follows page 182.

COOKING WITH

David Burke

THE MAKING OF AN AMERICAN CHEF

Several years ago, at the age of twenty-six, David Burke, a meteor on the American cooking scene, was chosen as the sole representative of his country at the Second International Cooking Festival in Tokyo. He had decided long in advance to prepare Cinnamon-Smoked Quail in Pecan Consommé with Apple Raviolis, and Lobster with Black-Olive Noodles and Lobster Oil. One of the demands of the competition was that chefs prepare one dish with ingredients native to Japan. After some indecision, and at virtually the last minute, David decided to cook sea bream, a fish similar to American carp, served with asparagus butter and lotus-root chips.

"The lotus chips certainly intrigued and evidently impressed the judges," recalls David. "I peeled and sliced the lotus roots into thin rounds and deep-fried them. In Japan, lotus roots are pickled, and no one had ever seen them prepared that way. Of course, neither had I until the day I made them." (Soon afterward, a Tokyo television station ran a show on David and his chips.)

For dessert, he prepared a Chocolate Whiskey Torte served on a plate spray-painted with chocolate. A staunch advocate of cake *and* ice cream, David arranged beside the cake an edible cabin of chocolate logs filled with chocolate ice cream. A chocolate butterfly perched on the roof.

When the judging was over, David had won from the Japanese government the Nippon Award of Excellence for Distinguished Skill and Technique, and from the French, Les Meilleurs Ouvriers de France, a prize never previously awarded to an American.

It was a great moment of triumph—both for David and for his breathtaking new approach to cooking. The Burke style is both innovative and inventive. Blending the principles of haute cuisine, French country cooking, American regional specialties, and ethnic details, David has taken to new heights the concept of *building* a dish, first introduced in Europe—rather than displaying food flat upon a plate, he uses various elements the way a child uses blocks, building up, creating layers of food, and at the same time presenting a remarkable mélange of tastes, colors, and textures.

Here, for the first time, David shares his secrets. The comments and anecdotes preceding the recipes are by David. His version of the New American Cuisine is bursting with imagination, infused with a genuine affection for the beauty of food. In teaching the concept of building a dish, he breaks down seemingly complex creations into their component parts, adapting them easily for the home chef (two of his award-winning Japanese entries are included here), while teaching a new way of looking at and preparing food. He makes brilliant use of foods we often discard—celery leaves, broad green leaves of leek, peelings from ginger or horseradish, apple and pear peelings—while emphasizing the twin goals of taste and beauty. Not only are his endless variations exciting but, if you can master his way of *thinking* about food, your own creativity in the kitchen will be notably enhanced. He has created a new aesthetic in food.

The story of how David achieved his success is instructive, for it demonstrates the evolution of his thinking and learning about food, from simple beginnings, to apprenticeships in both restaurants and private homes in the U.S. and Europe, to work with the great masters like Pierre Troisgros and Gaston Lenôtre. The knowledge David acquired along the way is valuable information for any chef, and a fitting prelude to the recipes that follow.

DAVID BURKE DECIDED to become a chef nine years prior to the Japanese competition, but his interest began earlier. Having grown up in Hazlet, a small New Jersey town, where he ate the simplest food at home, David can't explain the seemingly atavistic impulse that propelled him into the world of cuisine, but he remembers being intrigued by the white-toqued chefs he saw working in a small New Jersey hotel where, at fourteen, he had an after-school job as a dishwasher. The head chef and his associates exhibited a striking economy of movement and handled food items David thought of as rare and unusual.

"I had never even seen a whole chicken before," he says. "I hadn't spent a moment inside a supermarket or a butcher shop, and my mother purchased chicken parts. Now I saw a chef cut a chicken neatly into quarters or eighths, and apportion the pieces into a variety of dishes."

If a whole chicken was unfamiliar to David, a leg of veal was even more so. He would watch transfixed as the chef transformed the veal into a roast, chops, and translucent slices that he learned were called scaloppine.

The chef enjoyed David's interest, and while others of the kitchen staff were served stews and pastas, David was given tastings of the dinners prepared for customers. He tried scaloppine for the first time, the rosy veal slices sautéed in olive oil and flavored with lemon, and filet mignon topped with a dollop of mahogany-colored sauce he found especially exotic.

He was impressed with the knowledge displayed by the kitchen professionals and with their serious concern for ingredients. Veal was returned to the purveyor if the color was not a pale rose; asparagus were unacceptable if the tips were broken or the stalks limp.

"Asparagus were completely new to me," he says. "At home all vegetables, except for corn and potatoes, came from cans—peas, green beans, spinach, baked beans, but never asparagus."

Soup in the Burke household was always canned, either tomato with rice or chicken with noodles. David was fascinated by the twelve-quart soup pot he saw in the restaurant kitchen and its creamily bubbling contents, soft beige with flecks of brown and bits of green: a cream-of-mushroom soup.

"The chef ladled out a generous bowlful for me," says David. "I had never tasted anything so delicious or so rich—a richness that I identified as luxury."

When the school year ended, a new restaurant opened in David's area, the family-owned Lakeside Manor. David felt it might be a more sophisticated place to work. His lack of any serious kitchen experience didn't deter him from applying for a summer job as a "prep cook," the person designated to peel and slice vegetables, trim meats, beat eggs, and, in general, ready foods to be cooked. David spent much of the summer breading onion rings, fish fillets, veal cutlets, and chicken pieces, all robed in the simplest of crusts. The atmosphere was far different from the one at his previous job; the restaurant was busy and the chef was uninterested in letting the "prep cook" taste any of

his dishes. The chef worked hard and fast, and when through with a sauté pan he would scale it down the length of the kitchen toward the sink, a distance of twenty feet. Sometimes the pan hit the sink with a splash; sometimes it hit the hapless dishwasher. It was a long summer, and during those months the budding chef was learning to differentiate between the fine and the ordinary.

"I wouldn't touch breaded and fried foods for a long while afterward, but that experience formed part of my cooking education," says David. "I appreciated the crisp texture that a crust imparts, but I was determined to avoid the predictable breading I was so tired of."

Remembering his summer of crusts and crumbs, years later David experimented, finally coming to combine bread crumbs with such spices as ground mustard, caraway, poppy, fennel, cumin, or coriander seeds, and occasionally adding chestnut flour or cornmeal to the bread crumbs.

The unpleasant summer experience didn't deter David, and he told his father that after high school he wanted to continue his education at cooking school. At that time, unlike now, becoming a cook was not considered a prestigious career move, and David's father was determined to discourage him. Under the guise of "Well, if that's what you really want," he enrolled David in a cooking class given at a local shopping mall. David's fellow students were housewives, and his father felt this would indicate how inappropriate was his choice.

Miriam Brickman owned the culinary-equipment shop where the cooking classes were given, and David was fascinated by the shop's assortment of kitchen gadgets, chef's tools, and cookbooks. Miriam became David's friend and mentor, and they worked out a fair exchange: David cleaned up after cooking classes, and in turn was allowed to sit in on as many classes as time allowed. Paula Wolfert came and talked about Mediterranean cuisine, Marcella Hazan prepared a number of Italian dishes, Miriam Brickman made dishes using fresh salmon, John Clancy demonstrated bread baking, and Henry Hugh discussed Asian specialties.

"It was a wonderful, eye-opening time for me," says David. "I realized that spaghetti sauce didn't have to be red, and that there was more to salmon than the pink stuff that came in cans."

After his first class, David bought a notebook and entered information on how to buy, prepare, serve, and garnish foods; recipes were carefully inscribed with his comments, and preferences noted in the margin. He has that notebook still, and has remained true to those first lessons. (Leafing through that book once, I saw underlined and written in capital letters: NEVER WASH ENDIVE and DON'T EAT GARLIC GERM. Water washes away the subtle intensity of the endive flavor, David pointed out, and that tiny touch of green found in budding garlic cloves has a bitter aftertaste.)

Impressed by the professional chefs who came to that small cooking school, and envying the cache of tools they carried, David acquired his own assortment of knives, sharpeners, and peelers, and, for lack of a more dignified carrying case, he wrapped each item separately and packed them all in a box that had once held a large cleaver—the word "cleaver" imprinted in red letters on the top and ends of the box, which he carried with pride.

Afternoons at Miriam Brickman's were fol-lowed by evenings at La Crêpe, a small New Jersey restaurant, where David prepared crêpe fillings, working there until he broke his shoulder playing football. Shortly after, Miriam closed her school and David was out of work. It was time, his father decided, that David forget that nonsense about learning to cook and enter college. Still determined to become a chef, David was faced with his father's insistence that he return to school or get a job immediately. Day after day he looked for work, and one morning his father said, "Come home with a job tonight, or don't come home."

David can laugh at that today, but when he was seventeen his father's words were not to be ignored. He left home that morning carrying his box of chef's tools, hoping to hitchhike, but the box marked "cleaver" carried by an athletic teenager caused drivers to accelerate past him. David called at every restaurant, bar and grill, roadhouse, and luncheonette near and around Hazlet, walking about twenty miles, and he was depressed and discouraged when he arrived at the Molly Pitcher Inn in Red Bank. There were no jobs, but a *sous-chef* mentioned a possible opening at the Navesink Country Club, and rec-ommended that he ask for José, the head chef. It was dark when David left the Inn, and luckily a driver stopped and took him to his destination. He introduced himself to José and showed him his box of tools, hoping José would see them as an earnest of his intentions. Pleading for a job, he told José he was ready to do anything and everything in the kitchen. He would never have to be shown anything more than once, and he was eager to learn all the chef was willing to teach him.

José was ready to hire him halfway through

his speech, but David never gave him a chance to talk. David was to be the new broiler-cook, and though he has gone on to more prestigious positions, nothing, he says, has thrilled him as much.

Returning home, David strolled casually into the house, not willing to admit that he had been job hunting for twelve hours. When his father asked where he had been all day, David said he had been hired for a wonderful job first thing in the morning, and that he had taken the rest of the day off to play touch football. To his parents' questions as to how much he was being paid, however, David had no rejoinder—so excited to find work, he had failed to inquire about the salary. The next morning, David walked into the country-club kitchen and was given his first white, double-breasted cook's jacket. He was a cook, not a dishwasher or a prep cook, but a real cook, and so proud of his uniform that he wore it everywhere.

Hired to prepare broiled steaks, chops, and hamburgers, he learned much more, receiving his first lessons in butchering meat, boning chicken, and filleting fish. He was exposed to new foods: sweetbreads, calves' liver, shad roe, and scallops. It was his first experience with a truly disciplined kitchen environment that operated from a clean, organized, and efficient kitchen.

"José's watchword was 'organized,'" David says. "Before I could broil a steak, my work table had to be spotless, tools ready, fry pan and grill available, spices and oils at hand, meat cut into serving portions. I learned what every cook—professional or at home—must learn. The proper presentation of a dish is the final step of many in the logistics of a kitchen."

David picked up kitchen *lingua franca* and felt like an insider when he could say that he knew how to "jam when slammed" (i.e., he could move quickly when the dining room was exceptionally busy). He was so caught up in the excitement of the work that it was three more days before he settled the matter of salary, and was stunned to learn he would be earning more than he expected.

The lessons learned on that first job were invaluable: neatness and organization took precedence over all else. Working in a professional kitchen *before* attending cooking school was incredibly instructive, and he learned that a chef must take many less public steps before his beautifully plated food is presented in a dining room. Today, David's chefs hear him repeat the gospel according to José: organize your work station, clean up as you go, if you drop something pick it up at once, do not let your part of the kitchen become a disaster area. After six happy months in Navesink, he decided that country-club food was too traditional, and he moved on to the Turning Point Restaurant in Holmdel, New Jersey.

The Turning Point offered David his first glimpse of Italian and French cuisine. The head chef, Sammy, was Italian; his assistant, Jean, French. The men vied in stressing the importance of their native cuisines. Sammy was most proud of his minestrone, and David's version is based on that early experience (see page 86). Jean gave David his first taste of French cuisine when he prepared steamed striped bass with Anisette and Pernod.

"His presentation was different from any I had seen," says David. "The fish was served in a shallow soup bowl, and the sauce had the consistency of bouillon. I saw that a chef who understands his ingredients can depart from convention, and offer a dish in a new, distinctive way."

At that small restaurant, the cooks often did more than one job. Occasionally, David, garbed in a clean cook's coat, a toque placed on his head, would be sent into the dining room to aid a captain in preparing and serving cherries jubilee or *crêpe suzette*.

"I saw how the drama of the moment, flames shooting high, hot brandy poured over ice cream or delicate crêpes, pleased guests. I began to see that dinner was more than delicious food nicely served; it was also a special event, similar to an evening at the theater."

David remained at the Turning Point until he could prepare every dish on the menu, his notebook filled with recipes, and he gloated over each new dish, seeing them all as an extension of his repertoire. When he had become thoroughly familiar with the cuisine and techniques of the restaurant, he knew it was time to move on—he hoped to a school that would train him to be a professional chef. He applied and was admitted to the Culinary Institute of America in Hyde Park, New York, familiarly known as the C.I.A.

The school offered an important contrast to David's mélange of jobs. He had worked with chefs and gained practical experience. Now, at the C.I.A., he would attend lectures to learn the "why"s before being shown the "how"s in cooking demonstrations. Many of the students compared the C.I.A. to the army and nicknamed it Camp Culinary. All were uniformly garbed in white toques and chef's coats with names embroidered over the pockets, and yellow kerchiefs tied about the throat. They were meant to look like the professional chefs they hoped to become. A good student in high school, David attended lectures on nutrition, sanitation, cost control, and French culinary terms, and discovered he had the capacity to be a great student when the subject interested him. A new course began every three weeks, and he thrived on hours in the library, researching the nutritive properties of vegetables, writing a paper on the history of ice cream, analyzing the differences among the many Chinese cuisines.

After four weeks, the lectures incorporated demonstrations, and the students were taught such basics as knife skills and cooking parlance, and were allowed hands-on work: julienning, dicing, poaching, and sautéing. David was familiar with much of the work, and he enjoyed learning about wine, ethnic cuisines, and ice carving—all subjects new to him. At the end of his first year, he began his required externship, a six-month stint as a working chef. The C.I.A. posted a number of openings, and he applied for a position at the Fairmont Hotel in Dallas, wanting to experience the unfamiliar.

The Fairmont was proud of its French menu; the dishes were not innovative, but they were classically correct. The best ingredients were used, and the chefs took a small step away from Escoffier only in using vegetables not known in eighteenth- or nineteenth-century France. New types of lettuce from California found their way into salads, mushrooms originally known in the Orient went into sauces, nut oils substituted for olive oil in vinaigrettes. Working for the first time with chefs who had actually been schooled in French cooking, David was struck by how much more formal they were than José, Sammy, or Jean, who had learned their craft on the job.

The Fairmont had the largest kitchens David had ever worked in, and they were attended by a huge staff. Assisting in the preparation of elaborate dishes which he had only read about, David ground fish for *terrine de poisson,* whipped egg whites for soufflés, wrapped salt dough around individual clay pots to seal *faisan en croûte,* and shaped croutons to perfect size for *tournedos Rossini.* This last rich dish inspired him to some slight mimicry years later, when he created a more up-to-date version, substituting swordfish for beef (see page 119).

A few weeks into his externship, David took on a second job, working as a sauté chef at Ratcliff's, a seafood restaurant, making grits, hush puppies, crayfish, gulf shrimp, and fried catfish.

At the end of his six months in Texas, David had filled another notebook, and, with another free month before starting his second year at the C.I.A., he accepted a job as a broiler-cook at La Fromagerie, in Rumson, New Jersey. Despite its name, the specialty of the restaurant was not dishes made with cheese but, rather, those wrapped in envelopes of pastry. Sausages were encased in brioche dough, fish in puff pastry, beef filets in *pâte brisée.* Diners seemed to be charmed by this wrinkle, and David gained an important insight: people love a surprise, and a pastry casing is reminiscent of a beautifully wrapped gift.

The owners of La Fromagerie, Hubert and Marcus Peters, were true restaurateurs, open to culinary innovation. When David developed new dishes, they added his successful creations to their menu. One favorite was his version of the classic *poularde demi-deuil,* roast chicken with slices of black truffle placed between the skin and the meat of the chicken, which had been served at the Fairmont. David tucked a stuffing of ricotta cheese mixed with chopped spinach and beaten egg over the chicken breast, and roasted the bird until the breast puffed and turned a succulent brown. When it was carved, there were three appetizing layers: crispy skin, creamy cheese and spinach, and ivory chicken. This was David's first featured dish, and it was a smash.

The head chef at La Fromagerie was Indonesian, and though he prepared none of his specialties for the restaurant, he was happy to cook them for the staff. It was David's first experience with curried foods, which he liked but found too heavy. The memory of those aromatic dishes stayed with him, however, and inspired him later to create a curry-infused oil which offers a way to experience the redolent spice without a heavy carapace of sauce (see page 121).

On returning to the C.I.A. for his second year, David cooked, waited tables at the C.I.A. restaurant, and was a member of a team that designed a restaurant—an important school assignment. He was taught "Russian Service," which means serving a large number of people, be it at a banquet or on a cruise ship. And though the school stressed French cuisine, there were also classes in Chinese cooking. He participated in his first cooking competition, traveling to Philadelphia with a professor and five other students to compete against other American cooking schools. The C.I.A. group worked around the clock for thirty-six hours, preparing a tasting menu of thirty hors d'oeuvres, and was awarded eight gold medals and one silver. That experience, says David, hardened him to pressure, and built his confidence.

At graduation, the students wore white

chef's jackets and more elaborate toques. David was named most likely to succeed. He accepted a summer job working for the Stolt-Nielsen family in Fredrikstad, a small resort town in Norway. He was intrigued by the idea of living and working in a foreign country, and pleased that Mrs. Stolt-Nielsen had hired him rather than a French chef, her usual choice.

That summer was a time of epiphanies for David. He learned the boundaries of a chef working in a private household and decided this was a career he would not pursue. More important, he began to appreciate the flavor and variety of fish, an ingredient he had heretofore accepted without a great deal of enthusiasm. Gravlax, the cured salmon of Norway that is as ubiquitous in Norwegian households as peanut butter is in American homes, was the first fish that David genuinely enjoyed. In Scandinavia, he was exposed to the wonderful qualities of the freshest of fish. He would go to the harbor when the fishing boats put in, to purchase silvery salmon, slender mackerel, and just-caught shrimp. The flavors and textures were an inspiration, as was the fare offered at the open-air markets where he would stop for a steaming bowl of fish soup, fish cakes, or fish dumplings. He purchased smoked fish to round out his menu and set about learning the smoking technique.

The Stolt-Nielsens took David midnight fishing on their thirty-foot sailboat, and some afternoons their two sons and David would take a smaller motorboat and dive for mussels. They would sail to a rocky cove and go over the side into green, crystalline waters to pry mussels from the rocks below. When buckets were piled high, they would sail back to the boathouse, where David would prepare his own version of *moules marinière.*

"I cooked the mussels in white wine, added shallots," David explains, "and, rather than finishing the sauce with the traditional olive oil, added a chunk of Norwegian butter [which has a much higher fat content than American butter]. After the butter and wine blended, I'd toss in handfuls of chopped dill and tomatoes. We'd carry the pot and a basket of bread to a wooden table on the beach and we'd feast, dipping the bread into the sauce, pulling the orange mussels from their shells."

Mrs. Stolt-Nielsen had not hired David to serve anything as simple as mussels to her guests, however. French cooking was expected, and since fish was so commonplace, dishes prepared with fowl, meat, and game were preferred. There was a paucity of vegetables in Fredrikstad, but David discovered a variety of berries in the outdoor market and would add lingonberries, cloudberries, and currants to sauces; though this was not a traditional approach, Mrs. Stolt-Nielsen appreciated new flavors, and labeled these diversions *nouvelle cuisine.* The Stolt-Nielsens had guests frequently, so David would work for three weeks at a time and then have four or five days off. Inge, the family cook, would take over at that point and prepare more familiar Norwegian fare, like Bergen fish soup, pork roast, and gravlax.

Watching her work one day, David saw her finish a sauce for a roast with a wedge of cheese rather than butter. This was his introduction to creamy, *café-au-lait*-colored Gjetost. He sampled the cheese, enjoyed the mild, sweet flavor, and decided to follow Inge's lead. When he next prepared a sauce containing berries, he spooned off a small amount and added a bit of Gjetost. Tasting the sauce as the cheese was absorbed, he was pleased with the way the flavors married. The sauce complemented game nicely, and today David substitutes Gjetost for butter when preparing sauce for wild fowl (see page 31).

After David's summer stint in Norway, he had two weeks remaining until his return plane ticket would send him back to the States. He set out for France—his lodestar—and decided to pause in Strasbourg to sample that city's specialty: *foie gras*. Remembering that experience, David says, "I finally saw the ingredient that had been so graphically described to me. The chefs at the Fairmont had said that the best *foie gras* was light beige in color, almost blonde, and there it was."

That wasn't all Strasbourg had to offer: there were cheese shops with wheels and wedges of cheeses, *patisseries* with thumb-sized éclairs covered in chocolate so dark and rich that they looked more black than brown, *épiceries* featuring ducks and hams nestled in aspic and decorated with truffles or fruits. Most impressive were the chefs, wearing their white coats, strolling along the streets after lunch, clearly proud of their profession. All that, and he had not yet arrived in Paris. Once there, David purchased a Michelin Guide and located two- and three-star restaurants, but the visits were limited to viewing them from the street: he stared at the Tour d'Argent, tried to peer through the curtained windows of Le Grand Véfour, and strolled down the Rue Royale to watch the elegant enter Maxim's. The cost, for him, was prohibitive.

Working as a chef in Norway had given him confidence, and it had taught him that his years at the C.I.A. and working in American restau-

rants were necessary steps but not the final one. There were secrets of cuisine only the French masters could reveal to him. But before that, he had to return to the United States to earn some money. Many restaurants in New Jersey wanted to hire him as executive chef, but those restaurants did not present the challenge of haute cuisine, and he chose, instead, to take a job as *saucier* at La Crémaillière, a renowned restaurant in Banksville, New York.

Waldy Malouf, the executive chef there, was classically trained, and became an important mentor. After just three months, he promoted David to *sous-chef,* and his years under Malouf's tutelage were another important learning experience. Malouf used analogies, such as: "Hold that fish as though it were a wounded bird, carefully, delicately."

"I still remember his instructions on preparing a sauce for game," David says. " 'That sauce should be reduced until it has the qualities of sangría.' Did that mean it should *taste* like sangría? No, he meant the sauce should contain many elements—spicy, fruity, tart, sweet—*like* a sangría."

Nouvelle cuisine was then surfacing in America, and many techniques of that style were taught David by Malouf. "He would paint a plate with sauce," David says, "and then place elements of the dish on the sauce. It was a far more interesting presentation than spooning sauce over meat or fish."

Malouf also expanded David's knowledge of classic French cooking technique; this may seem unnecessary to some, especially since many notable chefs today neglect such methods, but David believes that learning time-honored techniques is valuable, because they provide a chef at any level with a sanctuary, a comfort zone from which to experiment, customize, and modify.

After two and a half years at La Crémaillière, David asked Malouf for an assessment of his talents. The chef felt that David had the ability and background to be a great *saucier* or a fine *sous-chef* in an important New York City restaurant, but he advised a return to France for further training if David aspired to be an executive chef. He offered David a letter of recommendation to André Daguin, owner of the Hôtel de France, a Michelin two-starred restaurant in Auch. With that in hand, David set off once more for France.

In Auch, Daguin informed him that there were no openings. Accepting the chef's generous offer of lunch, however, David stayed, and started a conversation with one of Daguin's employees, a young woman from New York, who told him about a job at a restaurant in the countryside, about ten miles from Auch. Daguin kindly made an introductory phone call, and gave David directions. After a twenty-minute bus ride, David arrived at the village of Mauvezin, and had no trouble finding La Rapière, the only restaurant there. Introducing himself to Michel Fourreau, the owner-chef, he was hired as an all-around helper.

David's first job on his pilgrimage through France honed his appreciation for regional specialties, especially those made with duck. La Rapière served roast duck, smoked duck legs, duck crackling, duck *lardons,* duck *pâté* prepared in a casing made from the skin of duck neck, duck *foie gras,* and, best of all, duck *confit.* The pantries of homes and restaurants in that region were stocked with *confit,* which was served with fried potatoes, beans, or cabbage. *Cassoulet* contained *confit,* as did bean soup, salad, and omelettes.

Whenever possible, David would lunch at the Hôtel de France, his first repeated experience with a traditional, important restaurant. He began to see why Michelin had awarded Daguin his stars. The restaurant was beautiful, the tables decorated with flowers and widely spaced; the dishes were unique—for example, brochette of grilled salmon nestled beside slices of *foie gras,* a combination that would not then have been found in an American restaurant. David saw that, if a chef truly understood food, was well versed in technique, he could move ahead in an innovative manner. His experiences in France encouraged him to gamble and invent once he became an executive chef and was master of a kitchen.

A colleague from La Rapière introduced David to another Michelin-starred establishment: Vanel, in Toulouse. One of Lucien Vanel's specialties was a casserole of snails prepared with walnuts. The snails were local and were resting on a bed of lettuce; because they were fresh, their texture was perfect. Other dishes were cooked in the regional young red wine of Cahors.

David's stay in southwestern France increased his appreciation for the reality, the naturalness of regional cooking. Until his stay in Mauvezin, he had been inclined to extol haute cuisine and relegate a provincial kitchen to a lower status, but working at La Rapière and visiting nearby restaurants forced him to reconsider his ideas. Regional cooking, as David explains it today, relies on family, history, memory—a combination that results in dishes equal to those created on more rarefied heights. There is no abyss between regional and haute cuisine, and the latter frequently searches regionally for new ideas.

Once David was exposed to the joys of Michelin-starred restaurants, he knew where the lessons were to be learned—he had to visit more of them and, he hoped, meet their chefs. After a reluctant farewell to friends in Mauvezin and Auch, he went directly to Paul Bocuse's world-famous three-star restaurant in Lyon. Though more than ten years have passed, David vividly remembers the *menu de dégustation* he ate there. (The experience impelled him, when he became an executive chef, to provide a tasting menu for guests who wanted to sample the variety of dishes he offered.)

"I started with a glass of Côtes-du-Rhône and a warm, sweetbread *pâté* enclosed in pastry," David recalls. "The maître d' could see that I was enjoying the meal, and when I asked about the preparation of a soup of truffles, he disappeared into the kitchen and brought out Bocuse himself."

The great chef sat at David's table and asked about his interest in cooking. David explained that he was just starting his career as a chef, and that dining at Bocuse's restaurant was an experience he had been waiting for. With that, Bocuse joined him for a glass of wine, and as they spoke plates were placed before David with beautifully timed regularity. The *menu de dégustation* had been considerably extended, and Bocuse waved away David's thanks with, "But we are colleagues."

Those words thrilled David even more than the meal, and he was tempted to leave France immediately, so anxious was he to return to a restaurant kitchen and start cooking, but he remained in Lyon and visited Alain Chappel's restaurant, where he had his second *menu de dégustation*. He remembers two dishes most vividly: *beignets de grenouilles,* frog's-leg fritters, and *crêtes de coq,* stuffed cockscombs. The cockscombs, rarely used even in France, helped establish Chappel for David as one of the most original and creative of the great chefs. When he returned to the States, he researched and found a recipe for *crêtes de coq* in an antique French cookbook. Today, cockscombs stuffed with crayfish, chicken, or wild mushrooms can be found occasionally on David's tasting menu.

Before leaving Lyon, David made a reservation at the famed restaurant of the Troisgros brothers in Roanne. He arrived there straight from the train, suitcase in hand. Ordering the *menu de dégustation,* David chose an especially fine white Burgundy to complement what he knew would be a very special meal. The waiter looked at the young American seated in front of him and asked in the kindest way, "Are you sure?" David appreciated the man's concern, because the wine was very expensive, but he explained that he was celebrating his return to New York as well as his dinner with the Troisgros brothers. Course after course of wonderful food arrived in measured cadence, yet David wanted more. Staring at every plate that came out of the kitchen, he asked the waiter or maître d' the name of the dish, unable to resist ordering dishes that did not come with the *menu de dégustation.* One favorite was oysters Gloria, warm oysters with a julienne of vegetables strewn over the shellfish.

Already served incredible pastries, he couldn't resist the sorbets that were being served from specially constructed carts that circulated around the room. Part of a rainbow of colors, each *sorbet* was offered from an etched silver container. Waiters paused at tables and, deftly using two large spoons, placed quenelles of the chilled dessert on plates, topping it with a lightly whipped *crème fleurette.* When the maître d' heard that the young guest wanted to taste every sorbet, he asked a few questions, went into the kitchen, and returned with an invitation from Pierre Troisgros: would David care to meet him and see where he worked? David followed the maître d' into the kitchen, where the white-toqued chefs looked at him with curiosity. In his broken French, he told Troisgros how honored he was to be allowed into the atelier of a great artist. Waving away the compliment, Troisgros questioned David about his background and future plans, and showed him around his splendidly organized kitchen.

After leaving Roanne the following day, David stopped at Cahors to lunch at La Taverne, a restaurant recommended by a friend from Mauvezin. When the chef learned David was a colleague from the States, he prepared an exotic and expensive dish: a large, whole black truffle, baked in a crust of salt, and served in a pool of truffle oil. Developing an assortment of infused oils some years later, David created a truffle oil which he uses to add aroma and flavor to salads, shellfish, and baked potatoes.

With just one day left to spend in France, David returned to Paris and a farewell dinner at Taillevent, a three-star restaurant he had looked at longingly a few years before. The atmosphere at Taillevent was serious, almost hushed, and the service was the finest he had yet experienced. He understood that he was in the home, the temple, of classical French cuisine, and he remembers dining on a delicate seafood sausage, striped bass in *beurre blanc,* and a pear soufflé perfumed with pear liqueur. It was wonderful, it was correct, and, given the opportunity, he knew he would use such classical dishes as a springboard into more innovative cooking.

When he returned to the United States, David needed to work off debts incurred in France as quickly as possible, and he went to work as a fish cook for Daniel Boulud, then executive chef at the Hotel Plaza Athénée in New York City. The hotel restaurant had a dichotomous personality: At dinner, dishes were laved in cream and garnished with caviar and truffles. The emphasis was on opulence rather than imagination. At lunch, the watchword was *cuisine minceur,* and David was required to do nothing more interesting than steam Dover sole over which he placed a lattice of steamed asparagus, and steam gray sole which he accented with spinach—also steamed. Recognizing the importance of low-fat, low-calorie cooking, David believed at the same time that such dishes would have been better if heightened with spices, herbs, and unusual vegetables. His philosophy and that of the Plaza Athénée were at odds, and he knew he had to move on; the restaurant did not allow him the creative space he needed to do his best work. Waldy Malouf came to his aid, recommending him to Charlie Palmer, then executive chef at The River Café, located near the Brooklyn Bridge. Palmer hired David as one of his *sous-chefs,* and the rapport between the two was immediate, with David's experiments welcomed and encouraged. Many of his dishes were added to the menu, and guests were laudatory about such inventions as Shrimp and Ginger Wontons, quail eggs Benedict, and Oysters with Watercress on Roasted Peppercorns; David felt that his personal view of cuisine was taking form.

Describing it, he says, "I was reaching toward a cuisine that would combine French classical technique with regional French and American cooking, woven together with ethnic touches. The vision was still amorphous, but I felt that if I could knit all those strands together the result would be imaginative and, I hoped, remarkable."

Not completely satisfied with his knowledge of classical technique, and sensing that his inventiveness needed a more solid base, David decided to do more work in France, and after one year at The River Café he took a six-week leave of absence and returned to Europe. It was to be six weeks crammed with experiences. A professional chef who is serious about his craft becomes a member of an unofficial international club that has no officers or dues. It was this "organization" that welcomed David, and gained him entrée into the kitchens of some of France's finest restaurants.

Wherever he worked, David was paid only in priceless knowledge and experience, and he dedicatedly committed to paper ideas, recipes, and impressions. His first stop was Chez la Mère Blanc, a two-star restaurant in Vonnas. Georges Blanc, the owner-chef, had created a small and elegant restaurant that mirrored his approach to food presentation, or "plating," the word used in the trade. Blanc transformed pastry and bread dough into a variety of shapes: a *croûte* intended as a platform for a bit of meat or fish was never cut into a simple round, but appeared on the plate as a wedge or heart. A roll, round and puffy, would be hollowed to form a *croustade,* an edible container for an

offering of shrimp cooked with broth and a dice of fresh vegetables. Dessert crêpes were filled with flavored cream, rolled pencil-thin, and arranged in a pyramid. Blanc *styled* his plates; there was a sense of architecture to his presentations.

David remained at Chez la Mère Blanc for two weeks, welcomed as that extra pair of hands always needed in a restaurant kitchen. He cleaned vegetables, sliced potatoes, chopped parsley, filled small squares of dough with puréed chicken; mostly, however, he watched the chef as he garnished, cut, and shaped, his imagination adding beauty to every meal. Each night he would transcribe impressions into his notebook, and many pages were filled before he moved on to the Troisgros restaurant in Roanne.

Troisgros greeted him with, "I knew you would come back to us," and David was back, not as a guest who ordered every dish, but as a kitchen helper whose day started at eight in the morning and who did everything: removed stems from spinach, peeled oranges, carved potato roses. He worked until three in the afternoon, then returned at five for the dinner shift, and stayed as long as needed. In the Troisgros system, the kitchen was organized as a team, with many chefs working on each dish. If turbot was ordered, one chef sautéed the fish, another prepared the sauce, still another cooked the vegetables, and a fourth readied the garnish. The fifth chef assembled all the elements and did the plating according to Troisgros's idea of perfection. David was afforded that privilege, upon his request, under Troisgros's supervision.

The food at the restaurant was regional, and *foie gras* was on the lunch and dinner menus, frequently served with potatoes cut into slices so thin they were translucent. The potatoes were sautéed quickly in butter, and resembled hot potato chips, garnished with minced parsley and a scattering of *gros sel.* Those potatoes gave David the idea for Fresh-Herb Wafers, where he captures minced herbs between two thinly sliced discs of potato (see page 31).

Working for the Troisgros family gave David the opportunity to sample every one of the desserts he had so admired. A few years earlier, he had been enchanted with the sorbet carts; they still made the rounds, offering a rainbow of chilled delights, but now he had a new favorite: *crème brûlée,* with a flavor that he enjoyed but could not divine. For a few days, he played a guessing game with the chef who prepared the rich custard dish with its brittle caramel lid. Finally, the chef divulged the secret: jasmine, a flavor David associated with tea, imparted that unusual taste and aroma. A few years later, David created a dessert with a Jasmine Caramel based on his experience at the Troisgros restaurant (see page 193).

David's next stop in his culinary pilgrimage was at L'Espérance, Marc Meneau's restaurant in Vézelay, Burgundy. All of Meneau's dishes were based on classical cuisine, which was his reference point; from there he flew daringly into the twentieth century. He knew all the rules, but, rather than follow them slavishly, he adapted and changed recipes that had been created more than a century before. As David worked with him, his own ideas began to crystallize. Meneau and his kitchen totally absorbed him. The way Meneau worked with stock was an example: beef, bones, and vegetables were cooked for hours; the cooked meat was removed from the pot, and fresh beef added; the liquid was reduced, strained, and cleared; and the result was a large pot of strong, rich, beautifully burnished liquid, ready to use according to most chefs' standards, but not according to Meneau's. The stock was cooled, and all fat removed (now a technique of David's), and then reduced still further. The entire process took three days, and the result was a double consommé that held the essence, but not the fat, of the ingredients. *Cuisine minceur?* No, the consommé was served with a healthy dollop of *crème fraîche* and a garnish of fresh Beluga caviar.

Meneau owned a large collection of books on cuisine from the seventeenth through the nineteenth centuries, and he consulted this library frequently. His idea for *cromesquis* was based on a recipe in an eighteenth-century volume that described tidbits of leftover meats, vegetables, or purées cooked in crêpes or a pig's caul; his *cromesquis* were made with *foie gras* or sweetbreads, carried in tiny crêpes or miniature vegetables.

Meneau kept one chef on staff whose job it was to experiment and create. He developed one or two dishes each day, and Meneau would taste and suggest, discarding more ideas than he kept. David enjoyed many of the dishes thus dismissed, and tried to understand Meneau's criteria. "You like that," Meneau explained, "but will a guest be happy finding something so unfamiliar on his plate? When you prepare something new, always ask yourself, 'Will my customers like that?' " A martinet compared with other chefs David had assisted, he would not allow David to don an apron when he arrived at the kitchen wearing black sneakers, but sent David out to purchase proper work shoes, saying, "I will not have tennis shoes in my kitchen. Too frivolous."

The kitchen at L'Espérance was clean, new,

and beautiful, and Meneau had his own ideas about keeping it so. Each work counter was covered with a stretch of paper. Cutting boards, pots, knives, all equipment was placed on top of the paper. If sauce spilled or fat splattered, the paper was removed and discarded, and fresh paper laid. It was more efficient than constantly cleaning counters, he explained. Elegance, beauty, comfort—all that must work in combination with food that was both classical and daring. In the dining room, tables were large and perfectly spaced, napery gleamed, crystal sparkled. The porcelain dinnerware was Limoges, the pattern created expressly for the restaurant. Lighting was subdued, but not so dim that the food was obscured; cream-colored beeswax candles presented everyone in a flattering light. The ambience and every course confirmed Meneau's idea of *raffinement*. All dishes were plated with tiny, unusual touches: a few drops of tomato water or basil water circled a halibut steak, individual black-truffle soufflés appeared between courses, and when a plate of miniature petits fours were served with coffee each tiny pastry was decorated with as much care as a five-tiered wedding cake. From the C.I.A. onward, David had heard chefs speak of the importance of the *look* of a dish, but Meneau, more than anyone, understood that the eye as well as the palate must be delighted.

When David left L'Espérance, he returned to the United States bubbling with energy and brimming with ideas: some were incorporated into The River Café menu; others remained in his notebook, ready for future use. The six weeks in France confirmed that there were no boundaries to creativity or imagination in his profession.

After his return from France, other fine restaurants offered him positions as executive chef. The offers were flattering, but David felt that, before accepting a job with a great deal of responsibility, he still had a lot to learn. Specifically, he wanted to return to France and study the fine art of preparing desserts and breads. Six months later, he did so, taking another leave from The River Café to enroll in the cooking school of the great *traiteur* and pastry chef Gaston Lenôtre.

David arrived in France a month before classes were to start, in order to acclimate himself and improve his French. He was drinking a *café au lait* in a small café one morning when he started talking to a man standing beside him, a baker named Basil. Basil introduced David to José Lampreia, a young chef then lauded in Paris for his dramatic food presentations at Maison Blanche, a restaurant on the very edge of the city (distance doesn't matter to the French, who follow fine chefs the way groupies trail rock stars). On learning David's background and the reason for his coming to France, Lampreia asked if he'd like to work with him until the start of classes. David accepted eagerly.

Lampreia originated the idea of building a dish, which David would later explore further. Lampreia looked at each dish as a cake, a pastry; his plating technique was joyous and celebratory. This style represents the cornerstone of David's cooking.

José and David appreciated each other's talents: David was a trained chef willing to do anything and everything in the kitchen, no task too menial; and David had the opportunity to observe another master of presentation. Lampreia enjoyed creating new food combinations, such as fish served with puréed potatoes.

"Today, many chefs place a fillet of fish atop

a mound of whipped potatoes," says David, "but it was Lampreia who first removed mashed potatoes from the dominion of steak and chicken."

Though he worked at Maison Blanche from four in the afternoon until eleven at night, David took on a second job at the Fauchon bakery, working from five in the morning until two in the afternoon. Fauchon, one of the world's great purveyors of fine food, employed twenty bakers, dispersing them among four large rooms. Croissants and brioches were prepared in one room; another room, in which the temperature was deliberately colder, was dedicated to puff pastries and cookies; specialists in tarts and cakes reigned in the third room; and the fourth contained giant mixers and ovens. As an inexperienced newcomer (he was a chef but not a pastry chef), David was assigned to the second room, where he prepared macaroons and nothing but for an entire month. (Unlike those popular in the States, French macaroons are delicate mouthfuls combining almond paste, egg white, sugar, and flavorings. Two macaroons are joined by a cream filling, and the result is one ethereal mouthful.) Each macaroon, like every other Fauchon pastry, had to be perfect. If a macaroon was ever-so-slightly cracked, it was discarded. A macaroon is evanescent, consumed in one bite, two at the most, and nothing was allowed to disturb the symmetry of those cookies. Whenever David could escape from the endless array of macaroons, he would visit the third room and observe the kings of pastry: the chefs neatly filling miniature tarts with lemon cream, carefully placing scarlet raspberries into pastry shells, and gently alternating layers of chocolate and meringue

until a small square tower of *gâteau* took shape.

Then classes began. The large Lenôtre facility included a laboratory for creating and experimenting, and a factory where food was prepared for the many Lenôtre shops all over Paris. David had registered for three courses, each lasting two very concentrated weeks. The first course was on the uses of chocolate and sugar; there were eight in the class, with David the only American. Each course consisted of demonstration followed by hands-on work by the students.

The first day, a professor named Laurent prepared blown sugar, which resembled fragile blown glass and had many of the same superficial properties: it was crystal-clear, pliable when hot, brittle and breakable when cold. Laurent did amazing things with sugar threads, working with unbelievable speed to create apples, bananas, and elegantly long-necked swans. This was followed by a demonstration on the uses of poured sugar; the thick, viscous liquid was formed into plates, vases, and sculpture reminiscent of works of ice. David looked forward to trying what the professor had so ably demonstrated, but the next day the eight students were allowed only to cook sugar, over and over again, while the professor repeated how important it was to get the consistency just right before starting to form the sugar.

David was unfamiliar with the French terminology for cooking sugar, and the professor had to stop class from time to time to make his explanations clear, but by the end of that day David had all the terms inscribed in his notebook, and he memorized them. The next day, the class went back to cooking sugar, moving more familiarly from stage to stage. The students were beginning to understand the quality of the ingredient as it metamorphosed from a liquid to a thread to a pliable ball. The final days of that week were dedicated to making sugar objects. David recalls that his first sugar apple was a sugar mess, but the second day a somewhat awkward sugar swan took shape, and he went on to make a nest of sugar threads to give his swan a resting place. The last day, he concentrated on using poured sugar, creating plates on which he visualized serving petits fours and glazed fruit. Remembering Marc Meneau and his credo—the happiness of the guest must come first—he was sure that tiny pastries served on a sugar plate would please.

The sugar week segued into work with chocolate, an ingredient David was more familiar with. He had worked with chocolate at the C.I.A. and at various restaurants, and, knowing chocolate as a ubiquitous favorite, he wanted to acquire more techniques for its use. The professor recommended the French bittersweet chocolate, Valrhona, a chocolate David still prefers, and demonstrated spray-painting a plate with liquid chocolate which dried to provide a wonderful base for a chocolate dessert. The remainder of the week was taken up with making molded or hand-dipped chocolate candies and preparing chocolate decorations.

A two-week hiatus after the chocolate studies gave David the opportunity to read books he had found in stalls along the Seine. Not completely literate in French, he purchased books that were heavily illustrated and dealt with *fin-de-siècle* customs and manners, and was especially fascinated with volumes picturing elegant nineteenth-century restaurants decorated with crystal chandeliers and Oriental carpets and Gobelin wall hangings. He also explored the restaurant scene in the Parisian suburbs, stopping one day in Bougival at the Michelin-starred restaurant La Camélia. The owner-chef, Jean Delaveyne, was well known; heralded chefs such as Joël Robuchon of Jamin and Michel Guérard of Eugénie-les-Bains had worked for him. Guérard was famous for *cuisine minceur,* which in part was originated by Delaveyne. After David introduced himself, Delaveyne agreed that he could work at La Camélia until classes resumed. The cuisine at the restaurant was eclectic, weighted toward dishes made with lobsters, oysters, and clams, and Delaveyne's imagination took him far afield. Tomatoes and strawberries were combined in a sauce which added a piquant touch to grilled fish. Rigatoni pasta was tossed in a curry vinaigrette along with sautéed calves' brains. The chef had a special way of serving smoked salmon—placing an entire side of fish on a slightly oiled block of ice; the salmon was always properly chilled, and the platform of ice facilitated slicing—a method David has adopted.

Two weeks later, David returned to Lenôtre for a course in bread baking. It was August, the month when France vacations, and he was the only student, but the class was held nevertheless. He learned about different grains, and how they were milled into a variety of flours; he studied fermentation, flavoring, and the art of creating all types of bread. The professor and his lone student would bake as much bread as might have been prepared by a class of eight. A favorite was a slim baguette baked in a metal pipe very similar to that used by plumbers. Dough was prepared, wrapped in parchment, and inserted in the pipe. The baked bread had perfect symmetry. (This is the method David uses today when preparing a rye-potato bread that's served with his Pastrami Salmon.) A souvenir from that course was a gift from David's professor: a container of sourdough starter that was twenty-two years old. David carried it back to the United States, and it is the basis of the sourdough bread he bakes today.

After the class in bread baking, David had a few free weeks before his next course began; wanting to practice what he had just learned, he found a job at a small and very elegant bakery and pastry shop in the suburb of St.-Germain-en-Laye. For three weeks, he baked bread, made pastries, and had a fine time working with chocolate. His day began at six in the morning and finished at noon. Noticing a wholesale *charcuterie* next door, he asked if he could work there in the afternoons. The owners were welcoming, and David would go from the bakery to the *charcuterie,* helping with the brining, smoking, and curing of meats; he employs what he learned then when he smokes and cures fish and meat today.

His jobs at the bakery and the *charcuterie* ended when his final course began: the preparation of desserts for restaurants. At last he could concentrate on dishes—part food, part fantasy—that so intrigue guests. "A chef may serve unique starters," says David, "imaginative main courses, but gasps of pleasure are heard when desserts are brought to the table. I often tell people that, if they are preparing a special dinner at home, they should serve two desserts and chocolates with after-dinner coffee."

For two weeks, David worked on soufflés, individual cakes, beignets, mousses, tarts large and small, *gâteaux,* and the sauces that went with them. He prepared elaborately decorated petits fours, miniature éclairs and profiteroles as well as their larger relatives, and edible chocolate containers that partnered individual fruit sorbets. Certainly he had studied dessert preparation at the C.I.A. and worked on desserts at restaurants, but Lenôtre carried dessert-making to a sublime level. His soufflés contained tiny surprises: bits of chocolate, or a spoonful of crushed fruit that had been marinated in *eau-de-vie.* David was familiar with praline, and at Lenôtre he learned to create a *marmite* of praline to be used as a container for fruit sorbets. Greatly influenced by Lenôtre, David combines two, often three elements in one dessert: a cake is served with a sorbet or ice cream and a sauce. "I want to create a feeling of opulence at the end of a meal," says David.

In December 1987, David returned to The River Café to find that Charlie Palmer was leaving to open his own restaurant, Aureole. Palmer asked David to join him, but David felt it was time for him to work as an executive chef, and when the café's owner, Buzzy O'Keefe, offered him that position, he eagerly accepted. David remained there until 1992, establishing his own style and moving in his own direction. Guests were offered the choice of a regular or a tasting menu, the latter because he wanted to share the enjoyment he had experienced in France with the *menu de dégustation.* The café offered David a venue that encouraged experimentation and a clientele that was responsive to the new and imaginative. When guests first sat at their tables, they were presented with a special welcome in the form of an *amuse-gueule,* a little tidbit that gave them time to study the menu at their leisure. The tiny treats varied: some evenings a few tablespoons of lobster consommé were served in a brandy snifter or demitasse cup, other nights there would be small pastries filled with a vegetable flan, lobster salad, or mascarpone mousse.

Today, co-owner, with Alan Stillman, of the Park Avenue Cafe, David continues that welcoming custom, serving wild-mushroom custard in an eggshell, miniature croques, or quail eggs Benedict to newly seated guests. And just as he begins each meal with a little gift, he ends dinners with a lagniappe of petits fours or chocolates. Desserts, often combining ice cream, cake, and sauce, emulate the lavish Lenôtre style, and his dessert menu is larger than those proffered by most restaurants. Presentations are reminders of Meneau and Lampreia; David plates with drama and verve, offering combinations with unusual contrasts of shapes, textures, and flavors.

Painters such as Hockney and Johns may intellectualize, explaining their work in cerebral terms, but when Michelangelo was asked for an explanation of his *David* sculpture, that great artist averred that all he did was chip away at the marble, ridding the stone of excrescence, until his vision was realized. In his profession, David Burke is of the Michelangelo school. He was taught, and certainly he can trace many influences, but his learning is one layer, centered between instinct and an artist's eye.

There is a Burke *look* that informs his meals; plates—from person to person or course to course—do not necessarily match. "Some dishes, such as *confit* or chili, look better on pottery," he says. "Whole fillets of fish or breasts of chicken are enhanced by porcelain." There is no reason why the pattern that marches around the perimeter of a soup plate has to copycat the pattern of a plate used for a main course or a salad. He urges home cooks to mix dinnerware, and learn to look at objects not necessarily intended for the dining table with a fresh eye. In his restaurant, lacquer-glossed decorative boxes hold warm oysters on the half-shell, and small wicker baskets embrace tiny pots of hot butterscotch sauce. "Every home has objects tucked away on a shelf that can be used to grace a table." A tabletop ornament such as a clear glass box is a fine container for chocolates, petits fours look elegant on a marble square, tiny cookies can be arranged in a jewelry box, and antique toys may double as table decorations. "Look at what you already own, see boxes, bookends, antiques, in terms of dining."

David recommends a fearless insouciance to the cook at home: new recipes should be tried when guests are invited; imagination is as much appreciated as a well-prepared dish that is familiar. He advises reading recipes through more than once, until the steps are understood, and when a dish calls for slicing, chopping, or dicing, it's best that work be completed in advance. The behind-the-scenes word is "organization": ingredients and equipment should be right at hand, herbs and spices easy to reach, knives sharpened and available. Presuming that those who cook are hoping to please, he suggests that hosts do as he does at his restaurant: "I keep notes, and I don't serve the same thing twice unless a dish is requested." Guests frequently ask how often they'll be able to dine with him without repeating a meal, and he says, "I tell them they can come forever, I'll just create new dishes for them."

I've functioned as David's Boswell in this

chapter, but the remainder of this work speaks in David's voice. Page through this book before you start cooking and you'll get to know David. You'll learn directly from him as he describes his favorite dishes and presents the recipes that have made him one of America's most famous chefs. You'll find that his imagination will engage yours as he leads you down new and intriguing culinary paths.

Brillat-Savarin, in *The Physiology of Taste,* wrote in 1825 that "The discovery of a new dish does more for human happiness than the discovery of a star." If what the great gastronome said is true, David Burke has created more happiness than a dozen astronomers. And he can help you do the same.

CARMEL BERMAN REINGOLD

Chapter 2

SMALL THINGS/LARGE FLAVORS

 "Small Things/Large Flavors" expresses the feeling I have for cooking and entertaining. A potpourri of ideas and information is presented in this section, including recipes for such small treasures as Vegetable Chips, Almond Wafers, Purées, and Savory Mousses—all of which can play a part in more intricate dishes. (Don't recoil at the word "intricate." It is not synonymous with "difficult." I've worked hard to break every recipe down into easy-to-follow steps.) Ingredients are plaited and interwoven to achieve delicious results.

This is a somewhat unorthodox chapter for a cookbook, but, then, I'm not an orthodox, go-by-the-book chef. I know the book, of course; by that I mean the basic tenets of classical (mainly French) cuisine. But having that background has allowed me to move forward, to break the envelope—as I've heard astronauts say—and to go further when creating my cuisine. Small culinary touches can make all the difference in a meal.

These pages are best read before planning a dinner, because so many recipes in later chapters call for ingredients prepared here.

Almond Wafers

YIELD: ABOUT 30 WAFERS

Almond Wafers are actually potato-with-almond wafers. I developed them when creating a Middle Eastern lamb dish. I seasoned roast lamb with freshly ground cumin seeds and added couscous with black olives and coriander, but something was still missing.

To add texture, I peeled several large baking potatoes and cut them into the thinnest slices possible. The potato slices were placed on a baking sheet and coated with Clarified Butter. I combined peeled and sliced almonds with beaten egg white and spooned the almonds over the potato slices, which were baked in a slow oven. The almonds browned as the potatoes cooked, and each wafer resembled an almond cluster or almond brittle. When you prepare these wafers, you'll notice that the potato slice isn't visible and comes as a pleasing surprise with the first bite.

Serve Almond Wafers with lamb or fish or cheese. These wafers make a fine snack and can also be prepared with pumpkin seeds, chopped pistachios, or chopped cashews.

> 3 tablespoons Clarified Butter (see page 26) or vegetable oil
> 2 large baking potatoes, peeled and thinly sliced
> 2 cups sliced almonds, peeled and lightly toasted
> 2 lightly beaten egg whites
> 1 tablespoon coarse or kosher salt

1. Preheat oven to 325°.
2. Brush a cookie sheet or sheet pan with Clarified Butter or vegetable oil. Place potato slices on the cookie-sheet pan.
3. Place almonds in a small bowl. Add egg whites and salt and mix until combined.
4. Spoon almond–egg-white mixture over potato slices and bake for 10 to 15 minutes, or until potatoes are crisp and almonds are nicely browned.
5. Serve Almond Wafers with drinks, as a garnish, with salads, and as an accompaniment to a lamb dish.

Variation: For Pistachio Wafers, substitute 2 cups coarsely chopped pistachios or pumpkin seeds. Do not toast pistachios or pumpkin seeds.

APPLE AND PEAR CRACKLING

Say "crackling" and people think of a dish prepared with duck or pork skin. But crackling made of apple and pear peelings can be used to top ice cream or fruit tarts or may be served with cheese or a salad.

Fruit crackling is simple to prepare: Peel apples and/or pears and cut the peel into ribbons. Fry the ribbons in vegetable oil, and, if used with dessert, toss with powdered sugar. Try them the next time you're serving ice cream or cheese.

Black-Olive Crackers

*T*he idea for Black-Olive Crackers occurred to me when I prepared a dish of artichoke bottoms, goat cheese, and roast eggplant. The ingredients had much the same texture, and I wanted a crisp counterpoint, preferably with an olive flavor.

That's when I devised a cracker combining pasta dough with Black-Olive Purée. The dough is rolled very thin, cut into triangles, and fried. The crackers resemble nachos and also go well with Southwestern dishes.

1½ cups Black-Olive Purée (see page 35)
1 cup semolina flour
1 cup all-purpose flour
1 egg
1 egg yolk
1 tablespoon freshly ground pepper
Additional all-purpose flour for board
4 cups vegetable oil
Coarse or kosher salt to taste

1. Place Black-Olive Purée in a fine strainer or sieve, and, using the back of a spoon, press out as much oil as possible into a small bowl. Pour oil into a jar, cover, and keep for future use. Reserve Black-Olive Purée.

2. Combine semolina flour, all-purpose flour, egg, egg yolk, and pepper in a food processor or an electric mixer. Process or mix for 2 to 3 minutes.

3. Add Black-Olive Purée to flour mixture, 2 tablespoons at a time, and continue mixing until purée is thoroughly combined. If mixture is sticky, add flour a tablespoon at a time.

4. Turn olive mixture out on a floured board. Knead dough and roll out into a thin sheet. Let dough rest on board for 3 minutes.

5. Using a sharp knife or pastry cutter, cut dough into small rectangles, triangles, or squares.

6. Heat oil in an electric deep fryer to 325° to 350° (if you prefer, Black-Olive Crackers can be sautéed in a large pan, using ¼ inch of oil).

7. Place Black-Olive Crackers in basket of fryer and cook until crackers are crisp.

8. Using a slotted spoon, remove crackers from oil and drain on paper towels. Add salt to taste.

CELERY LEAVES

Celery leaves are too often discarded, a terrible waste of a flavorful ingredient. Think of these pale-green leaves as a fresh herb containing the essence of celery flavor, and use them in soups or sauces, as a garnish for fish or seafood, or to prepare Celery Oil (see page 161). Fried crisply, celery leaves can be added to soups, salads, scrambled eggs, or omelettes.

CHESTNUT MEAL

In the past, chestnut meal was used in various areas of Italy to prepare polenta. Chestnut meal has a nutty flavor and adds an especially crispy texture to fried foods. Combine chestnut meal and freshly made bread crumbs in equal parts to coat veal, chicken, fish, and sweetbreads. You can prepare chestnut meal in a food processor, using dried chestnuts, or purchase chestnut flour in stores that specialize in Italian products.

Clarified Butter

YIELD: ABOUT 1½ PINTS

C larified Butter belongs in the kitchen of any serious or even halfway serious cook. When butter is clarified, water and milk solids are cooked off, and the result is butter that won't burn quickly during cooking.

Clarified Butter is simple to make and can keep, refrigerated, for two months. Use Clarified Butter when sautéing meats, searing fish over high heat, or stir-frying.

2 pounds butter

1. Place butter in a heavy saucepan. Allow butter to melt over very low heat. As the butter heats, the water will evaporate and the milk solids will leave a white film on the bottom and sides of the saucepan. After milk solids form, remove pan from heat immediately. If milk solids are allowed to brown, butter will have a burnt taste.

2. Allow Clarified Butter to cool for 15 minutes.

3. Carefully pour butter into jars, making sure to leave white residue in the pan. Cover jars and refrigerate.

SPECIAL NOTE: When preparing Clarified Butter or using butter in any of my recipes, I prefer sweet (unsalted) butter.

CRUSTS

Many people enjoy the crispy texture of food robed in a crust, and a bread-crumb crust can be made more interesting with the addition of spices. Combine freshly ground crumbs with ground mustard seeds, caraway seeds, poppy seeds, fennel seeds, cumin seeds, or coriander seeds. These crusts will have a subtle flavor which substantially enhances a dish.

I sometimes combine bread crumbs with chestnut meal or cornmeal, and I always make crumbs from *fresh* bread. Dried bread crumbs act as a sponge and absorb more oil, whereas fresh crumbs are less absorbent and use less oil.

GARLIC AND ITS MANY USES

The use of garlic in cooking is infinite. I prepare Garlic Chips (from elephant garlic), Pickled Garlic, Roast-Garlic Purée, and even Candied Garlic.

Roast-Garlic Purée

YIELD: ABOUT 2 CUPS

One of the best ways of using garlic is in a purée. This tamed, slightly quieter version of garlic can be added to Light Chicken Stock or canned broth, and then used as a base for many sauces.

I combine puréed garlic with the pan juices from a roast chicken and then spoon it over the chicken, or an accompanying dish of mashed or baked potatoes. This is easily prepared at home. You can also combine puréed garlic with a bit of softened butter and add it to a risotto or spoon it over a filet of beef; it's also delicious spread over rye toast and served as an hors d'oeuvre, or with another appetizer.

Puréed garlic can be made in advance, refrigerated for about two weeks, or frozen in an ice-cube tray, where it will keep for many months, ready to use when you pop it out, a cube at a time.

6 heads of garlic, separated into cloves
½ cup olive oil
Coarse or kosher salt to taste
Freshly ground pepper to taste

1. Preheat oven to 325°.
2. Place garlic cloves in a single layer in a baking pan. Spoon 2 tablespoons of olive oil over garlic. Bake until tender, 20 to 30 minutes.
3. Allow cloves to cool until they're easy to handle, and pop cloves out of garlic skins.

4. Place cloves in a food processor and purée, adding remaining olive oil gradually. Season to taste.

Pickled Garlic

YIELD: 24 GARLIC CLOVES

I use Pickled Garlic with duck, smoked meats, in a salad, or on top of a steak. Pickled Garlic can also be added to a risotto or baked or mashed potatoes. A small skewer of Pickled Garlic makes a fine hors d'oeuvre, especially with one or two scallops or shrimp added to the skewer.

24 cloves garlic, peeled
1 quart water
2 cups Clove-Oil Pickling Liquid (see page 181)

1. Add garlic cloves to 1 quart boiling water and cook for 1 minute. Drain and reserve garlic.
2. Bring Clove-Oil Pickling Liquid to a boil in a nonreactive saucepan. Add garlic and allow to return to a boil.
3. Remove from heat and allow garlic to steep in liquid for 15 minutes.
4. Serve garlic by removing from liquid with a slotted spoon, or store garlic in pickling liquid for later use. Garlic will keep, refrigerated, for 2 weeks.

Candied Garlic

YIELD: 24 GARLIC CLOVES

I originally tried *confit* of garlic in a restaurant in southwestern France. The recipe has been changed to create a sweet-and-sour balance, and renamed Candied Garlic. Serve Candied Garlic with roast chicken, salmon, and game, or spread on rye or sourdough toast and serve with drinks.

Candied Garlic can be kept refrigerated for a week. Heat gently until just warm before serving.

> *2 cups Light Chicken Stock (see page 76) or*
>   *canned chicken broth*
> *4 tablespoons sugar*
> *Juice of 2 oranges*
> *Juice of 2 lemons*
> *4 tablespoons butter*
> *24 large cloves garlic, peeled*

1. Combine all ingredients except garlic cloves in a saucepan. Bring to a simmer and cook, stirring, for 3 minutes.

2. Add garlic cloves to sauce, and simmer over low heat. Cook for 20 to 40 minutes, or until garlic has absorbed most of the sauce and cloves are glazed and very tender.

GINGER

Following garlic, ginger root is the most versatile ingredient, and easily used by the cook at home. Ginger can be candied, pickled, puréed, used in a court bouillon, sauces, oils, and marinades.

I peel ginger root—save the peelings—and blanch the root in water for several hours until the sharpness is tamed. The ginger is then puréed and used in vinaigrettes, sauces, marinades, or soups.

Try broiling shrimp with a bit of purée, or adding a dollop to baked fillet of fish. Combine a teaspoonful of Ginger Purée with a small amount of oil and spoon it over a fillet of salmon or tuna. Sear the fish fillet in Ginger Oil and the purée will become a spicy crust.

Ginger peelings may be steeped in oil, and

the oil whipped into a sauce, or droplets of it can garnish salmon or shellfish. The flavor is intense, the look that of an abstract painting.

I've also blended Ginger Purée with sour cream or *crème fraîche* to build a dish of apple slices, crisp potato pancakes, and the ginger-flavored cream. The cream melts into the pancake, and the entire dish is redolent with the flavor of ginger.

Pickled ginger can be added to a sauce, soup, or salad, and the pickling liquid (see pages 180–1) combines beautifully with pan drippings from roast duck, roast pork, or roast fresh ham for an easy sauce.

RIBBONS OF LEEK

Too many good foods are discarded by those unaware of the intense flavors inherent in vegetable leaves and tops. Recipes calling for leeks often read, "Use only the white part of the leek." But if the white part is used in a creamed soup, the green of the leek can be used in another recipe.

I wash the green tops of leeks thoroughly, and cut them into slim strands. The strands are placed on a baking sheet, brushed with a little Clarified Butter or olive oil, and baked in a slow oven until they're slightly crisp. I use these Leek Ribbons to build a curving bridge over a fillet of fish, medallions of lobster, or a filet mignon. Leek Ribbons add height and texture, are visually appealing, and have a delicate flavor. They can also be added to custards and potato purées.

GJETOST CHEESE

Gjetost is caramel-colored sheep cheese from Norway. It's slightly sweet, has a nutty flavor and a silky texture. I learned to use this cheese in Norway when I was chef to a family of shipbuilders, and I add it to sauces as a final emulsifier and to give a sauce a glossy finish and an unctuous quality. You can replace the final touch of butter in a sauce, and add flavor and interest to a familiar sauce with an ounce or two of Gjetost.

Gjetost may also be added to pan drippings in roasting pheasant or chicken. Most Americans have yet to discover Gjetost; because of its natural sweetness, people think that sugar has been added—it hasn't; and because of its color, people think it's like peanut butter—it isn't.

Fresh-Herb Wafers

YIELD: ABOUT 35 TO 40 WAFERS

3 tablespoons Clarified Butter or vegetable oil
2 large baking potatoes, approximately 1 pound, peeled and cut into thin, translucent slices
2 tablespoons finely chopped fresh herbs or whole herb leaves (tarragon, coriander, chives, sage, basil, rosemary, or other available fresh herbs)
Coarse or kosher salt to taste

1. Preheat oven to 325°.
2. Brush a cookie sheet or sheet pan with Clarified Butter or vegetable oil. Place half the potato slices on the cookie sheet or sheet pan.
3. Place 3 leaves or ½ teaspoon chopped herbs on each potato slice.
4. Cover each potato slice with another potato slice, and press to seal.
5. Bake 10 to 15 minutes, or until potatoes are cooked, lightly browned, and crisp. Season and serve as hors d'oeuvres or with grilled fish or meat.

PRESERVED LEMON RINGS

My inspiration for these Lemon Rings came from the fried onion rings that are served with steak. Wanting to decorate fish with edible rings, I decided to make them of lemon rinds—the perfect accompaniment. I liked the idea of something that fooled the eye and added fun to the meal—people expected an onion flavor, took a bite, and were surprised by the fragrant, acidic flavor of lemon.

I first prepared Lemon Rings when I was at a cooking competition in Chicago. Assigned a lobster dish, I wanted to create a dish representing current American cooking trends. What's more American than a steak with onion rings? And what's more current than the idea of eating more fish and shellfish and less meat? That gave me the idea of creating a lobster steak topped with Lemon Rings.

Since then I've served Lemon Rings on a Provençal tart of olives, anchovies, basil, tomatoes, and crayfish. I've also used them with a smaller eggplant tartlet, and garnished many fish dishes with them.

Lemon Rings are marinated overnight in a combination of salt and sugar, rinsed thoroughly, and poached in a sugar syrup. They're then dipped in a tempura batter and deep-fried. When I'm preparing a dish with Provençal overtones, I often add a touch of anchovy paste to the batter.

If you're using lemons for juice, save the rinds—you'll have the main ingredient for Lemon Rings. If Lemon Rings break after poaching, mince the pieces and use on a lemon tart or in a sauce. Use Lemon Rings on grilled fish, shellfish, veal, or duck.

Preserved Lemon Rings in Tempura Batter

YIELD: ABOUT 30 LEMON RINGS

5 lemons
¼ cup coarse or kosher salt
1¼ cups sugar
1 quart water
1 cup seltzer or club soda
1 cup all-purpose flour
1 egg
Oil for frying

1. Cut tips off both ends of lemons. Insert a grapefruit or serrated knife into each lemon and detach pulp from lemon skin. Slice each lemon into ¼-inch slices, and remove pulp. (Lemon pulp may be used for lemonade.)

2. Combine salt and ¼ cup sugar, toss lemon rings in salt-sugar combination, and marinate rings overnight in refrigerator.

3. Combine water and remaining sugar in a saucepan. Bring to a boil and remove from heat.

4. Remove lemon rings from marinade and rinse thoroughly. Add lemon rings to syrup, return to heat, and bring to a simmer. Cook for 1 hour, or until rings are tender.

5. Drain lemon rings and place on a cookie sheet to chill. Lemon rings will be very soft. Any broken rings can be chopped fine and used in tarts or sauces.

6. Combine seltzer or club soda, flour, and egg in a bowl to make tempura batter. Mix very lightly with a fork. Do not overbeat, or mixture will be lumpy.

7. Place approximately 5 rings on tines of fork and dip into tempura batter. Continue until all lemon rings are dipped.

8. Heat oil in a deep fryer to 300° to 325°.

9. Place lemon rings in basket of fryer and fry until rings are golden and crisp. Remove rings from fryer and drain on paper towels.

ONION RINGS

There are fried onion rings—and then there are fried onion rings. Many people turn away from the very idea of onion rings because they can be heavy and greasy, but a well-made onion ring is a fine touch with grilled meat or fish and adds texture to game birds, calves' liver, or a mound of mashed potatoes.

A simple preparation is to slice a Bermuda or Vidalia onion into thin rings, dip rings into a little flour, and deep-fry. At home I prepare onion rings in a Beer Batter, stack them in threes, and then fill each stack with salad.

Beer Batter for Onion Rings, Fish, and Shellfish

YIELD: ABOUT 2½ CUPS

*B*eer Batter is excellent for onion rings, shrimp, scallops, fish fillets, squid, and vegetables such as broccoli florets, mushrooms, and asparagus. Ingredients cooked in Beer Batter stay crisp longer than those prepared in other batters—as much as 20 to 30 minutes.

> *½ cup dark beer*
> *½ cup seltzer or club soda*
> *1 tablespoon mustard oil*
> *1 egg white*
> *1 teaspoon cayenne pepper*
> *1 teaspoon coarse or kosher salt*
> *1 cup finely milled flour, such as Wondra*
>   *brand*

Place beer, seltzer or club soda, mustard oil, egg white, cayenne pepper, and salt in a large bowl. Whisk until ingredients are mixed. Gradually add flour until all ingredients are thoroughly combined.

LEFTOVER PASTA

Don't throw out leftover pasta. Fry cooked spaghetti or noodles into small noodle cakes and serve with fish or chicken. If you think the pasta is too crunchy after you've fried it, toss in a little tomato sauce to soften. Small noodle cakes are also excellent with sautéed shrimp.

PURÉES

A purée is a classic French filling of fish, meat, chicken, or vegetables that can be used in tortes, sausages, pastas, strudels, and croque sandwiches. The main ingredient of a purée is combined with eggs and heavy cream to create a rich—and highly caloric—filling.

I've developed another method, which eliminates the cream and substitutes olive oil or cold stock from which all fat has been removed. I call these dishes purées. If I use stock, I choose one to complement the basic purée ingredient: fish stock with fish, chicken stock with chicken, meat stock with meat purée. There is no loss of flavor when the cream is eliminated, because the stock intensifies the flavor of the purée.

Purées made with oil have a consistency similar to mayonnaise, and chefs may refer to such purées as "mayonnaise."

Purées appear in many different courses, from hors d'oeuvres through entrées, and they are referred to frequently throughout this book. Purées of fish and shellfish must be cooked before they are eaten, and purées made with chicken must be cooked thoroughly.

Purées can also be prepared with duck, shrimp, or lobster.

Black-Olive Purée

YIELD: ABOUT I CUP

1 cup small pitted California ripe black olives
1 clove garlic, cut in half
2 teaspoons lemon juice, or to taste
¼ cup olive oil
Coarse or kosher salt and freshly ground pepper
*   to taste*

Place all ingredients in a food processor and purée until smooth.

CHICKEN PURÉE PREPARED THREE WAYS

Chicken Purée can be prepared with heavy cream, olive oil, or chicken stock—the calories are in descending order. Chicken Purée is simple to prepare and can be used to stuff mushrooms, chicken wings, strudels, and croque sandwiches. A Chicken Purée must be thoroughly cooked before it is eaten, and should be used within three days of preparation.

Chicken Purée with Cream

YIELD: 2½ CUPS

10 ounces skinned and boned chicken (the best
*   combination is 1 chicken breast and meat*
*   from 1 leg of chicken)*
1 tablespoon coarse or kosher salt
1 teaspoon freshly ground pepper
1 egg
1 cup heavy sweet cream

Cut chicken into large pieces and place in a food processor. Add salt, pepper, and egg. While processing, gradually add heavy sweet cream. Continue processing until all ingredients are combined into a smooth purée.

Chicken Purée with Olive Oil

YIELD: 3 TO 3½ CUPS

10 ounces skinned and boned chicken (the best combination is 1 chicken breast and meat from 1 leg of chicken)
3 egg whites
1 tablespoon coarse or kosher salt
1 teaspoon freshly ground pepper
2 cups olive oil
½ cup crushed ice

Cut chicken into large pieces and place in a food processor. Add egg whites, salt, and pepper. While processing, gradually add olive oil. Then gradually add crushed ice (this adds the necessary moisture and keeps the mixture from becoming too thick). Continue processing until all ingredients are combined into a smooth purée.

Chicken Purée with Chicken Stock

YIELD: 3½ CUPS

10 ounces skinned and boned chicken (the best combination is 1 chicken breast and meat from 1 leg of chicken)
3 egg whites
1 tablespoon coarse or kosher salt
1 teaspoon freshly ground pepper
1 cup Light Chicken Stock (see page 76) or canned chicken broth

Cut chicken into large pieces and place in a food processor. Add egg whites, salt, and pepper. While processing, gradually add stock or canned broth. Continue processing until all ingredients are combined into a smooth purée.

SALMON PURÉES

You can purchase a fillet of salmon to prepare Salmon Purée. However, if you are cooking salmon for dinner, you may have salmon trimmings. Use these scraps to prepare a purée. Salmon purées can fill wontons, ravioli, strudels, and croque sandwiches. A salmon purée should be used within three days of preparation. (Other fish such as sole, cod, or snapper may also be used.)

Salmon Purée with Cream

YIELD: 2 CUPS

½ pound salmon, without skin or bones
1 tablespoon coarse or kosher salt
1 teaspoon freshly ground pepper
1 egg
¾ cup heavy sweet cream

Cut salmon into pieces and place in a food processor. Add salt, pepper, and egg. While processing, gradually add heavy sweet cream. Continue processing until all ingredients are combined into a smooth purée. Once cream has been added, do not process too long: the cream may whip and separate.

Salmon Purée with Olive Oil

YIELD: 2 CUPS

½ pound salmon, without skin or bones
1 egg
1 tablespoon coarse or kosher salt
1 teaspoon freshly ground pepper
1 cup olive oil
½ cup crushed ice or ice water

Cut salmon into pieces and place in a food processor. Add egg, salt, and pepper. While processing, gradually add olive oil. Then gradually add crushed ice or ice water (this adds the necessary moisture and keeps the mixture from becoming too thick). Continue processing until all ingredients are combined into a smooth purée

Scallop Purée

YIELD: ABOUT 2 CUPS

Scallop Purée can be used as a filling for ravioli, terrines, and as a binder with crab meat for stuffed shells and crab cakes.

½ pound bay or sea scallops
2 teaspoons coarse or kosher salt
1 teaspoon freshly ground pepper
Zest and juice of 1 lemon
1 cup olive oil

Place scallops, salt, pepper, zest, and lemon juice in a food processor. While processing, gradually add olive oil and continue processing until all ingredients are combined into a smooth purée.

Ginger Purée

YIELD: ABOUT 1 PINT

Ginger Purée may be used in marinades, sauces, and vinaigrettes. It can serve as a condiment with a fish carpaccio, and it's part of my recipe for Seared Salmon (see page 84). Ginger Purée will keep for ten to twelve days, refrigerated.

2 pounds ginger root, peeled and cut into 1-inch
    pieces
2 quarts water
4 ounces olive oil

1. Place ginger root in water and bring to a boil. Lower to a simmer and cook ginger about 3 hours or until tender, changing the water every ½ hour.
2. Drain ginger and place in a food processor. While processing, add olive oil gradually and process until ginger is finely puréed.

Roast-Shallot and Armagnac Purée

YIELD: APPROXIMATELY 1½ CUPS

There are myriad uses for Roast-Shallot Purée. It may be used as filling for tiny ravioli which I serve as an appetizer combined with a salad or smoked fish, can be spread on roast chicken, added to mayonnaise, or served with fried oysters. Roast-Shallot Purée, combined with an equal amount of Chicken Purée, makes an excellent filling for strudel. It can also be stirred into a vinaigrette or spooned over a sautéed salmon steak.

4 tablespoons butter
20 shallots, peeled
2 tablespoons Armagnac (or other brandy)
1 tablespoon coarse or kosher salt
1 tablespoon freshly ground pepper

1. Preheat oven to 350°.
2. Heat butter in a sauté pan, preferably with a nonstick surface. Sauté shallots over low heat for 15 to 20 minutes, or until shallots are golden brown.

3. Add Armagnac or other brandy to pan and stir to combine. Spoon shallot mixture into a baking dish. Bake for 30 minutes, stirring every 5 minutes.

4. Allow shallot mixture to cool slightly and place in a food processor. Add salt and pepper and purée.

SPECIAL NOTE: I can't stop thinking about all the things you can do with versatile Shallot Purée: combine 1½ cups of purée with 4 cups Light Chicken Stock or canned chicken broth in a saucepan. Bring to a simmer, heat for 3 or 4 minutes, and you have a fantastic soup. If you wish, add a lid of Gruyère cheese and bake in a crock, or you can also serve a dollop of Shallot Purée with sautéed calves' liver.

Potato Purée

YIELD: 4 TO 6 SERVINGS

*P*otato Purée can accompany both meat and fish dishes. Many people find a Potato Purée with fish unusual. They're so accustomed to boiled potatoes decorated with sprigs of parsley that Potato Purée accompanying cod or halibut presents a surprise. This purée is prepared with both butter and olive oil, more intriguing than purée prepared with butter alone—a proven winner, time after time.

4 medium baking potatoes, peeled and cut into quarters
4 tablespoons butter
4 tablespoons extra-virgin olive oil
½ cup milk (or more to taste)
1 tablespoon coarse or kosher salt, or to taste
1 teaspoon freshly ground white pepper, or to taste

1. Cook potatoes in boiling, salted water for 30 minutes, or until tender. Drain and, using a potato masher, food mill, fork, or food processor, purée, adding all ingredients gradually.

2. If using a processor, put potatoes and all ingredients in processor bowl simultaneously and pulse machine on and off quickly, or potatoes will have a gluey-starchy consistency.

Variations

Saffron Potatoes: Dissolve 1½ teaspoons of saffron threads in 1 teaspoon of hot water and stir into Potato Purée.

Black-Olive Potatoes: Stir 3 tablespoons of Black-Olive Purée (see page 35) into Potato Purée. Potatoes will take on a gray color which I find appealing: it reminds me of Beluga caviar.

Roquefort Potatoes: Stir ½ cup of crumbled Roquefort cheese into Potato Purée.

Coarse Salt and Sea Salt

I prefer coarse salt to finely milled salt. In France, coarse salt is called *gros sel,* and in the United States it's often sold as kosher salt. The flavor of coarse salt is much truer, and I recommend a taste test. Place a little coarse salt and regular table salt in small plates and taste the difference. I think you'll find the coarse salt is somehow *saltier* and does not leave an aftertaste.

I also prefer coarse salt when cooking, because fine salt dissolves too quickly and absorbs moisture. Fish or meat that's been salted won't sear if you use fine salt.

I don't cook with sea salt, but I do use it as a final garnish on fish carpaccio. It adds texture and an ever-so-slight flavor of the sea.

Cold Savory Mousses

Hearing "mousse," many people think of a sweet dessert, but the following recipes are for cold savory mousses, which combine a tart vegetable such as tomato or an herb or a spice—horseradish or mustard—with *crème fraîche,* heavy cream, or olive oil. Savory mousses are used in place of sauces or as fillings for puff pastry, may be added to soups, or are served as a dip for raw vegetables.

A favorite savory mousse of mine combines whipped cream with finely chopped fresh basil and is added to gazpacho. *Crème fraîche* laced with a tiny bit of caviar or other fish roe creates a snow cap for a fish soup or bouillabaisse. A small amount of savory mousse won't thicken a soup but it will add a pleasing flavor and texture. I serve Pastrami Salmon with Mustard Mousse—nothing complicated, just *crème fraîche* that has been whipped with mustard.

There's no end to the variety of savory mousses. To name a few: cayenne mousse, Black-Olive Mousse, smoked-cod mousse, smoked-salmon mousse, celery mousse, Cumin Mousse—all flavorful, intriguing, and simple to prepare.

Horseradish Mousse

YIELD: 1½ CUPS

Horseradish Mousse is especially fine with warm oysters or grilled salmon, and can be served with a meat casserole or stew. It also adds the proper sharpness to a carpaccio of beef or tuna.

1 cup crème fraîche
½ cup prepared horseradish
Coarse or kosher salt and ground white pepper
    to taste

1. Whip *crème fraîche* until thick, and stiff peaks have formed.
2. Gradually fold horseradish into *crème fraîche.* Season to taste.

Black-Olive Mousse

YIELD: ABOUT 2 CUPS

*B*lack-Olive Mousse is delicious floated on top of a tomato soup or added to a tomato salad. I also use it to finish grilled vegetables, and a tuna or swordfish steak. When I serve it with fish, I first place a tablespoonful of Tomato Concasse (see page 43) on the fish steak, and then top with Black-Olive Mousse. It can also be swirled into Artichoke Soup with Bay Scallops (see page 79).

1 cup crème fraîche
½ cup Black-Olive Purée (see page 35)
Coarse or kosher salt and freshly ground pepper
    to taste

1. Whip *crème fraîche* until thick, and stiff peaks have formed.
2. Fold Black-Olive Purée into *crème fraîche.* Season to taste.

Mustard Mousse

YIELD: 1½ CUPS

I use Mustard Mousse with Pastrami Salmon (see page 69). What is more fitting than mustard and pastrami—even though my pastrami is made with fish, not meat? I also spoon a tablespoonful of Mustard Mousse over grilled vegetables, and it's a fine dip with grilled prawns.

1 cup crème fraîche
½ cup whole-grain mustard
1 teaspoon freshly ground pepper, or
    to taste

1. Whip *crème fraîche* until thick, and stiff peaks are formed.
2. Fold mustard into *crème fraîche.* Season to taste.

Tomato Mousse

Serve Tomato Mousse with cold lobster or with a shrimp cocktail instead of cocktail sauce. Float dollops of Tomato Mousse on hot or chilled watercress soup, or spoon into a Black-Olive Puff (see page 54) for an hors d'oeuvre.

½ cup Tomato Fondue (see page 44)
2 tablespoons minced sun-dried tomatoes
¾ cup crème fraîche
1 tablespoon coarse or kosher salt
Freshly ground pepper to taste

1. Combine Tomato Fondue and sun-dried tomatoes in a saucepan. Cook over low heat, stirring, until fondue is reduced by half. Mixture will have the consistency of paste. Chill tomato mixture.

2. Whip *crème fraîche* until thick, and stiff peaks are formed.

3. Gently fold tomato mixture into *crème fraîche*. Add salt and season with pepper to taste.

SPICE MILLS

There's more to freshly ground spices than black or white peppercorns, and I keep a whole shelf of spice mills in my kitchen. Buy five or six spice mills and use them for mustard seeds, fennel seeds, cumin seeds, coriander seeds, cloves, anise. Freshly ground spices have an aroma and a flavor that are never found in ground spices.

Once you have fresh spices available, you'll find many uses for them. A bread-crumb crust for fish or chicken will take on new dimensions with the addition of freshly ground mustard or caraway seeds. A mild, soft goat cheese benefits from the addition of freshly ground cumin, as do shrimp, scallops, peas, and cabbage. Try mashed potatoes with freshly ground fennel seeds and olive oil. Ground cumin or fennel goes well on salads, and ground cloves are delicious on a baked-ham sandwich. Freshly ground coriander is an interesting addition to a honey or sweet-wine marinade for duck.

Many people want to cut down on salt, and that's easier to do when substituting freshly ground spices.

Most of my recipes do not specify "white" pepper or "black" pepper. White pepper is slightly stronger than black, and I use it when I want a sharper flavor. I do not match the color of the pepper to the color of the food.

CONCASSE, FONDUE, AND COULIS OF TOMATOES

I use tomatoes in three basic ways: as a concasse, a fondue, and a coulis. Each is a step in the preparation of tomatoes for use in other dishes.

To begin: Tomato Concasse is a fresh tomato that's been peeled, seeded, and chopped. A Tomato Concasse is used in salads and soups, and as a garnish in cold dishes such as fish carpaccio.

Tomato Fondue is a tomato relish that has been reduced by cooking tomatoes to a thick paste. I add a small amount of Tomato Fondue to some purées and mousses, and I use this fondue in timbales or sauces, or as a garnish for steamed fish, grilled steak, broiled chicken, or pasta salads.

Tomato Coulis is a sauce used for pastas and pizzas or any dish requiring tomato sauce. Coulis is made by combining Tomato Fondue with chicken stock or water, and olive oil or butter.

Tomato Concasse

YIELD: I CUP

2 fresh, ripe tomatoes
1 quart boiling water

1. Make a small incision in the bottom of each tomato. Drop tomatoes into boiling water. Remove after 1 minute.

2. Place tomatoes under cold running water for ½ minute.

3. Peel tomatoes. Cut each tomato in half and squeeze out seeds and juice into a small bowl. Reserve seeds and juice.★

4. Place tomatoes on a cutting board and cut into a small dice.

★ Tomato seeds and juice can be used for a Tomato Vinaigrette by combining with ¼ cup olive oil, 3 tablespoons tarragon vinegar, and salt and pepper to taste.

Tomato Fondue

YIELD: ABOUT 2 TO 2½ PINTS

½ cup olive oil
1 small onion, chopped
2 stalks celery, chopped
3 cloves garlic, chopped
3 pounds canned Italian plum tomatoes, peeled
    and seeded; reserve juice
1 tablespoon freshly ground pepper
1 tablespoon coarse or kosher salt
½ cup freshly chopped basil
1 pint chicken stock

1. Heat olive oil in a saucepan. Add onion, celery, and garlic, and cook over low heat for 3 minutes, stirring occasionally.

2. Add tomatoes and remaining ingredients, including reserved tomato juice. Simmer over low heat for 2 to 3 hours, or until tomato mixture has a thick, almost pastelike consistency.

3. Allow to cool and spoon into food processor. Process for 30 seconds. Mixture should not be completely smooth.

Tomato Coulis

YIELD: ABOUT 1 QUART

2 cups Tomato Fondue (see previous recipe)
2 cups or more Light Chicken Stock (see page 76)
    or canned chicken broth
¼ pound butter
½ cup olive oil
Coarse or kosher salt and freshly ground pepper
    to taste

1. Combine Tomato Fondue and Light Chicken Stock or broth in a saucepan. Bring to a simmer and cook, stirring, until ingredients are combined and slightly thickened. If necessary, add more chicken stock.

2. Add butter to sauce, stirring to combine. Gradually stir in olive oil. Adjust seasoning. Simmer for an additional 2 minutes, or until all ingredients are thoroughly combined.

VEGETABLE CHIPS

Chips can mean much more than potato chips. I prepare chips from a variety of vegetables: mushrooms, parsnips, carrots, chestnuts, garlic, lotus root. They are fun to eat and add texture, and the flavor of a vegetable intensifies when it's prepared as a chip. Water evaporates, emphasizing the pure essence of the vegetable.

The chips can be used as garnish or a side

dish; Mushroom Chips can be served with drinks rather than nuts, pretzels, or potato chips (they also combine with lamb and other meats). Pumpkin Chips can be served with desserts.

Of all the vegetable chips I've prepared, Lotus-Root Chips are the most unusual. I developed the recipe when participating in an international cooking competition in Tokyo for which I was required to prepare a dish with ingredients indigenous to Japan. I took a lotus root and turned it into Lotus-Root Chips.

The judges loved the chips. They had never tasted them before (neither had I), and they admired the way the design of each lotus slice became more evident. The flavor was deep and rich, and the semi-hard root had acquired a wonderful crisp texture. The Lotus-Root Chips were unique and delicious, and helped me win a prize at the competition.

Carrot Chips

YIELD ABOUT 40 CHIPS

Carrot Chips take on a wonderfully abstract—almost surreal appearance after they're cooked. Cut into long strips, they twist into imaginative shapes when fried, adding a crisp texture and a sweet flavor to baked chicken, grilled fish, or heartier dishes such as beef or venison stew.

2 large carrots (approximately 1 pound)
4 cups vegetable oil
Coarse or kosher salt to taste

1. Using a vegetable peeler, scrape carrots. Continuing with the peeler, cut carrots into ribbons or strands until the core is reached, and discard core.
2. Heat oil in an electric deep fryer to 300° to 325°.
3. Place carrot chips in basket of fryer, and cook until chips are golden and crisp.
4. Using a slotted spoon, remove chips from fryer and drain on paper towels. Salt to taste.

Garlic Chips

YIELD: ABOUT I CUP

1 head elephant garlic, separated into cloves
1 quart water
½ cup olive oil
Coarse or kosher salt to taste

1. Add garlic cloves to 1 quart boiling water, cook for 1 minute, and drain. Allow cloves to cool; peel and thinly slice each clove.

2. Heat oil in a sauté pan and add sliced cloves. Cook, stirring over low heat, for 1 to 2 minutes, or until slices are light tan.

3. Using a slotted spoon, remove garlic slices from pan and drain on paper towels. Salt to taste and serve with shrimp or roast meat, or toss with a warm spinach salad.

4. Save oil, and use in Roast-Garlic Oil (see page 122).

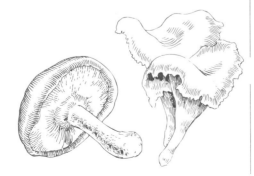

Chestnut Chips

YIELD: ABOUT 2 CUPS

Chestnut Chips have a flavor somewhere between a nut and a vegetable. They can be used with sweetbreads, chicken livers, or roast turkey, or added to soups. I also sauté a combination of mushrooms—shiitake, morels, portobello, or oyster mushrooms—and serve them with Chestnut Chips on top.

1 pound chestnuts
1 cup all-purpose flour
4 cups vegetable oil
Coarse or kosher salt to taste

1. Preheat oven to 400°.

2. Cut a cross in each chestnut and place chestnuts on a baking sheet. Bake chestnuts for 10 minutes, or until shells open slightly. Remove from oven and allow to cool until they can be handled easily.

3. Peel chestnuts and slice carefully. Do not try to make the slices too thin or chestnuts will break into pieces.

4. Toss chestnuts in flour.

5. Heat oil in electric deep fryer to 300° to 325°. Place chestnuts in basket of fryer and cook until chips are lightly browned and crisp.

6. Using a slotted spoon, remove chestnuts from fryer and drain on paper towels. Salt to taste.

Mushroom Chips

*M*ushroom Chips may be my favorite vegetable chip. Try just one and you'll find them addictive. They're marvelous hand food, and can replace nuts or potato chips when you are serving drinks. They can also be added to other dishes to great effect: use in a salad instead of croutons, float in clear soup, combine with scrambled eggs, spoon over warm oysters, or sprinkle liberally over a steak.

*1 pound large white mushrooms or portobello
    mushrooms
2 cups Clarified Butter or vegetable oil
Coarse or kosher salt to taste*

1. Hold mushrooms by stems and, using a sharp slicing knife or a mandoline, slice each mushroom cap crosswise or horizontally into thin, almost translucent, slices. Reserve stems for another dish.

2. Heat butter or vegetable oil in a small saucepan (do not allow butter or oil to smoke; a perfect mushroom chip is crisp and tender, but not burned).

3. Add mushroom slices to hot butter or oil and cook over medium heat, stirring occasionally, until golden brown, about 6 minutes. Using a slotted spoon, remove mushroom slices from saucepan and drain on paper towels.

4. Season Mushroom Chips with salt and allow to rest. They will become crisp after 1 to 2 hours.

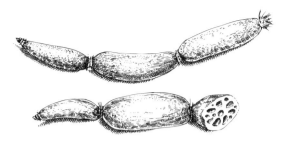

Lotus-Root Chips

YIELD: ABOUT 40 TO 45 CHIPS

*H*ere's one of the prize-winning recipes that I prepared at the International Cooking Festival in Tokyo. Lotus root is available in Oriental markets around the country.

½ pound lotus roots (approximately 3 roots),
peeled, rinsed, and thinly sliced
4 cups vegetable oil
Coarse or kosher salt to taste

1. Heat oil in an electric deep fryer to 300° to 325°.
2. Place lotus-root slices in basket of fryer and cook until slices are golden and crisp.
3. Using a slotted spoon, remove chips from fryer and drain on paper towels. Salt to taste.

Pumpkin Chips

YIELD: ABOUT 3 CUPS

1 miniature pumpkin, about ½ pound
4 cups vegetable oil
Coarse or kosher salt to taste or confectioners'
sugar to taste

1. Cut top off pumpkin; remove and discard all seeds. Carefully cut pulp from pumpkin and thinly slice.
2. Heat oil in an electric deep fryer to 300° to 325°.
3. Place pumpkin slices in basket of fryer and cook until golden and crisp.
4. Using a slotted spoon, remove chips from fryer and drain on paper towels.
5. Salt to taste if serving with meat, soups, or sandwiches, or sprinkle with confectioners' sugar if serving with a dessert such as Pumpkin Brûlée (see page 204).

Sweet-Potato Chips

YIELD: ABOUT 3 CUPS

3 large sweet potatoes, about 1 pound, peeled and
*   thinly sliced*
4 cups vegetable oil
Coarse or kosher salt to taste

1. Heat oil in an electric deep fryer to 300° to 325°.

2. Place potato slices in basket of fryer and cook until golden and crisp.

3. Using a slotted spatula, remove chips from fryer and drain on paper towels. Salt to taste and serve with sandwiches or game dishes, or use as a cracker for caviar.

Chapter 3

STARTERS AND SMALL MEALS

The recipes in this chapter can be used in a variety of ways: one or two can be presented as starter courses, three or four can form a small meal, and more than four can be served buffet-style at small or large gatherings.

Consult this chapter if you're planning a party. If you're inviting friends for drinks and want to serve hand food, check the recipes for Cherry Tomatoes Filled with Duck-Liver Mousse, Croque Sandwiches, and Pastrami Salmon. For parties that start with drinks and require a light supper, Shrimp and Jalapeño Jack Cheese Quesadillas, Ratatouille, and Croque with Shrimp will ensure that no one goes hungry. Begin a seated dinner with Shiitake-Mushroom Caps on Mousse Stems, and create a small meal by preparing Parfait of Artichoke, Goat Cheese, and Marinated Vegetables, Smoked-Fish Falafel, Rigatoni Filled with Scallop Purée and Crabmeat, and Celery-Root Napoleons.

Most of these dishes can be prepared in advance. They're not difficult, and directions are in easy-to-follow steps. I recommend that you ready more starters than you think you'll need—there won't be many leftovers.

Parfait of Artichoke, Goat Cheese, and Marinated Vegetables

YIELD: 6 SERVINGS

½ pound soft, ripe goat cheese (not hard or aged)
2 ounces extra-virgin olive oil*
2 tablespoons chopped chives
Coarse or kosher salt to taste
Freshly ground pepper to taste
1 cup extra-virgin olive oil*
3 ounces tarragon vinegar
1 ounce mustard oil
2 tablespoons chopped fresh basil
1 teaspoon coarse or kosher salt
6 cooked artichoke bottoms
1 small zucchini
1 small yellow squash
3 stalks asparagus
2 tablespoons extra-virgin olive oil*
Watercress sprigs

*I use extra-virgin olive oil in this dish because the strong flavor of the cheese and the subtle flavor of the artichoke require an assertive oil.

1. Blend goat cheese with 2 ounces olive oil. Add chives, salt, and pepper, and continue mixing until all ingredients are combined. Reserve.

2. Prepare a vinaigrette by combining 1 cup olive oil, vinegar, and mustard oil. Whisk until combined. Stir in basil, add 1 teaspoon salt and pepper to taste, and mix again.

3. Place artichoke bottoms in a shallow dish, and spoon vinaigrette over artichokes. Reserve.

4. Cut zucchini and yellow squash in half (lengthwise) and discard seeds. Slice and mince.

5. Peel asparagus and cut stalks into narrow rounds. Cut asparagus tips into fine juliennes.

6. Heat 2 tablespoons olive oil in a sauté pan. Add minced zucchini and squash and cook for 1 minute, stirring. Add asparagus and cook an additional 15 seconds, stirring. Spoon vegetable mixture into a small bowl and chill.

To Assemble: Remove artichoke bottoms from vinaigrette and place on a platter or on 6 individual plates. Using a pastry bag or a spoon, place equal amounts of goat-cheese mixture onto asparagus bottoms. Smooth cheese with a knife. Add chilled vegetables to remaining vinaigrette and spoon mixture over cheese. Garnish with watercress, and serve with sourdough toast or Black-Olive Crackers (see page 25).

White-Bean Purée with Caviar

A dish should intrigue by look as well as by taste. I serve White-Bean Purée with Osetra caviar in an egg cup. There's something special about an egg cup when it's not used strictly for medium-cooked eggs. This dish can be prepared at home with such less expensive roe as American golden caviar, from whitefish, or salmon roe.

½ pound Great Northern white beans
1 quart Light Chicken Stock (see page 76), canned chicken broth, or water
1 carrot
1 stalk celery
1 small onion
1 bay leaf
5 ounces extra-virgin olive oil
2 ounces tarragon vinegar
3 tablespoons coarse or kosher salt
1 tablespoon freshly ground pepper
4 teaspoons caviar (Osetra or other roe)
4 fried or poached quail eggs (optional)

1. Place beans in a saucepan with water to cover. Soak beans for 8 hours or overnight.

2. Drain beans. Add Light Chicken Stock, canned chicken broth, or water, vegetables, and bay leaf to beans (leave vegetables whole; they'll be easier to discard after beans are cooked).

3. Bring beans to a boil, remove from heat, and allow to rest for 1 hour. Return to heat and cook over medium heat, adding water to cover if necessary. Cook for 20 to 30 minutes, or until beans are tender. Allow beans to rest for 10 minutes.

4. Drain beans, discarding any liquid, vegetables, and bay leaf. Place beans in a food processor and purée.* Gradually add olive oil, vinegar, and seasonings, and continue processing until all ingredients are thoroughly combined.

To Serve: Using four egg cups, fill each egg cup about three-quarters full with bean purée. Smooth purée with back of spoon and top with 1 teaspoonful of your favorite caviar or fish roe. Serve with toast. I often top the caviar with a fried or poached quail egg (there you have it, an egg in the egg cup after all).

---

*Save leftover bean purée and use in soups or as a side dish with grilled or roast meat or fish.

Black-Olive Pastry for Puff Shells, Éclairs, Sticks

YIELD: ABOUT 20 PIECES

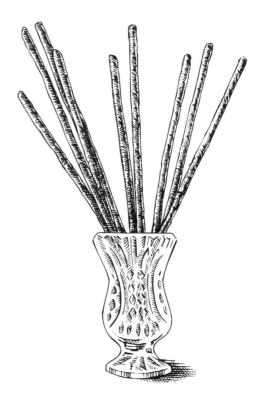

Black-Olive Pastry is easy to prepare and has many uses: the pastry can be formed into tiny puffs or éclairs and filled with a mixture of fish, seafood, or cheese. The pastry can also be baked in long strips and served as breadsticks with soups and pasta dishes.

BLACK-OLIVE PASTRY

1 cup water
4 tablespoons butter
½ cup all-purpose flour
1 teaspoon coarse or kosher salt
¼ teaspoon freshly ground pepper
2 eggs
1 tablespoon Black-Olive Purée (see page 35)
2 tablespoons grated Parmesan cheese

1. Place water and butter in a saucepan and heat to boiling point. Using a wooden spoon, quickly stir in flour, salt, and pepper. Cook over low heat for about 2 minutes, or until mixture coats the bottom of the pan and begins to move away from the sides. Cool slightly.

2. Place mixture in a food processor. Add eggs, one at a time, pulsing on and off, add Black-Olive Purée and cheese, and continue pulsing on and off until pastry is shiny and smooth.

To Bake and Form

1. Preheat oven to 425°.

2. *For Black-Olive Puffs:* Drop pastry mixture by heaping teaspoonfuls onto a lightly oiled baking sheet.

For Black-Olive Éclairs: Using a pastry bag, pipe out small éclairs onto a lightly oiled baking sheet.

For Black-Olive Breadsticks: Using a pastry bag, pipe narrow strips of pastry onto a lightly oiled baking sheet.

3. Bake for 15 minutes.

4. Lower temperature to 375° and continue baking for approximately 5 minutes, or until pastry is crusty. Remove from oven and cool. Cut tops off puffs or éclairs, and spoon out and discard uncooked dough from within.

Fillings for Puffs or Éclairs

Goat-Cheese Filling: Combine ¾ cup soft goat cheese with 4 tablespoons olive oil in a food processor and purée. Season to taste and stir in 1 tablespoon chopped fresh basil.

Lobster Filling: Combine ½ cup cooked lobster with 1 tablespoon olive oil and 4 tablespoons mascarpone cheese in food processor and chop finely. Season to taste.

Blue-Cheese Filling: Combine ¾ cup blue cheese with 3 tablespoons olive oil and 1 tablespoon softened butter in a food processor and purée. Add ⅓ cup toasted pine nuts or walnut halves and pulse once or twice in processor (nuts should be in pieces, not ground too fine). Season to taste.

Smoked-Salmon Filling: Combine ¾ cup chopped smoked salmon with 6 tablespoons mascarpone cheese, or soft French cheese such as St.-André, in a food processor and purée. Season to taste and stir in ½ tablespoon chopped fresh dill.

SPOON PREFERRED FILLING into bottom halves of puffs or éclairs and cover with tops of pastries. Serve as hors d'oeuvres or as a starter.

AN ASSORTMENT OF CROQUE SANDWICHES

"Croque" means "crispy" or "crusty," and Croque Monsieur is a cheese-and-ham sandwich sautéed in butter until crisp. A Croque Madame is a more delicate variation on the same theme—the ingredients are much the same, but for Madame the sandwich is open-faced.

In France, I was served croque sandwiches for lunch or cut into quarters with an apéritif. I like these crispy tidbits, but to vary the filling I took the basic croque a step further and decided to fill the sandwiches with shrimp purée, thinly sliced yellowfin tuna, or chicken mousse. The fillings are spread on white bread—a French-type *pain de mie,* not a soft or mushy bread—or on slices of brioche, and a mayonnaise is prepared that complements each croque. With yellowfin tuna, for example, the mayonnaise contains wasabi—the Japanese horseradish powder—and Ginger Oil.

Croque with Shrimp

YIELD: 4 SERVINGS

½ pound shrimp, peeled and deveined
Zest and juice of 1 lemon
1 tablespoon coarse or kosher salt
1 teaspoon freshly ground pepper
1 tablespoon chopped fresh tarragon
1 tablespoon chopped fresh parsley
1 cup olive oil
8 slices white bread
Butter or Shrimp Oil (see variation, page 168)
    for sautéing

1. Place half of shrimp (¼ pound) in a food processor and purée.
2. Add lemon zest and juice, salt, pepper, and herbs. Gradually add olive oil and continue processing until all ingredients are puréed. Spoon purée into a bowl.
3. Cut remaining shrimp into a small dice and fold into shrimp purée.
4. Spoon shrimp mixture on four slices of bread. Cover with remaining bread slices. Heat butter or Shrimp Oil in a sauté pan, preferably with a nonstick surface. Sauté sandwiches over

low heat, turning so that bread is golden brown and shrimp are hot and completely cooked.

5. Remove sandwiches from pan, using a slotted spatula, and drain on paper towels. Add salt to taste. Cut each sandwich into quarters.

Variation: Prepare a Horseradish Mayonnaise by combining ½ tablespoon ground horseradish and 2 tablespoons mayonnaise. Mix thoroughly and spread on bread slices before adding shrimp mixture.

Croque with Yellowfin Tuna and Wasabi Mayonnaise

YIELD: 4 SERVINGS

2 tablespoons water
2 tablespoons wasabi powder*
1 egg yolk
½ cup Ginger Oil (see page 124)
8 slices white bread or brioche slices
½ pound yellowfin tuna, cut into 4 slices,
    approximately the same size as bread
    slices
Coarse or kosher salt and freshly ground pepper
    to taste
Ginger Oil for sautéing

*Wasabi powder can be purchased in supermarkets, gourmet stores, and shops specializing in Oriental ingredients.

1. Combine water and wasabi powder in a bowl and mix. Add egg yolk and whisk. Slowly add Ginger Oil, whisking together until mixture thickens into a mayonnaise.

2. Spread Wasabi Mayonnaise on 8 slices of bread.

3. Place a slice of tuna each on 4 of the bread slices. Season to taste. Cover with remaining bread slices.

4. Heat Ginger Oil in a sauté pan, preferably with a nonstick surface. Sauté sandwiches over low heat, turning so that bread is a golden brown. Do not overcook. Tuna should be rare or, at most, medium-rare.

5. Remove sandwiches from pan, using a slotted spatula, and drain on paper towels. Salt to taste. Cut sandwiches into quarters.

1. Combine Chicken Purée, blue cheese, and bacon in a bowl. Mix until thoroughly combined.

2. Combine mayonnaise and cayenne pepper in another bowl and mix until thoroughly combined.

3. Spread mayonnaise on 8 slices of bread. Spoon chicken mixture on 4 of the bread slices. Cover with remaining bread slices.

4. Heat butter in a sauté pan, preferably with a nonstick surface. Sauté sandwiches over low heat, turning so that bread is golden brown and chicken mixture is hot and thoroughly cooked.

5. Remove sandwiches from pan, using a slotted spatula, and drain on paper towels. Add salt to taste; there is bacon in the mixture, so you won't need too much. Cut sandwiches into quarters.

Chicken, Bacon, Blue-Cheese Croque with Cayenne Mayonnaise

YIELD: 4 SERVINGS

1 cup Chicken Purée with Cream (see page 35)
½ cup crumbled blue cheese
6 slices bacon, sautéed, drained, and crumbled
4 tablespoons mayonnaise
½ teaspoon cayenne pepper
8 slices bread
Butter for sautéing
Coarse or kosher salt to taste

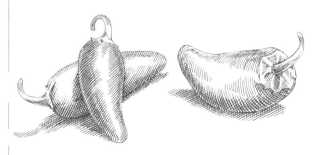

Celery-Root Napoleons

YIELD: ABOUT 12 NAPOLEONS

Celery root—possibly more familiar as *céleri rave*—is not as appreciated in the United States as it should be. This root vegetable—not to be confused with stalks of celery—can be made into chips, and combines beautifully with potatoes in a purée. Celery root adds a fine flavor to chicken or beef stock and can also be prepared with a vinaigrette or mayonnaise for an hors d'oeuvre. In this recipe, celery root is prepared two ways: as a chip and as a purée. I recommend serving it with roast fowl or grilled shellfish.

1 or 2 celery roots (about 1½ to 2 pounds),
*   peeled*
1 large baking potato, peeled and cubed
⅓ cup olive oil
⅓ cup butter
Coarse or kosher salt and freshly ground white
*   pepper to taste*
4 cups vegetable oil
⅓ cup Tomato Concasse (see page 43)

1. Cut half of total celery root into large cubes.
2. Place celery root and potato cubes in saucepan, cover with water, and cook for 20 minutes, or until ingredients are tender.
3. Drain and purée in a food processor; gradually add olive oil, butter, salt, and pepper. Reserve.
4. Cut remaining celery root into thin slices (you should have about 24 slices). Heat oil in an electric deep fryer to 300° to 325°. Place celery-root slices in basket of fryer and cook until golden and crisp.
5. Using a slotted spoon, remove chips from fryer and drain on paper towels.

To Assemble: Place a celery-root chip on a plate. Top with a spoonful of purée. Cover with another chip. Garnish with Tomato Concasse. Four layers equal one napoleon. Continue until all ingredients are used.

Crabmeat-Scallop Zucchini Rolls

YIELD: 4 SERVINGS

*1 cup fresh lump crabmeat, picked clean of
    cartilage*
¼ cup Scallop Purée (see page 37)
1 teaspoon coarse or kosher salt
½ teaspoon freshly ground pepper
2 medium zucchini, thinly sliced lengthwise
2 eggs, lightly beaten
¾ cup all-purpose flour
*2 cups bread crumbs or 1 cup bread crumbs
    combined with ¼ cup ground caraway
    seeds★*
*Clarified Butter or vegetable oil for
    sautéing*

*★I like to use a variety of ingredients to create crusts. Expecting
plain bread crumbs, everyone is happily surprised by new flavors
when bread crumbs are combined with spices. Caraway seeds can be
ground in a small food processor or in a spice mill, and ground fennel seeds can be substituted for the caraway.*

1. Place crabmeat, Scallop Purée, salt, and
pepper in a bowl. Mix until thoroughly combined.

2. Place a small amount of crabmeat-scallop
mixture on one end of a zucchini slice. Roll slice
tightly. Brush end of zucchini slice with egg to
seal. Dredge zucchini roll in flour and dip in
egg. Place on rack to drain for 5 minutes. Repeat
until all ingredients are used.

3. Roll zucchini rolls in bread crumbs or
crumb-and-caraway-seed mixture.

4. Heat Clarified Butter or vegetable oil in a
sauté pan, preferably with a nonstick surface.
Saute zucchini rolls over medium heat, a few at
a time, turning until rolls are golden brown and
crisp. Remove from pan with a slotted spatula
and drain on paper towels.

5. Serve as an appetizer with Salsa (see
page 179) or Mustard Mousse (see page 41).
Crabmeat-Scallop Zucchini Rolls are an excellent accompaniment to soft-shell crabs or grilled
fish, and I also like them with salad.

Duck-Liver Mousse

YIELD: 2 CUPS

2 shallots, peeled and chopped
1 cup dry vermouth or dry white wine
1 tablespoon peppercorns
¼ cup heavy sweet cream
2 eggs, lightly beaten
½ pound duck livers
½ pound butter, melted
3 tablespoons coarse or kosher salt
2 teaspoons freshly ground pepper
2 tablespoons Madeira wine

1. Preheat oven to 325°.

2. Combine shallots, vermouth, and peppercorns in a small saucepan. Bring to a boil and reduce until liquid has consistency of a syrup. Strain and allow to cool.

3. Stir in cream gradually, and slowly add eggs, stirring to combine. Reserve.

4. Wash duck livers and cut off any visible fat. Place duck livers in a food processor and purée, gradually adding cream-egg mixture. Add butter gradually and continue processing just until ingredients are incorporated.

5. Season duck mixture with salt, pepper, and wine and process until ingredients are just mixed.

6. Strain mixture through a very fine strainer or *chinois* to eliminate any liver fibers or sinews. Spoon mixture into a 2-cup ovenproof ramekin or small terrine.*

7. Place ramekin or terrine in a *bain-marie* and bake mousse for 25 to 30 minutes, or until middle is slightly firm to the touch and skewer comes out clean when mousse is pierced.

8. Allow mousse to cool, and refrigerate overnight.

9. Serve mousse with toast and thinly sliced raw Bermuda onions, or use as a filling for ravioli, strudels, or cherry tomatoes (see page 73).

*Mousse can also be spooned into 2-ounce individual ramekins and baked for 10 to 15 minutes, or until just set.

Shiitake-Mushroom Caps on Mousse Stems

YIELD: 4 SERVINGS

I was about to stuff a shiitake-mushroom cap with duck-liver mousse when the ingredients suggested a new presentation. The mushrooms, I decided, would look more appealing resting on a stem of mousse. Using a pastry bag with a Number 5 tip, I piped a two-inch stem of mousse on a plate and placed the mushroom cap on top. I surrounded the stem with shreds of assorted delicate lettuce, and I piped four dots of Thick Walnut-Oil Vinaigrette on top of each mushroom cap. It looked—and tasted—magnificent.

To prepare this dish successfully, you must make sure that the plates you'll be using are

1. Heat olive oil in a sauté pan. Add shallot and cook, stirring, for 2 minutes. Add mushroom caps and continue cooking, stirring occasionally, for 2 to 3 minutes.

2. Season mushrooms and, using a slotted spoon, remove from pan and refrigerate.

3. Add vinegar to pan and reduce, stirring, for 2 minutes. Spoon into a bowl and allow oil-vinegar mixture to cool completely. Toss lettuce in mixture.

4. Spoon very cold Duck-Liver Mousse into a pastry bag. Remove 4 chilled plates from the refrigerator and pipe a 2-inch cylinder of mousse to stand upright on each plate. Place a mushroom cap on the top of each mousse stem and surround with lettuce. If you wish, pipe 4 dots of Thick Walnut-Oil Vinaigrette on each mushroom cap.

5. Add Mushroom Chips to each plate and serve with toast.

chilled and that the mousse is very cold. If the mousse is not cold enough, the mushroom stem will collapse. Start out by chilling the plates and the mousse in the refrigerator, and then go from there.

6 tablespoons olive oil
1 shallot, minced
8 shiitake-mushroom caps
Coarse or kosher salt and freshly ground pepper
  to taste
2½ tablespoons sherry-wine vinegar or balsamic
  vinegar
Lettuce combination: may be frisée, curly endive,
  arugula, watercress, torn into small pieces,
  approximately 2 cups
1½ cups Duck-Liver Mousse (see previous
  recipe)
¼ cup Thick Walnut-Oil Vinaigrette (see page
  173), optional
1 cup Mushroom Chips (see page 47)

Smoked-Fish Falafel

YIELD: ABOUT 75
SMOKED-FISH FALAFELS

Falafel is usually a fried ball of chick-pea purée, but a lot more can be done with the basic recipe. I season the chick-pea purée with coriander, cumin, or curry and add smoked fish. Shrimp, lobster, or crabmeat may also be used. Smoked-Fish Falafel can be served at a cocktail party, tucked into pita bread, or offered with a salad of radicchio and arugula as a first course.

1 pound cooked chick-peas (follow procedure
    in recipe for White-Bean Purée and
    Caviar, page 53) or canned, drained
    chick-peas
3 tablespoons tahini paste
3 tablespoons Ginger Purée (see page
    38)
1 cup toasted sesame seeds
1½ teaspoons cayenne pepper
½ cup chopped coriander
½ cup chopped parsley
1 tablespoon sesame oil
2 eggs
2 tablespoons coarse or kosher salt
1 teaspoon freshly ground pepper
1 pound smoked fish, may be whitefish, trout,
    or salmon
½ cup all-purpose flour
Clarified Butter or vegetable oil for
    sautéing

1. Place chick-peas in a food processor and purée, gradually adding all other ingredients up to smoked fish. Depending on the size of your processor, you may have to do this in 2 or more steps.

2. After ingredients are puréed, add smoked fish and process just until smoked fish is incorporated into chick-pea mixture.

3. Place a sheet of parchment paper or waxed paper on a cookie sheet and lightly dust with flour. Place remaining flour in a shallow bowl. Using a small ice-cream scoop or spoon, make 1-inch balls from chick-pea–smoked-fish mixture. Roll each ball in flour and place on parchment paper.

4. Heat Clarified Butter or vegetable oil in a large sauté pan, preferably with a nonstick surface. Over medium heat, sauté falafels a few at a time. Do not overcrowd pan. Turn falafels so that they brown and crisp on all sides and, using a slotted spoon, remove from pan and drain on paper towels.

Variation: Substitute crabmeat or peeled, deveined shrimp for smoked fish.

Warm Oysters with Sweet Corn and Mushroom Chips

YIELD: 6 SERVINGS

*T*his combination of oysters, corn, and earthy mushrooms brings together the taste of the earth and the sea.

1 quart Light Chicken Stock (see page 76) or canned chicken broth

4 ears fresh corn or 2 cups cooked corn kernels

¼ pound butter

Coarse or kosher salt and freshly ground pepper to taste

1 cup chopped chives

36 oysters on the half-shell

1 cup Mushroom Chips (see page 47)

1. Prepare a corn stock by combining Light Chicken Stock or broth and ears of corn. Bring to a boil. Reduce heat and simmer for 10 to 12 minutes, or until corn is tender. (If using cooked corn kernels, simmer for only 3 minutes.)

2. Strain stock and cut kernels from corncobs. Return cobs to stock and cook over low heat for 15 minutes, until stock is reduced to approximately 1 pint. (If corn kernels are used, strain and reserve kernels, and cook stock over low heat for 15 minutes, until stock is reduced to approximately 1 pint.)

3. Preheat oven to 350°.

4. Return kernels to the stock and bring to a simmer. Add butter and whisk until stock and butter are combined. Sauce will be thick.

5. Season to taste and stir in chives. Keep sauce warm over low heat.

6. Place oysters on a cookie sheet or in a shallow baking pan. Heat in oven for 4 minutes.

7. Place oysters on a serving platter or on 6 individual plates. Pour sauce over oysters and serve with Mushroom Chips.

Oysters with Watercress on Roasted Peppercorns

YIELD: 4 SERVINGS

I like to present oysters on a bed of warm peppercorns. It's an attractive presentation that creates a surprise, and the aroma adds a wonderful spicy scent to the surroundings, piquing the appetite. I recommend that you purchase peppercorns at a market where they're sold by the pound. If you can't, you'll need one pound of white and one pound of black peppercorns in one- or two-ounce jars. Save the peppercorns after the oysters are eaten. They can be heated again or used in a pepper mill to flavor other dishes.

1 bunch watercress
¼ pound butter, cut into 8 pieces
2 shallots, peeled and minced
4 tablespoons Riesling wine
24 oysters, shucked, shells and oyster liquid
*   reserved*
Coarse or kosher salt and freshly ground pepper
*   to taste*
1 pound black peppercorns
1 pound white peppercorns

1. Preheat oven to 350°.
2. Blanch watercress in boiling salted water for 20 seconds. Drain and run under cold water to stop cooking. Place watercress in a food processor and purée. Reserve.
3. Heat 1 piece of butter in a saucepan. Add shallots and cook, stirring, for 1 minute. Add wine and cook for another minute. Add liquid from oysters and continue cooking until liquid is reduced by approximately half.
4. Slowly add remaining butter, one piece at a time, and whisk until ingredients are combined. Season to taste. Reserve and keep warm.
5. Combine black and white peppercorns and mix. Place in a shallow pan and bake for about 8 minutes, or until the peppercorns release a spicy aroma.
6. Add oysters and watercress to butter sauce, stir, and heat until oysters are just warm. Oysters should not cook. Correct seasoning.

To Assemble: Divide peppercorns among 4 shallow soup plates. Smooth surface of peppercorns. Place 6 oyster shells on each plate. Place an oyster in each shell and top with sauce. (Do not throw out peppercorns after oysters are consumed.)

Variations: You can substitute clams for the oysters if you wish, and the watercress-butter sauce can be used for other fish dishes. Substitute Light Chicken Stock or canned broth for the liquid from oysters or clams when preparing fish.

Potato Pancakes

YIELD: ABOUT 8 TO 10 PANCAKES

Potato Pancakes can be combined with other ingredients, and may be served as hors d'oeuvres or appetizers, at brunch, lunch, or dinner; in fact, there's no time when a Potato Pancake isn't welcome. A recipe for Potato Pancakes with apples and ginger cream follows, and Potato Pancakes may also be served with smoked salmon, grilled fish, and squab.

Neither flour nor eggs are used; the starch in the potatoes holds the pancake together. I make pancakes fairly thick when they're used as a base for fried eggs, grilled fish, or barbecued breast of squab. When pancakes are more than a quarter of an inch thick, they're transferred from the sauté pan to a baking sheet and baked in a 325° oven for five to ten minutes.

2 large baking potatoes, peeled
3 shallots, peeled
1 egg
Coarse or kosher salt and freshly ground
    pepper to taste
Clarified Butter or olive oil for sautéing

1. Combine potatoes, shallots, and egg in a food processor and grate.

2. Spoon grated-potato mixture into a bowl and add salt and pepper. Heat Clarified Butter or olive oil in a large sauté pan, preferably with a nonstick surface.

3. Spoon 2 or more tablespoons of potato mixture into pan for each pancake. The thickness and diameter of the pancakes will depend on how they are to be used. Cook pancakes until golden brown, turning frequently.

Potato Pancakes with Apples, Ginger Cream, and Apple Crackling

YIELD: 4 SERVINGS

½ cup crème fraîche
¼ cup Ginger Purée (see page 38)
2 Granny Smith or other tart apples, each cut in
    half, cored, and sliced
8 Potato Pancakes (see previous recipe)
Apple Crackling (see page 24)

1. Make Ginger Cream: Whip *crème fraîche* until thick, and stiff peaks are formed. Fold in Ginger Purée.

2. Divide apple slices into 4 portions and place them in a fan shape on 4 plates. Place 2 Potato Pancakes on each plate. Spoon Ginger Cream over pancakes and top with Apple Crackling.

Crabmeat Stuffed Rigatoni

YIELD: 8 TO 10 SERVINGS

*T*hese filled rigatoni are simple to prepare and can be made ahead of time. Rigatoni may be filled with scallop, shrimp, chicken purée, or a shellfish combination such as the one used in this recipe.

½ pound rigatoni, cooked al dente, or firm to the bite

1 cup Scallop Purée (see page 37)

1 cup cooked lump crabmeat, cleaned of cartilage

2 teaspoons coarse or kosher salt

1 teaspoon freshly ground pepper

2 teaspoons curry powder

1 tablespoon butter, softened

2 cups Light Chicken Stock (see page 76) or canned chicken broth

¼ cup Tomato Fondue (see page 44)

4 tablespoons butter, softened

1. Preheat oven to 350°.

2. After rigatoni are cooked, allow to cool until they can be easily handled.

3. Combine Scallop Purée, crabmeat, salt, pepper, and curry powder in a large bowl. Mix until thoroughly combined. Place mixture in a pastry bag with a Number 5 tip and carefully fill each rigatoni. (A small spoon can be used instead of a pastry bag.)

4. Spread 1 tablespoon softened butter over the bottom of a large baking pan. Place filled rigatoni in pan. Add Light Chicken Stock or broth.

5. Cover pan with foil and bake for 10 minutes, or until rigatoni are completely heated through and filling is hot and cooked.

6. Using a slotted spoon, remove rigatoni carefully from pan. Place on a serving platter and keep warm.

7. Pour sauce from baking pan into a saucepan. Add Tomato Fondue and 4 tablespoons butter. Bring to a simmer and cook for 2 to 3 minutes, until ingredients are combined. Correct seasoning. Pour sauce over rigatoni.

Ratatouille

YIELD: ABOUT 1 QUART

*S*poon Ratatouille into the center of a dinner plate and top with steamed fish, or serve this vegetable mélange with shrimp or sweetbreads. Don't peel the eggplant. The color and slightly bitter flavor of the skin adds an interesting note to the dish.

½ cup olive oil

2 cloves garlic, finely minced

1 small onion, diced

1 red bell pepper, diced

1 yellow bell pepper, diced (use green pepper if
    yellow pepper is not available)

1 small eggplant, about ¼ pound

1 small zucchini

1 small yellow squash

Tomato Concasse, made with 1 tomato (see
    page 43)

½ cup Tomato Fondue (see page 44)

½ cup minced fresh basil leaves

Coarse or kosher salt and freshly ground pepper
    to taste

1. Heat ¼ cup olive oil in a large sauté pan. Add garlic, onion, and peppers and sauté over moderate heat until ingredients are tender. Remove vegetables from pan and reserve.

2. Using only outer layers of vegetables, cut eggplant, zucchini, and squash into a dice (discard seeds and pulp around seeds). Heat remaining olive oil and add eggplant, zucchini, and squash to pan. Cook over moderate heat. The vegetables must cook quickly, so that water from vegetables evaporates and they retain their bright colors. The vegetables are not steamed, they are seared.

3. Add Tomato Concasse, Tomato Fondue, basil, and reserved onion-pepper-garlic mixture to pan. Season and cook an additional 1 to 2 minutes, stirring, until all ingredients are thoroughly combined.

Salmon Ham

YIELD: 10 TO 15 SERVINGS,
DEPENDING ON USE

*T*his dish is named Salmon Ham because the marinade and the technique are similar to those used in curing a ham. The same method can be used with monkfish, halibut, or sturgeon. I like to serve Salmon Ham at brunch or lunch, because it's especially good with an omelette or scrambled eggs. It's also delicious in a "ham-and-cheese sandwich" made with mascarpone cheese on a baguette. Serve Salmon Ham as an hors d'oeuvre or a first course with a drizzle of Mustard Oil. After Salmon Ham is removed from the marinade, it will keep for four to five days, refrigerated.

1 side salmon, about 2 to 2½ pounds, skin and
    bones removed

2 cups soy sauce

¾ cup honey

6 tablespoons water

3 cloves garlic, minced

2 teaspoons freshly ground pepper

1. Place fish on a platter. Combine all other ingredients and spoon over fish. Cover and refrigerate.

2. Marinate fish for 36 to 48 hours. Turn fish once in marinade.

3. Remove salmon from marinade. Pat dry and cut into thin slices diagonally.

Parfait of Salmon and Tuna Tartars with Crème Fraîche

YIELD: 10 SERVINGS

*T*his is one of my favorite dishes and one of the most popular in my restaurant. It offers a counterpoint of flavors and a presentation to delight the eye. The parfait is composed of alternating layers of salmon tartar, tuna tartar, and *crème fraîche* topped, if you wish, with caviar.

To form the parfait, you will need cylindrical rings that are approximately two inches high and two inches in diameter. When I devised this dish, I went to a hardware store that specialized in construction material and had them cut steel pipes into two-inch rings. However, any circular object can be used: pastry rings, cookie cutters, biscuit cutters, pancake rings, and even bracelets. The parfait can also be prepared in a ramekin or demitasse cup, but then the impact of viewing the parfait in its entirety is lost.

1 cup crème fraîche
2 shallots, peeled and minced
4 tablespoons olive oil
2 tablespoons chopped capers
2 teaspoons lemon zest
4 teaspoons soy sauce
2 teaspoons ground horseradish
2 tablespoons chopped coriander
2 tablespoons chopped chervil
10 ounces yellowfin tuna, diced
10 ounces salmon, ground
2 teaspoons coarse or kosher salt
2 teaspoons freshly ground pepper
Olive oil for rings
10 ounces Osetra or other caviar (optional)*

1. Whip *crème fraîche* until thick, and stiff peaks are formed. Reserve in refrigerator.

2. Combine shallots and olive oil in a small saucepan and sauté until shallots are translucent. Place shallots in a bowl and add capers, lemon zest, soy sauce, horseradish, coriander, and chervil. Mix until combined.

3. Divide shallot mixture into two equal parts. Combine one half with diced tuna; combine the other half with ground salmon. Add 1 teaspoon salt and 1 teaspoon pepper to tuna mixture and mix until all ingredients are combined. Add 1 teaspoon salt and 1 teaspoon pepper to salmon mixture and mix until all ingredients are combined.

4. Lightly brush inside of 10 rings or molds with olive oil.

5. Place waxed paper on a cookie sheet. Place molds on the cookie sheet.

To Assemble

1. Place 2 tablespoons of tuna mixture in each mold. Smooth tuna mixture with back of spoon. Place 2 tablespoons of salmon mixture on top of tuna mixture. Smooth salmon mixture with back of spoon.

**If you wish, you may spoon 2 tablespoons of caviar on top of salmon mixture before topping with *crème fraîche*. You will then have 4 layers.

2. Add 2 tablespoons of *crème fraîche*. Smooth with blade of flat knife, making sure that *crème fraîche* is level with top of mold. You should have 3 equal layers.

3. Chill in refrigerator for 2 to 3 hours. Place each ring or mold on a plate and gently remove mold, leaving parfait on plate. Serve with toast.

Pastrami Salmon

YIELD: 10 SERVINGS AS A STARTER
OR MORE AS HORS D'OEUVRES

After my stay in Norway, I experimented with gravlax recipes and developed this spicier version, which I named after the American delicatessen favorite.

*1 side salmon, about 2 to 2½ pounds, skin and
    bones removed*
1 cup coarse or kosher salt
½ cup sugar
2 bunches fresh coriander
1 bunch fresh Italian parsley
½ pound shallots, peeled
½ cup molasses
2 tablespoons cayenne pepper
5 bay leaves
4 tablespoons paprika
4 tablespoons ground coriander seed
4 tablespoons freshly ground black pepper
4 tablespoons cracked pepper
Mustard Oil
Rye toast
Potato Pancakes (optional)

1. Place salmon on a platter. Combine salt and sugar. Mix well, and coat both sides of salmon with salt mixture.

2. Combine coriander, parsley, and shallots in a food processor and purée. Coat both sides of salmon with purée.

3. Refrigerate salmon for 2 to 3 days.

4. Scrape marinade from fish and discard. Dry fish with paper towels.

5. Combine molasses, cayenne pepper, and bay leaves in a saucepan. Bring to a boil and simmer for 1 minute. Allow molasses mixture to cool and, using a brush, paint fish on both sides with molasses mixture.

6. Sprinkle paprika, coriander, ground black pepper, and cracked pepper on both sides of fish. Refrigerate salmon overnight.

To Serve: Cut Pastrami Salmon into thin slices on the bias, or diagonally, and serve with Mustard Oil, rye toast, and (if you wish) Potato Pancakes (see page 65).

Sautéed Sea Scallops with Morels and Pistachios

YIELD: 6 SERVINGS

¾ pound white mushrooms, thinly sliced
2 cups Dark Chicken Stock (see page 77) or
    canned beef broth
6 tablespoons butter
1 shallot, minced
18 morel mushrooms
½ cup toasted pistachio nuts*
½ cup chopped chives
Coarse or kosher salt and freshly ground pepper
    to taste
¼ cup olive oil
12 large sea scallops

1. Prepare a mushroom stock by combining white mushrooms and Dark Chicken Stock or canned beef broth. Cook until reduced to approximately 1 cup. Strain stock and discard solids.

2. Heat 2 tablespoons butter in a sauté pan. Add shallot and morel mushrooms. Sauté for 2 minutes, stirring. Add mushroom stock and continue cooking, stirring, for 3 minutes. (You're deglazing the pan with the mushroom stock.)

3. Add remaining butter, pistachios, and chopped chives. Season to taste and cook for another minute, or until all ingredients are combined. Reserve.

* To toast pistachio nuts: Preheat oven to 325°. Place shelled nuts on a baking sheet and toast for approximately 5 minutes. Pistachio nuts should be a light brown.

4. Heat olive oil in a sauté pan, preferably with a nonstick surface. Pat scallops dry with paper towels and season with salt and pepper. Sauté scallops quickly over high heat for about 30 seconds on each side. Scallops will be medium-rare in the center. Cook an additional 15 seconds if you want them cooked through.

5. Using 6 medium-sized serving plates, place 2 scallops in the center of each plate. Spoon morel-pistachio sauce around scallops.

Shrimp and Jalapeño Jack Cheese Quesadillas

YIELD: 40 TO 50

Traditionally, quesadillas are flat tortillas with topping—almost like thick pizzas. I often serve them rolled and lay them across a bowl of Black-Bean Soup or Gazpacho. These quesadillas are miniature sandwiches and may be served with salads or as an hors d'oeuvre.

1 pound medium shrimp, peeled and deveined
    (about 20 to 25)
2 eggs
1 tablespoon coarse or kosher salt
1 teaspoon freshly ground pepper
½ cup shredded Jalapeño Jack cheese
16 6-inch flour or corn tortillas
Vegetable oil for cooking

1. Place shrimp in a food processor and purée roughly. Add eggs, salt, and pepper, and continue processing until purée is fairly smooth.

2. Spoon shrimp purée into a bowl and fold in cheese. Mix until all ingredients are combined. Reserve.

3. Using a 1½-inch cookie cutter, cut tortillas into small rounds.

4. Place half of the tortilla rounds on a board or platter and spoon 1 tablespoon of shrimp mixture on each of the tortillas. Top with remaining tortilla rounds. (You now have small tortilla sandwiches.) Place quesadillas in refrigerator and chill for 30 minutes.

5. Lightly oil a griddle or sauté pan, preferably with a nonstick surface. Cook quesadillas over low heat, turning until they're crisp and golden on both sides.

6. Using a slotted spatula, remove quesadillas from griddle or pan and drain on paper towels.

Shrimp and Jalapeño Jack Cheese Strudels

YIELD: 40 TO 50

Filling for Shrimp and Jalapeño Jack Cheese
Quesadillas (see previous recipe)
10 sheets phyllo dough
½ cup Clarified Butter
1 egg, beaten
Vegetable oil for cooking

1. Prepare filling for Shrimp and Jalapeño Jack Cheese Quesadillas.

2. Remove 2 sheets of phyllo dough from the package. Unfold 1 sheet of phyllo dough and generously butter one side with Clarified Butter. Cover with second sheet of phyllo dough and brush this sheet with butter as well.

3. Cut the sheets of phyllo dough lengthwise into 2 strips. Cut each strip crosswise into 8 or 9 pieces (each piece will be about 2½ inches wide).

4. Place a scant tablespoon of shrimp mixture at 1 end of each piece of phyllo dough. Roll halfway down, then tuck in sides and continue rolling. Seal ends of each roll with beaten egg.

5. Continue using sheets of phyllo dough, 2 at a time, until shrimp mixture is used up.

6. Heat ¼ inch of vegetable oil in a sauté pan, preferably with a nonstick surface. Sauté strudels a few at a time, being careful not to crowd pan, and turning until each strudel is crisp and golden brown.

7. Using a slotted spatula, remove strudels from pan and drain on paper towels.

Shrimp and Ginger Wontons

YIELD: 50 WONTONS

I got the idea for this dish when I was shopping in Chinatown and bought a package of ready-made wonton skins. Since then I've made this dish with my own pasta, but I recommend ready-made wonton skins for the cook at home.

Shrimp and Ginger Wontons can be served with Ginger Oil (see page 124), which intensifies the flavor, or they can be offered with Gazpacho (see page 83), and they add a crisp touch to a salad, especially one garnished with shrimp or prawns.

Keep wonton skins in your freezer. They can be filled with purées of shrimp, scallops, shallots, or vegetables.

1 pound medium shrimp, peeled and deveined
   (about 20 to 25)
3 tablespoons Ginger Purée (see page 38)
½ cup chopped chives
2 teaspoons lemon juice
1 tablespoon coarse or kosher salt
1 tablespoon soy sauce
1 teaspoon freshly ground pepper
1 package wonton skins (50 in a package)
1 egg, lightly beaten
Vegetable oil for cooking

1. Place shrimp in a food processor and purée until fairly smooth.

2. Spoon into a bowl and fold in Ginger Purée, chives, lemon juice, salt, soy sauce, and pepper. Mix until thoroughly combined.

3. Lay out wonton skins, 5 at a time. Place 1½ teaspoons of shrimp mixture in center of each wonton skin and fold over into a triangular shape. Brush edges with beaten egg to seal. Continue until all wonton skins are filled.

4. Heat ¼ inch of oil in a sauté pan, preferably with a nonstick surface. Sauté wontons, a few at a time, making sure not to overcrowd the pan. Turn wontons from side to side until they are crisp and golden.

5. Using a slotted spatula, remove wontons from pan and drain on paper towels.

Variation: This shrimp-and-ginger mixture can also be used as a filling for phyllo dough. See recipe for Shrimp and Jalapeño Jack Cheese Strudels (page 71), and follow directions.

Sweetbread and Raisin Terrine

YIELD: 6 SERVINGS

I serve this terrine in many different ways, including slightly chilled as an appetizer or warm as a foundation for medallions of veal. The terrine can also be the centerpiece of a dish built in layers: a Potato Pancake topped with a blanched slice of celery root, completed with a slice of terrine.

½ cup dark raisins

½ cup golden raisins

½ cup Calvados

1 small pair sweetbreads, about 1 pound

2 tablespoons white wine vinegar

2 cups Chicken Purée with Chicken Stock (see page 36)

½ cup chopped chives

Coarse or kosher salt and freshly ground pepper to taste

1 tablespoon butter

1. Combine raisins and Calvados in a bowl. Mix and allow to steep for 8 hours or overnight.

2. Soak sweetbreads in cold water for 1 hour. Drain.

3. Preheat oven to 350°.

4. Place sweetbreads in a saucepan with water to cover. Add vinegar. Bring to a boil, remove from heat, and allow sweetbreads to remain in water for 15 minutes. Drain and remove membrane and connective tubes. Separate sweetbreads into 8 to 10 nuggets.

5. Combine sweetbreads, drained raisins, Chicken Purée, chives, salt, and pepper in a bowl. Mix to combine. To test seasoning, sauté a teaspoonful of mixture in a sauté pan. Correct seasoning.

6. Butter a 1-quart terrine or loaf pan and spoon sweetbread mixture into it. Smooth top with a knife and cover with parchment paper or foil.

7. Place in a *bain-marie* and bake for 45 minutes to 1 hour, or until a knife inserted in center of terrine comes out clean.

8. Allow terrine to rest for 20 minutes before slicing. May be served warm or cold.

Cherry Tomatoes Filled with Duck-Liver Mousse

YIELD: 16 PIECES

*T*his excellent hors d'oeuvre is well worth the work of preparation. The hot *foie gras* becomes almost liquid when fried. Make sure the tomato is very cold before frying, and tell your guests to consume the tomato in one bite.

16 cherry tomatoes

1 cup Duck-Liver Mousse (see page 60), room temperature

1 cup all-purpose flour

3 eggs, lightly beaten

2 cups bread crumbs

Vegetable oil for sautéing

Coarse or kosher salt to taste

1. Remove stem end from each tomato and, with a very sharp paring knife, cut a small opening in top of each tomato. Gently squeeze out seeds and pulp.

2. Place Duck-Liver Mousse in a pastry bag with a tip small enough to fit into opening of

tomato. Fill each tomato with mousse and refrigerate tomatoes for 30 minutes.

3. Coat each tomato with flour, eggs, and bread crumbs. Repeat (each tomato must be breaded twice). Refrigerate breaded tomatoes.

4. Heat oil in a large sauté pan, preferably with a nonstick surface. Remove tomatoes from refrigerator and place in sauté pan. Do not crowd pan. Fry tomatoes in two batches if necessary. Turn tomatoes gently and cook until they're golden brown and crisp.

5. Using a slotted spoon, carefully remove tomatoes from pan. Drain on paper towels. Season with salt.

Chapter 4

SOUPS AND PAN STEWS

As I mentioned earlier, I've been especially fond of soups since the time I began working in a New Jersey restaurant when I was seventeen. I was an assistant-assistant-assistant chef—far below the formally titled *"sous-chef,"* and I was fascinated by the large cauldrons of soup that were bubbling on the range. How did the chef create such interesting concoctions? How did he know how much of each ingredient was called for? What I found especially intriguing were the rich soups heavily laced with cream—people were not then as worried about cholesterol and saturated fat.

Since then I've created soups that I often use as a base or carrier for other courses; I combine soup with an hors d'oeuvre, a salad, or a substantial garnish and serve this multifaceted course in one dish.

In addition to soups, I prepare pan stews combining small amounts of liquid with stir-fried shellfish or vegetables and finished with butter,

olive oil, Tomato Fondue, or Tomato Coulis. A pan stew can be served as a main course: Crab Minestrone with Crabmeat-Stuffed Shells, Gazpacho with Crabmeat Salad and Cumin Mousse, Cucumber Linguine with Manila-Clam Sauce. These dishes need nothing more than dessert to complete a meal.

Create your own combinations, adding a tablespoonful of pasta or white beans to Gazpacho, or using Tomato Soup as a liquid background for a swirl of Goat-Cheese Fondue, a small wedge of grilled salmon, or three or four grilled shrimp. You'll achieve a wonderful contrast of flavors, textures, and colors with a savory mousse added to Mushroom Soup or Sweet-Potato and Leek Soup.

A skewer of shellfish placed across a plate of soup makes a far more interesting addition than croutons or crackers. Serve Black-Olive Breadsticks on the side if you're looking for a crisp finish.

Soups originally combined simple ingredients: beans, potatoes, tomatoes. They answered the need to serve many people inexpensively, which is why every culture offers many soup recipes. Search out the bits and pieces in your own refrigerator—cooked meat, fish, extra vegetables—and combine with a stock to create your own original soup recipe.

This chapter includes recipes for a variety of stocks, but if you don't have the time or inclination to prepare them, dishes can be successfully prepared with canned broth. When using a canned product, check the flavor before adding salt.

LIGHT AND DARK CHICKEN STOCKS

A restaurant kitchen is never without soup stocks. They're used in soups, sauces, and stews, adding flavor to many dishes. Most useful are the chicken stocks. A Light Chicken Stock is used mainly in soups; though the flavor is rich, it is not strong enough to overpower other ingredients.

A Dark Chicken Stock is a Light Chicken Stock that has been reduced until it arrives at the very essence of chicken flavor. It's intense, and is used mainly in sauces. Many of the recipes in this book call for one of these stocks, but, as mentioned previously, canned broths may be substituted.

The following stock recipes have been adapted for the cook at home. I recommend

preparing stock, chilling it, and removing and discarding the fat that has risen to the top. The remaining stock can then be frozen in an ice-cube tray, the cubes of stock to be used as needed.

Light Chicken Stock

YIELD: ABOUT 3 QUARTS

5 pounds chicken bones: necks, backs, chicken
    carcasses
6 quarts water
2 onions, quartered
1 carrot, cut into 3 pieces
½ bunch celery, including leaves, roughly
    chopped
1 tablespoon peppercorns
1 bay leaf

1. Rinse chicken bones.
2. Place all ingredients in a large pot. Bring to a boil. Lower heat to a simmer and cook 3 hours. Skim foam every ½ hour and discard. Strain and discard all solids. Refrigerate, and remove and discard all surface fat.

Dark Chicken Stock

YIELD: ABOUT 2 CUPS

5 pounds chicken bones: necks, backs, chicken
  carcasses
6 quarts water
2 onions, quartered
1 carrot, cut into 3 pieces
½ bunch celery, including leaves, roughly
  chopped
1 tablespoon peppercorns
1 bay leaf

1. Rinse chicken bones.
2. Place all ingredients in a large pot. Bring to a boil. Lower heat to a simmer and cook 3 hours. Skim foam every ½ hour and discard.
3. Strain and discard all solids. Return liquid to pot. Simmer until liquid is reduced to approximately 2 cups, 40 minutes to 1 hour.
4. Refrigerate, and remove and discard all surface fat.

Variation: Smoked-Chicken Stock. Follow the same directions, adding either 1 smoked turkey breast or 1 smoked chicken during the last ½ hour of cooking. Reserve smoked turkey or chicken meat for a salad. Smoked stocks are used for soups or sauces that require an especially strong, smoky flavor.

Brown Stock Made with Veal Bones

YIELD: ABOUT 2 CUPS

Brown Stock is used in sauces for meat dishes. After the stock is prepared, I reduce it, discarding all bones and vegetables. A small amount of this reduced stock adds a wonderful, rich flavor to meat dishes. It can keep in your freezer for months, or in your refrigerator for approximately two weeks. Brown Stock Made with Veal Bones can be used in dishes calling for beef, lamb, chicken, duck, pork, and certain fish. When preparing lamb or venison, substitute lamb or venison bones to prepare stock.

5 pounds veal bones or veal trimmings, or
  combination
¼ cup vegetable oil
2 onions, quartered
1 carrot, cut into 3 pieces
1 bunch celery, including leaves, roughly
  chopped
2 cups Tomato Fondue (see page 44)
1 bay leaf
1 tablespoon peppercorns
6 quarts water

1. Preheat oven to 350°.
2. Place bones in a roasting pan, add vegetable oil, and roast until bones are nicely browned, about 30 to 45 minutes. Add vegeta-

bles and Tomato Fondue to roasting pan and cook an additional 15 minutes.

3. Place all ingredients in a large pot. Add bay leaf, peppercorns, and water. Bring to a boil. Lower heat to a simmer and cook 3 to 4 hours, depending on size of bones. Skim foam every ½ hour and discard.

4. Strain and discard all solids. Return liquid to pot. Simmer until liquid is reduced to approximately 2 cups.

5. Refrigerate, and remove and discard all surface fat.

FLAVORED STOCKS

I use flavored stocks to create a continuity of flavor in a dish. If I'm preparing chicken with turnips, for example, I want a chicken-turnip flavor to infuse the dish, and I'll prepare a chicken-turnip stock.

Use stocks when cooking vegetables. Instead of cooking vegetables in water and then discarding the water, cook your vegetables in a Light Chicken Stock. The vegetables and the stock will be enriched by each other, and the stock can be saved for future use.

Cauliflower-Flavored Light Chicken Stock

YIELD: ABOUT 3 CUPS

*C*auliflower-flavored stock can be used as a basis for a cauliflower cream soup, in sauces for pasta or fish, or as a bouillon served in a brandy snifter before dinner.

> *4 cups Light Chicken Stock (see page 76 or canned chicken broth*
> *1 pound cauliflower, separated into florets, stem and leaves retained*

1. Combine Light Chicken Stock or canned broth and cauliflower in a large pot. Bring to a simmer and cook until cauliflower florets are tender.

2. Using a slotted spoon, remove cauliflower from liquid. Discard stems and leaves and reserve florets to use as a vegetable side dish.

Variations: Vegetable-flavored stocks can be prepared with any and all vegetables, including artichoke, asparagus, mushroom, and corn. Follow directions above.

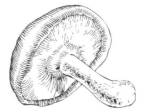

Shellfish-Flavored Stock

YIELD: ABOUT 1 QUART

1 pound shrimp or lobster shells, or shells from
*   hard crabs (shells may be cooked or raw)*
4 cups Light Chicken Stock (see page 76) or
*   canned chicken broth*
1 cup Tomato Fondue (see page 44

1. Combine all ingredients in a saucepan and bring to a boil. Lower heat to a simmer and cook for 20 minutes. This is the time needed to extract the flavor from seafood shells.

2. Strain stock, discarding shells.

Artichoke Soup with Bay Scallops

YIELD: 6 TO 8 SERVINGS

¼ pound butter
2 cups chopped leeks (white part only)
2 potatoes, peeled and chopped
2 quarts Light Chicken Stock (see page 76) or
*   canned chicken broth*
3 medium artichokes, stems removed
1 tablespoon coarse or kosher salt
1 teaspoon freshly ground pepper
¾ pound bay scallops
½ cup chopped chives

1. Heat butter in sauté pan. Add leeks and potatoes. Sauté for 10 minutes. Reserve.

2. Combine stock or broth and artichokes in a large soup pot and bring to a boil. Reduce to a simmer and cook for 35 minutes. Using a slotted spoon, remove artichokes from liquid and cool under running water until they can be easily handled.

3. Remove leaves from artichokes and return leaves to soup pot. Cut chokes from artichoke bottoms, and discard chokes. Dice artichoke bottoms and reserve.

4. Bring liquid with artichoke leaves to a simmer and cook an additional 15 minutes. Strain, and discard leaves.

5. Add sautéed leeks and potatoes to liquid and simmer for 25 minutes, or until potatoes are cooked. Season with salt and pepper.

6. Ladle soup into a food processor and purée. Depending on the size of your processor, you may have to do this in 2 or more steps. Return soup to pot.

7. Bring soup to a simmer and add artichoke bottoms and scallops. Cook for 2 to 3 minutes. Add chives and stir. Serve with cheese croutons, or garnish by placing 3 cooked scallops on bamboo skewers and then placing one skewer across each soup plate.

Black-Bean Soup with Shrimp and Jalapeño Jack Cheese Quesadillas

YIELD: 10 TO 12 SERVINGS

½ pound black turtle beans
3 slices bacon, chopped
4 cloves garlic, chopped
1 small onion, chopped
1 stalk celery, chopped
1 carrot, diced
2 quarts Light Chicken Stock (see page 76) or
    canned chicken broth
½ tablespoon ground cumin
¼ cup chopped fresh coriander or 1 tablespoon
    dried coriander
½ tablespoon cayenne pepper
1 tablespoon coarse or kosher salt
2 tablespoons butter
Shrimp and Jalapeño Jack Cheese
    Quesadillas (see page 70)
Salsa (see page 179), optional

1. Place black beans in a large pot. Cover with water and allow to soak for 8 hours or overnight. Drain and reserve beans.

2. In a soup pot, render the bacon over low heat.

3. Add garlic, onion, celery, and carrot to pot. Sauté over low heat, stirring, for 3 minutes, or until onion is wilted.

4. Add black beans and Light Chicken Stock or broth to pot. Cover and cook for about 1½ hours, or until beans are tender. Add more Light Chicken Stock, broth, or water if necessary, making sure beans are covered with liquid. Add cumin, coriander, cayenne pepper, and salt. Stir to combine.

5. Purée soup in a food processor. Depending on the size of your processor, you may have to do this in 2 or more steps. Return soup to pot. Add butter and whisk until ingredients are combined. Correct seasoning. Simmer until hot.

To Assemble: Ladle soup into individual soup bowls and serve with Shrimp and Jalapeño Jack Cheese Quesadillas and, if desired, Salsa.

White-Bean Soup

½ pound white beans

3 slices bacon, chopped

1 small onion, chopped

1 stalk celery, chopped

1 carrot, sliced

2 quarts Light Chicken Stock (see page 76) or
   canned chicken broth

1 tablespoon coarse or kosher salt

1 teaspoon freshly ground pepper

½ cup Roast-Garlic Purée (see page 28)

2 tablespoons butter

1. Place white beans in a large pot. Cover with water and allow to soak for 8 hours or overnight. Drain and reserve beans.

2. In a large soup pot, render the bacon over low heat. Add onion, celery, and carrot to pot. Sauté over low heat, stirring, for 3 minutes, or until onion is wilted.

3. Add white beans, Light Chicken Stock or broth, salt, and pepper to pot. Cover and cook for 1½ hours, or until beans are tender. Add more chicken stock or water if necessary, making sure beans are covered with liquid.

4. Purée soup in a food processor. Depending on the size of your processor, you may have to do this in 2 or more steps. Return soup to pot and stir in Roast-Garlic Purée. Add butter and whisk until ingredients are combined. Correct seasoning. Simmer until hot.

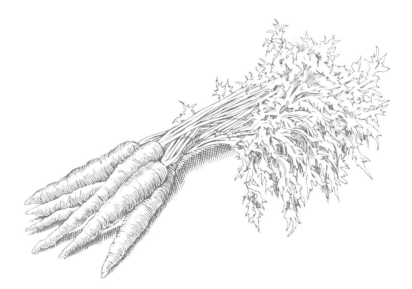

Roast-Eggplant and Roast-Garlic Soup

YIELD: 8 TO 10 SERVINGS

2 eggplants, each about 1 pound
2 tablespoons coarse or kosher salt
½ cup olive oil
4 tablespoons butter
1 onion, diced
¼ cup Roast-Garlic Purée (see page 28)
2 quarts Light Chicken Stock (see page 76) or
*   canned chicken broth*
1 tablespoon freshly ground pepper
Chorizo sausages (optional)

1. Cut each eggplant in half, lengthwise. Score the pulp with a sharp knife. Sprinkle salt over the eggplant pulp and allow eggplant to rest for 1 hour, pulp side down. Salt will draw out the bitter eggplant liquid.

2. Preheat oven to 350°.

3. Rinse eggplant halves and gently squeeze eggplant to drain additional liquid.

4. Spoon olive oil over cut side of eggplant halves. Place eggplant halves in a shallow baking pan and bake for 25 minutes, or until eggplant is brown and tender. Coarsely chop eggplant and reserve.

5. Heat butter in a large saucepan or soup pot. Sauté onion, stirring, for 2 minutes. Add eggplant, Roast-Garlic Purée, Light Chicken Stock or broth, and pepper.

6. Cover and simmer over low heat for 30 minutes.

7. Purée soup in a food processor. Depending on the size of your processor, you may have to do this in 2 or more steps. Return soup to pot.

8. Correct seasoning. Simmer until hot. Serve with sliced chorizo sausages, if desired.

Gazpacho with Crabmeat Salad and Cumin Mousse

YIELD: 10 SERVINGS

GAZPACHO

5 large ripe tomatoes, quartered
½ cucumber, peeled, seeded, chopped
½ red bell pepper, chopped
2 cloves garlic
2 tablespoons coarse or kosher salt
2 teaspoons freshly ground pepper
1 teaspoon cayenne pepper
*½ cup olive oil or Tomato Oil (see page
    169)*

Place all ingredients in a food processor and process until finely puréed. Depending on the size of your processor, you may have to do this in 2 or more steps. Reserve.

CRABMEAT SALAD

*1 pound cooked lump crabmeat, picked clean of
    cartilage*
3 tablespoons olive oil
*3 tablespoons Tomato Fondue (see page
    44)*
2 tablespoons tequila or brandy
2 tablespoons chopped fresh basil
1 tablespoon coarse or kosher salt
1 teaspoon freshly ground pepper

Place crabmeat in a bowl. Add all other ingredients and toss lightly. Reserve.

CUMIN MOUSSE

1 cup crème fraîche
1 tablespoon ground cumin
1½ teaspoons coarse or kosher salt

Place *crème fraîche* in a bowl. Add cumin and salt and whip until cream is stiff.

To Assemble: Place approximately 1½ tablespoons of Crabmeat Salad in each soup bowl. Ladle Gazpacho around crabmeat salad and top with a dollop of Cumin Mousse.

Variations: Gazpacho can be served with quesadillas (see page 70), and lobster or chicken salad can be substituted for the Crabmeat Salad.

Cucumber Linguine with Manila-Clam Sauce

YIELD: 6 SERVINGS

Small Manila clams imported from Canada are used for this pan stew, but if Manila clams are not available, other small clams, such as littlenecks, can be substituted. Cut the cucumber into linguine-like strands, or into batons, about the size of rigatoni. Long English or gourmet cucumbers are best for this recipe, or spaghetti squash may be substituted. The clam sauce can also be served with pasta.

2 red bell peppers

2 yellow bell peppers

3 English cucumbers (also called "gourmet cucumbers")

30 Manila or other small clams

2 cups Dark Chicken Stock (see page 77) or canned chicken broth

1 cup Tomato Concasse (see page 43)

2 cloves garlic, minced

4 shallots, minced

2 cups chopped parsley

6 ounces butter

Coarse or kosher salt and freshly ground pepper to taste

½ cup radish sprouts or chopped parsley

1. Preheat oven to 350°.

2. Broil the red and yellow peppers, turning every few minutes, until skin of peppers is partially black and has blistered. Remove peppers from oven and place in a paper bag. Close bag tightly and allow peppers to cool.

3. When peppers are cooled enough to handle, peel off outer skin. Peppers will peel more easily if they are under cold running water while being peeled.

4. Slice peppers and chop finely. Reserve.

5. Peel cucumbers and run lengthwise through a mandoline to create long linguinelike strands, or cut cucumbers into batons, similar in size to rigatoni. Reserve.

6. Wash clams.

7. Heat Dark Chicken Stock or broth in a large soup pot. Add clams and bring stock to a boil. Add peppers, Tomato Concasse, garlic, shallots, and parsley and *cook* about 2 minutes, or until clams start to open.

8. Add cucumber, butter, salt, and pepper and continue cooking until the cucumber linguine is slightly wilted but still crisp and the clams are completely open.

9. Spoon linguine and clams into 6 individual soup plates and twirl linguine with a fork to create the appearance of spaghetti before serving. Garnish with radish sprouts or chopped parsley.

Harlequin Soup

YIELD: 6 SERVINGS

Harlequin Soup is a combination of Black-Bean Soup and White-Bean Soup in one soup plate. You can either use White-Bean Soup base and then swirl Black-Bean Soup into the plate, or reverse it and have white on black. Whichever your color preference, the soup will look like an abstract work of art.

3 cups Black-Bean Soup (see page 80)
1½ cups White-Bean Soup (see page 81)

1. Heat both soups.

2. Divide Black-Bean Soup among 6 soup plates.

3. Using a large spoon, swirl White-Bean Soup on top of Black-Bean Soup, creating whatever pattern pleases you. Do not stir.

Variation: If you prefer a White-Bean Soup base, reverse the amounts of soup and proceed as above.

Crab Minestrone with Crabmeat-Stuffed Shells

YIELD: 6 TO 8 SERVINGS

ne of my first mentors, Sammy, the chef at the Turning Point Restaurant, inspired this dish. Today, I prepare it for Sammy, who says that it's not like his, but good nevertheless. Though my version is lighter, the historic intention of the original Minestrone is confirmed—a soup that doubles as a one-course meal served in a bowl.

MINESTRONE

½ cup olive oil
6 live hard-shell crabs
½ cup chopped celery
½ cup chopped leeks (white part only)
½ cup chopped fresh basil
6 cloves garlic
1 cup Tomato Fondue (see page 44)
2 quarts Light Chicken Stock (see page 76)
    or canned chicken broth
1 tablespoon coarse or kosher salt
1 tablespoon peppercorns
½ cup diced carrots
½ cup diced celery
½ cup diced green beans
½ cup Tomato Concasse (see page 43)
½ cup chopped spinach
1 cup white beans, cooked
2 cloves garlic, minced
Coarse or kosher salt and freshly ground pepper
    to taste

1. Heat olive oil in a large soup pot. Add crabs, celery, leeks, basil, and garlic. Sauté, stirring, for 5 minutes. Add Tomato Fondue, stock or broth, salt, and peppercorns.

2. Bring liquid to a boil and simmer for 30 minutes, skimming and discarding foam that rises to the top.

3. Drain broth and discard vegetables. (Crabs can be eaten if you wish, but then, obviously, they won't be used for this recipe.) Return broth to soup pot and bring to a simmer.

4. Reduce broth to approximately 1½ quarts. Add carrots, celery, and green beans and cook for about 5 minutes. Add Tomato Concasse, spinach, white beans, minced garlic, salt, and pepper, and simmer an additional 5 minutes.

CRABMEAT-STUFFED SHELLS

¼ pound small pasta shells
3 tablespoons olive oil
¼ cup Scallop Purée (see page 37)
¾ cup fresh lump crabmeat, picked clean of
    cartilage
½ teaspoon coarse or kosher salt
¼ teaspoon freshly ground pepper

1. Cook pasta shells in boiling, salted water until al dente, or firm to the bite. Drain, discard any broken shells, and toss remainder of shells with 1 tablespoon olive oil. Reserve.

2. Preheat oven to 350°.

3. Place Scallop Purée, crabmeat, salt, and pepper in a bowl and mix until thoroughly combined.

4. Spoon scallop-crabmeat mixture into a pastry bag and, using a small Number 3 tip, fill each shell. Coat a baking pan with remaining olive oil and place filled shells in pan. Bake for 10 minutes, or until Scallop Purée is cooked and heated through. (Scallop-crabmeat mixture can also be used to make "meatballs.")

To Assemble: Place 5 or 6 stuffed shells in individual soup plates. Ladle soup around shells. Serve with Italian bread and freshly grated Parmesan cheese, if desired.

Mushroom Soup with Stir-Fried Duck

YIELD: 6 TO 8 SERVINGS

ream-of-mushroom soup enchanted me when I first worked in a restaurant. My recipe is a lighter, more subtle version of an old favorite.

MUSHROOM SOUP

> 4 tablespoons butter
> 1 small onion, chopped
> 2 stalks celery, chopped
> ½ pound mushrooms, chopped
> 1 quart Light Chicken Stock (see page 76) or canned chicken broth
> ½ cup heavy sweet cream
> 1 tablespoon coarse or kosher salt
> ½ tablespoon freshly ground pepper

1. Heat 2 tablespoons butter in a large soup pot. Add onion and celery and sauté for 4 to 5 minutes, until onions are translucent.

2. Add mushrooms to pot and continue cooking for 5 minutes, or until mushroom liquid has been absorbed.

3. Add Light Chicken Stock or broth and bring to a simmer. Cook for 10 minutes. Ladle

soup into a food processor and purée. Depending on the size of your processor, you may have to do this in 2 or more steps. Return soup to pot.

4. Return soup to a simmer and whisk in cream. Add remaining butter and seasoning. Cook an additional 5 minutes, or until all ingredients are combined. Remove from heat and reserve.

STIR-FRIED DUCK

> 2 tablespoons sesame oil
> Duck Confit (see page 132), cut into strips,* approximately 2 cups
> 1 cup snow peas, cut into strips
> 1 cup carrot strips
> 1 cup quartered mushroom caps
> 2 cloves garlic, minced
> 1 teaspoon chopped ginger
> 1 tablespoon coarse or kosher salt
> 2 teaspoons freshly ground pepper

1. Heat oil in a wok or a large sauté pan, preferably with a nonstick surface. Add duck and cook over high heat, stirring, for 1 minute.

2. Add all other ingredients and cook, stirring, for 1 minute, or until ingredients are hot.

To Assemble: Spoon stir-fried duck mixture into 12 bowls. Ladle soup around mixture. An optional garnish could be Lotus-Root Chips, Mushroom Chips, or strands of Pickled Ginger.

*Duck strips and vegetable strips should be short enough to be eaten comfortably with a soup spoon.

Sweet-Potato and Leek Soup with Sage and Smoked Turkey

YIELD: 6 TO 8 SERVINGS

> ¼ pound butter
> 2 cups chopped leeks (white parts only)
> 4 large sweet potatoes, peeled and cubed
> 3 stalks celery, chopped
> 2 quarts Light Chicken Stock (see page 78) or canned chicken broth
> ¼ cup chopped fresh sage or 1 tablespoon dried sage
> 3 tablespoons coarse or kosher salt
> 1 tablespoon freshly ground pepper
> 4 tablespoons butter
> 1 pound smoked turkey, preferably breast of turkey, diced
> Fresh-Herb Wafers (see page 31), optional

1. Heat butter in a large saucepan or soup pot. Add leeks, sweet potatoes, and celery and sauté over low heat until leeks are wilted and lightly golden.

2. Add Light Chicken Stock or broth, sage, salt, and pepper. Cover and simmer for 30 to

40 minutes, or until potatoes are very tender.

3. Purée soup in a food processor. Depending on the size of your processor, you may have to do this in 2 or more steps.

4. Return soup to pot and bring to a boil. Reduce to a simmer and correct seasoning. Add butter and whisk until it is completely blended into soup. Add diced turkey.

5. Pour soup into a tureen or ladle into individual soup bowls. Serve with Fresh-Herb Wafers, if desired.

Variation: Substitute a savory Cumin Mousse for the sage.

Tomato Soup

YIELD: IO TO I2 SERVINGS

½ cup olive oil

2 onions, chopped

3 stalks celery, chopped

6 cloves garlic, chopped

3 pounds canned Italian plum tomatoes, peeled and seeded, with liquid

2 quarts Light Chicken Stock (see page 76) or canned chicken broth

2 tablespoons coarse or kosher salt

2 tablespoons freshly ground pepper

1 cup chopped fresh basil

4 tablespoons butter

Optional enrichment: melted mascarpone cheese, whipped crème fraîche, or Goat-Cheese Fondue (see page 134)

1. Heat olive oil in a large saucepan or soup pot. Add onions, celery, and garlic. Cook over low heat for 3 minutes, stirring occasionally.

2. Add all other ingredients, except butter and optional enrichments, to saucepan. Cover and simmer over low heat for 2 to 3 hours.

3. Purée soup in a food processor. Depending on the size of your processor, you may have to do this in 2 or more steps.

4. Return soup to pot and bring to a simmer. Add butter and whisk until butter is completely blended into soup. Cook for 30 minutes, or until soup has thickened. Correct seasoning.

5. Pour soup into a tureen or ladle into individual soup bowls. Serve with melted mascarpone cheese, whipped *creme fraîche,* or Goat-Cheese Fondue, if desired.

Variation: Add a small wedge of grilled salmon or 3 or 4 grilled shrimp to each serving of soup, and do not use any of the optional enrichments.

An Introduction to the Following Three Chapters: Building a Dish

THE FOLLOWING THREE CHAPTERS contain recipes for main courses prepared with fish, birds, and meat. The recipes include directions on how to build a dish. This is how I think of main courses—I build them, combining three complementary elements on one plate. There are no separate chapters in this book for vegetables or other side dishes, because they are important components of my main courses. For example, you won't find a recipe for grilled salmon in the following pages. What you will find is Seared Salmon with Ginger and Cracked Pepper in a Burgundy Butter Sauce served with Lotus-Root Chips. This is one of the ways I build a dish.

Another technique is to create a three-dimensional effect. I might form a column of polenta or spoon a mountain of couscous on a plate, and then build around this centerpiece, creating levels and layers of food. Layering permits a play of contrasts, textures, and colors—all brought together on one plate. The eye moves to the center of a plate and sees a meal analogous to a splendidly wrapped gift—it's a surprise on a dinner plate! There's excitement as a diner satisfies curiosity by unwrapping his or her own meal. There's also a practical advantage to building a dish: layers of food retain heat. No worry here of a potato's getting cold while you eat your steak.

Though I like to add dimension, I don't want a dish to be so elaborate or fussy that a diner is afraid to touch the food on the plate. I enjoy the pleasure that people derive from a beautiful presentation, but I also like to see someone pick up a crispy Almond Wafer and eat it without benefit of a fork.

I think of many of my dishes as abstract. I don't like a plate that's too organized, too evenly laid out. Years ago, in classic French cuisine, we were taught to place food in a fleur-de-lys or other exact pattern. Today, I prefer the vitality of the abstract, because I believe this may better express the emotions, attitudes, and intentions of the cook. I still *plate* a main dish—place component parts on a dinner plate—but my technique has a random touch and my designs are not rigid.

The abstract has another advantage: it offers a variety of views to those sitting around a table. A different angle gives each guest a unique perspective.

The dishes in the following chapters are created by combining two and sometimes three recipes. When I build a dish, I present the main ingredient with an appropriate side dish, sauce, and garnish. The directions for each main course are in the order in which they should be prepared. When a fish requires quick cooking, the sauce, vegetable, and garnish are prepared first. Recipes may appear lengthy, but they're easy to follow.

The following chapters contain a cornucopia of ideas, and side dishes can be served with other main ingredients. I serve Corn Crêpes with lobster, but the crêpes would also complement fish or pork; the Honey-Baked Turnips I suggest with lamb shanks would be equally effective with beef or chicken. The Shrimp and Ginger Strudel presented with salmon, and the Shrimp Falafels offered with mako shark, can be used as starters or hors d'oeuvres. Mix and match fearlessly to satisfy your own preferences.

Chapter 5

BUILDING A DISH WITH FISH AND SHELLFISH

 I began to appreciate fish cookery when I lived and worked in Norway, where I would buy fresh fish almost every day, purchasing the day's catch from local fishermen. First, the colors appealed to me: the deep red of wild salmon, the ivory white of halibut. Then I realized that the textures of fish also had special definition. Living on a fjord, surrounded by icy water—the waters that produce the tastiest, firmest fish—I began to understand the potential of cooking with fish.

Later, when I traveled around France, I was influenced by the way French chefs treated fish. They created sauces that enhanced delicate fish and shellfish flavors, and used side dishes that offered a surprisingly sharp counterpoint to a mildly flavored fish. When I became an executive chef at The River Café I emphasized fish on the menu, and Seared Salmon with Ginger and Cracked Pepper in Burgundy Butter Sauce became my signature fish dish.

I enjoy the versatility offered by fish cookery. There's such a variety of fish and shellfish, each with its own texture: there's tender and delicate sole, flaky cod, firm swordfish and tuna resembling cuts of meat. And fish can be steamed, poached, grilled, sautéed, baked, fried, and eaten raw in a carpaccio.

I like to combine fish with ingredients not usually served with them: duck livers with swordfish, or grilled fish over a bed of whipped or mashed potatoes. It's important to add texture to fish—the basic tenderness requires the contrast—so I wrap some fish in crusts and serve others with crisp vegetables. Many diners tell me they don't care too much for fish and eat it only because they believe it's healthier than meat, but these same people then say that my fish dishes are different—they enjoy eating the fish I prepare.

The secret of successful fish cookery is to purchase fresh fish and not to overcook it. Overcooked fish is dry, tasteless, inedible. I prefer fish rare or, at most, medium-rare. Its delicate flavor marries well with a variety of sauces and vegetables, and fish and seafood dishes can be the most elegant and satisfying part of a cook's repertoire.

Catfish and Crabsteak with Old Bay Polenta

YIELD: 6 SERVINGS

*D*uring an externship served while studying at the C.I.A., I worked in Texas, and this recipe is based on my experience as a sauté chef at Ratcliff's, a popular Dallas seafood restaurant. I like to serve this with either Caramelized-Bell-Pepper and Shellfish Sauce (see page 175) or Red-Pepper Butter (see page 178).

CATFISH AND FILLING

6 fillets of catfish, each about 4 to 5 ounces
*Coarse or kosher salt and freshly ground pepper
    to taste*
*4 tablespoons Light Chicken Stock (see page 76)
    or canned chicken broth*
1 teaspoon coarse or kosher salt

Freshly ground pepper to taste
*6 tablespoons butter, softened until almost
    liquid*
3 tablespoons chopped chives
*½ pound lump crabmeat, picked clean of
    cartilage*
*3 to 4 tablespoons Wondra or other finely milled
    flour*
2–3 tablespoons olive oil for sautéing

1. Cut away any dark or fatty parts of fish and discard. Cut each fillet in half lengthwise, reserving smaller halves of fillets.

2. Season larger fish-fillet halves with salt and pepper.

3. Using either a 2½-inch ring mold or 6- to 8-ounce ramekin, roll larger fillets into mold, pressing fish against the sides of the mold. (If a ring mold or ramekin is not available, use a coffee cup or small soufflé dish.)

4. Chop 3 or more of the reserved fish fillets until you have ½ cup chopped fish. (Reserve any remaining fish for another dish.)

Prepare a Catfish Purée

1. Place chopped fish in food processor. Add Light Chicken Stock or broth, salt, and pepper. While processing, add softened butter gradually.

2. Continue processing until all ingredients are combined into a smooth purée. (I call this purée a Catfish Buttercream, because it resembles a pastry buttercream in texture.)

3. Spoon catfish purée, or Catfish Buttercream, into a bowl. Add chives and crabmeat. Mix until Catfish Buttercream and crabmeat are thoroughly combined.

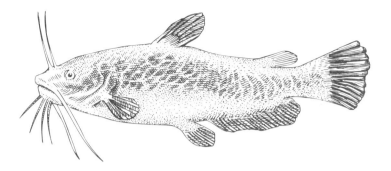

4. Pack mixture into center of molds or ramekins and refrigerate for 2 hours.

5. Coat baking sheet or pan with Wondra flour.

6. Remove molds or ramekins from refrigerator. Run a knife gently around the inside of each mold or ramekin. Unmold onto baking sheet. Each portion has the shape of a filet mignon. If ramekin does not unmold easily, place a hot cloth on bottom of ramekin for a few seconds.

7. Make band out of aluminum foil and wrap band around each portion of catfish fillet. (Unlike collars for soufflés, these bands should not be as high as the fish fillets.) Carefully tie bands with small lengths of butcher's twine. Dust tops of fillets with flour and refrigerate.

VEGETABLE GARNISH

4 tablespoons vegetable oil
1 red bell pepper, minced
1 yellow bell pepper, minced
½ cup cooked corn kernels
½ cup cooked green peas
4 cornichons, minced
Coarse or kosher salt and freshly ground pepper
*   to taste*

Combine all ingredients in a bowl and reserve.

POLENTA

1 tablespoon butter
½ small onion, minced
2 cups Corn Stock (see variations, page 78), Light Chicken Stock (see page 76) or canned chicken broth
½ cup instant polenta
1 cup cooked corn kernels
2 teaspoons Old Bay Seasoning
4 tablespoons butter
1 tablespoon chopped celery leaves
Coarse or kosher salt and freshly ground pepper to taste
Cornmeal for dredging
4 tablespoons olive oil

1. Heat 1 tablespoon butter in a large saucepan. Add onion and cook, stirring, for 2 minutes. Add Corn Stock, Light Chicken Stock, or broth. Bring to a boil and gradually stir in polenta. Cook, stirring, for 4 to 5 minutes, or until liquid is absorbed and polenta is cooked.

2. Add corn kernels, Old Bay Seasoning, 4 tablespoons butter, and celery leaves and

stir. Season to taste and continue cooking until all ingredients are thoroughly combined.

3. Spoon polenta into a square baking pan. Chill until firm.

4. After polenta has chilled, cut it into rectangular blocks. Dredge each portion in cornmeal.

5. Heat 4 tablespoons olive oil in a large sauté pan, preferably with a nonstick surface. Sauté polenta, turning each piece from side to side until golden brown. Drain on paper towels and keep warm.

To Cook Fish

1. Preheat oven to 350°.

2. Heat 2 to 3 tablespoons olive oil in a sauté pan, preferably with a nonstick surface. You may have to cook the catfish in 2 or more steps, depending on the size of your pan. Do not overcrowd pan.

3. Sauté catfish fillets over medium heat for 2 minutes on one side. Turn gently and sauté for 2 minutes on second side. Return catfish fillets to baking pan and continue cooking in oven for an additional 8 to 10 minutes. Carefully remove and discard aluminum-foil collars and string.

To Cook Vegetable Garnish

While catfish fillets are baking, heat 4 tablespoons olive oil in a sauté pan. Add Vegetable Garnish and cook, stirring occasionally, for 2 minutes, or until vegetables are heated through.

To Build This Dish

1. Place fish fillets on 6 dinner plates.

2. Cut each polenta rectangle in half diagonally.

3. Stand 2 pieces of polenta beside each fish fillet.

4. Spoon approximately 3 tablespoons Vegetable Garnish over each fish fillet, allowing it to cascade down sides of fish.

5. Spoon Caramelized-Bell-Pepper and Shellfish Sauce (see page 174) or Red-Pepper Butter (see page 178) around perimeter of plate.

Brandade of Fresh Cod, with Cod Fillets, Shrimp, and Vinaigrette of Sun-dried Tomatoes

YIELD: 4 SERVINGS

*B*randade is a purée traditionally made of salt cod and mashed potatoes, but I think that Brandade is too strong, too salty, and has the uninteresting appearance of oatmeal. I use fresh rather than salt cod for my Brandade, adding fillets of cod and shrimp and a sauce for additional texture and flavor.

You can use my version of Brandade as an appetizer or a spread, as well as the base on which to build the rest of this dish.

BRANDADE AND COD FILLETS

1½ pounds fillet of cod
12 large shrimp, peeled and deveined
¾ cup olive oil
2 teaspoons minced garlic
1 cup Potato Purée (see page 39) combined with
 Black-Olive Purée (see page 35, and use half
 of recipe)
Coarse or kosher salt and freshly ground pepper
 to taste

1. Cut cod into 5 equal portions. Reserve 4 portions and roughly chop remaining portion.

2. Roughly chop 4 shrimp.

3. Heat ½ cup olive oil in a large sauté pan. Add chopped cod and chopped shrimp to pan. Sauté, stirring, for 30 seconds. Stir in garlic. Add Potato Black-Olive Purée and stir until all ingredients are combined. Correct seasoning and reserve.

4. Preheat oven to 350°.

5. Lightly oil a baking pan with remaining olive oil. Season reserved cod fillets with salt and pepper. Place fillets in pan and spoon remaining olive oil over fish.

6. Bake fish fillets for about 8 to 9 minutes, depending on thickness of fillets. Fish should not be overcooked.

SHRIMP AND VINAIGRETTE

8 remaining shrimp
1 cup extra-virgin olive oil
4 tablespoons lemon juice
2 tablespoons minced sun-dried tomatoes
2 tablespoons minced red bell pepper
2 tablespoons minced yellow bell pepper
4 tablespoons thinly shredded fresh basil
 leaves
1 teaspoon coarse or kosher salt
Freshly ground pepper to taste

While fish is baking, combine all ingredients in a saucepan, stir, and bring to a simmer. Cook for about 3 minutes, or until shrimp are cooked.

To Build This Dish

1. Spoon Brandade mixture into four soup plates. Top with baked cod fillets.

2. Place 2 shrimp on top of each cod fillet. Spoon sauce over and around cod and Brandade of Cod.

Baked Cod with Roast-Shallot Crust on Asparagus Raft with Asparagus Sauce

YIELD: 4 SERVINGS

ASPARAGUS RAFT

12 asparagus spears, steamed (see Asparagus
*   Butter Sauce, page 174)*
½ cup all-purpose flour
2 eggs, lightly beaten
1 cup fresh bread crumbs
Olive oil for sautéing

1. Place 3 asparagus spears side-by-side and secure with toothpicks. Repeat with remaining asparagus.

2. Dredge each Asparagus Raft in flour, egg, and bread crumbs, and reserve.

BAKED COD WITH ROAST-SHALLOT CRUST

4 fillets of cod, about 5 to 6 ounces each
Coarse or kosher salt and freshly ground
*   pepper to taste*
4 tablespoons Roast-Shallot Purée (see page
*   38)*
¼ cup olive oil

1. Preheat oven to 350°.

2. Season cod fillets with salt and pepper. Place 1 tablespoon of Roast-Shallot Purée on top of each fillet and spread evenly with a knife.

3. Lightly oil a baking sheet. Place cod fillets on baking sheet and bake for 8 to 9 minutes. Fish will be medium-rare, and roast shallots will be a deep brown with a soft crust.

4. While fish is baking, heat olive oil in a large sauté pan, preferably with a nonstick surface. Place Asparagus Rafts in pan and sauté 1 minute on each side, until golden brown and heated through. Depending on the size of the pan, you may have to do this in 2 or more steps. Drain rafts on paper towels.

To Build This Dish

1. Place each raft on a dinner plate. Remove toothpicks.

2. Place 1 baked cod fillet on each raft. Spoon Asparagus Butter Sauce around perimeter of each plate, and serve with sautéed diced carrots and Onion Rings (see page 33), if desired.

Soft-Shell Crabs

YIELD: 3 SERVINGS AS A MAIN COURSE,
6 AS AN APPETIZER

Soft-Shell Crabs are a favorite of mine, and though there are many ways to cook and present them, I prefer the following technique, taught to me by one of my mentors, Waldy Malouf, when we worked together at La Crémaillière in Banksville, New York. Because crabs lose a lot of water while being cleaned and become scrawny, to plump them up and to emphasize their sweet flavor, I marinate them in heavy cream. If the crabs have even a small touch of bitterness, the cream will dispel it, and the cream helps form a tender crust.

After the crabs are cooked, I place them belly up—they look better that way—or I cut each crab in half and stand them on their cut sides so that their claws seem to be waving in the air. I serve them different ways, including on a pedestal of Old Bay Polenta (see page 94), or with Crabmeat-Scallop Zucchini Rolls (see page 59).

To add piquancy, I may add a dollop of Salsa (see page 179).

*6 medium soft-shell crabs, cleaned and ready to
    cook
2 cups heavy sweet cream
1 teaspoon Tabasco
2 teaspoons coarse or kosher salt
1 teaspoon freshly ground pepper
2 cups all-purpose or Wondra flour
½ cup Clarified Butter for sautéing
Coarse or kosher salt to taste*

1. Place crabs in a large shallow pan. Combine all remaining ingredients, except for flour and butter and final salt seasoning, and pour over crabs. Refrigerate and allow crabs to marinate for 2 hours.

2. Remove crabs from marinade—do not dry—and dredge in flour.

3. Heat Clarified Butter until almost smoking in a large sauté pan. Add crabs, belly side down, and sauté for 2 to 3 minutes. Turn crabs and cook an additional 1½ minutes on second side.

4. If crabs start to burn, lower heat and turn them immediately. Depending on the size of your pan, you may have to cook crabs in 2 or more steps.

5. Using a slotted spatula, remove crabs from pan and drain on paper towels. Season with salt.

6. Serve soft-shell crabs belly up, or cut each crab in half and stand on cut sides so that claws seem to be waving in the air.

Building a Dish with Fish and Shellfish   99

Crabcakes with Red-Pepper Butter

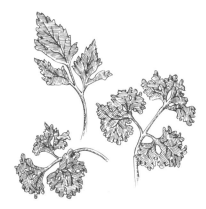

YIELD: 4 SERVINGS

¼ pound fillets of any white-meat fish, such as
    flounder, sole, catfish, scallops, or shrimp
    (cleaned and deveined)
4 tablespoons Light Chicken Stock (see
    page 76) or canned chicken broth
¼ pound butter, softened until almost
    liquid
3 tablespoons chopped chives
½ pound lump crabmeat, picked clean of
    cartilage
2 tablespoons chopped cornichon (optional)
⅛ teaspoon cayenne pepper
Coarse or kosher salt and freshly ground pepper
    to taste
Cornmeal for dredging
Olive oil for sautéing
Red-Pepper Butter (see page 178)
Fresh-Herb Wafers (see page 31)

1. Chop fish or shellfish into small pieces.
Place in food processor. Add Light Chicken
Stock or broth and purée. Add softened butter
gradually and continue processing until ingredients are combined. Spoon fish purée into a
bowl.

2. Add chives, crabmeat, cornichon, cayenne,
salt, and pepper to fish purée and mix thoroughly.

3. Form mixture into 8 cakes and dredge in
cornmeal.

4. Heat olive oil in sauté pan, preferably with
a nonstick surface. Sauté crabcakes, turning,
until golden brown and cooked through.

5. Place 2 crabcakes each on 4 dinner plates.
Spoon warm Red Pepper Butter beside crabcakes, and add 3 Fresh-Herb Wafers.

Variations: For a more dramatic presentation,
cut each crabcake into half-moon and stand on
cut side. Spoon Red-Pepper Butter around perimeter of plate and place Fresh-Herb Wafers
between the cakes.

Or: Bake 4 potatoes. Scoop out potato pulp
and prepare a Potato Purée (see page 39). Place
a serving of Potato Purée on 4 dinner plates.
Top Potato Purée with hollowed-out potato
shell. Spoon an inch of Red Pepper Butter into
shell and top with four half-moons of crabcakes. Garnish with a toothpick which holds
one cornichon, one cocktail onion, and a sprig
of fresh parsley or watercress.

Halibut Steamed in Foil with Prosciutto and Lemon

YIELD: 6 SERVINGS

I created this dish when I was invited to a friend's house for a barbecue. Instead of having to spend the day in the kitchen, I prepared these halibut steaks at home, brought them with me, and just placed them on a hot barbecue grill.

Everyone enjoyed unwrapping his or her own "gift package" of halibut. The vegetables, horseradish, and Horseradish Oil combined with the fish to create a sauce. I served the fish with potato salad and thick slices of bread grilled with a touch of whole-grain mustard.

If you're preparing this dish indoors, serve with Potato Purée (see page 39).

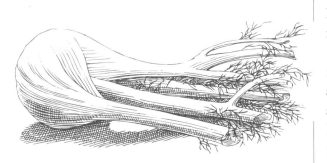

Horseradish Oil (see page 166)
Zest and juice of 2 lemons
1 fennel bulb, slivered
1 zucchini, cut into ½-inch slices
1 yellow squash, cut into ½-inch slices
Tomato Concasse, made with 1 large tomato (see page 43)
½ cup blanched green beans, cut into ½-inch lengths
1 bunch fresh basil, finely chopped
¼ pound prosciutto ham, cut into thin strips
4 tablespoons freshly ground horseradish (if not available, use bottled horseradish, first pressing out liquid)
6 halibut steaks or fillets, about 5 to 6 ounces each
3 teaspoons cracked black peppercorns
Coarse or kosher salt to taste
½ cup chopped fresh basil leaves
Whole-grain mustard

1. Preheat oven to 400°, or ready an outdoor barbecue grill.

2. Prepare 6 sheets of aluminum foil, each about 16 inches by 10 inches. Coat each sheet with a small amount of Horseradish Oil.

3. In a bowl, combine zest and juice of lemons, all vegetables, prosciutto, and horseradish, and mix until all ingredients are combined.

4. Place half of vegetable mixture on aluminum-foil sheets. Top with halibut steaks. Season fish with cracked black peppercorns and salt. Cover with remaining vegetable mixture. Fold foil over, closing all sides. You now have 6 packages of fish with vegetables.

5. Cook halibut by placing foil packages on a baking sheet and baking in oven, or place foil

packages on barbecue grill. Cook 5 minutes on first side, turn and cook an additional 5 minutes, depending on thickness of fish. (To test: pierce one package with knife or skewer; if knife or skewer comes out warm, fish is done.)

6. Place on a platter and present in foil, allowing guests to unwrap their own package.

7. Pass chopped basil leaves and mustard, and serve with potato salad or Potato Purée.

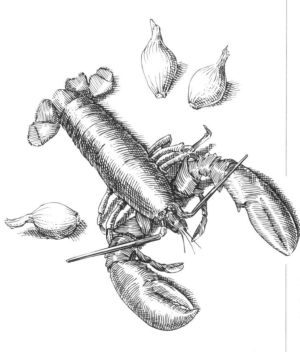

Braised Lobster with Corn Crêpes and Bacon

YIELD: 6 SERVINGS

*t*his dish resembles a pot pie. The corn crêpes are placed right over the braised lobster, creating the appearance of a crust. Prepare the batter for the corn crêpes first, because batter must rest for one hour before being used.

CORN CRÊPES

> *½ cup all-purpose flour*
> *¼ teaspoon sugar*
> *¼ teaspoon coarse or kosher salt*
> *1 egg*
> *¾ cup plus 2 tablespoons milk*
> *1 tablespoon butter, melted and browned*
> *6 tablespoons cooked corn kernels, finely*
>   *minced*
> *Clarified Butter for sautéing*

1. Combine all ingredients, except for corn and Clarified Butter, in a food processor. Mix until thoroughly combined. Pour crêpe mixture into a bowl and stir in corn kernels. Cover bowl and refrigerate for 1 hour before using.

2. Cook crêpes in a 6-inch crêpe or omelette pan with a nonstick surface. Heat Clarified Butter in pan and ladle a small amount of batter into pan. Tilt pan so that batter covers bottom

of pan. Cook crêpe until brown on one side. Turn over with spatula and cook on second side. Remove crêpes as they are cooked, drain on paper towels, and reserve.

3. If there are more than 6 crêpes, cut the additional crêpes into ½-inch strips. Bake until crisp in a 350° oven and add the strips to the braised lobster before topping the dishes with the corn crêpes.

LOBSTERS

2 2-pound lobsters
2 cups Light Chicken Stock (see page 76) or
*   canned chicken broth*
4 tablespoons Tomato Fondue (see page 44)
10 slices bacon, diced
Tomato Concasse (see page 43)
½ cup cooked corn kernels
2 green onions, cut on bias, white and green parts
*   reserved separately*
2 shallots, minced
6 tablespoons butter
Coarse or kosher salt and freshly ground pepper
*   to taste*
3 tablespoons Lobster Oil (see page 168)

1. Poach lobsters in boiling, salted water for 6 minutes. Drain and, when lobsters are cool enough to handle, remove lobster meat from lobster shells, reserving shells. Cut claw meat into 2 pieces and tail meat into 6 pieces. Reserve lobster meat.

2. Prepare a Lobster Stock by combining lobster shells with Light Chicken Stock or broth and Tomato Fondue in a saucepan. Bring to a simmer and reduce by approximately half.

3. Place diced bacon in a sauté pan and sauté until bacon fat is rendered. Using a slotted spoon, remove bacon from pan and drain on paper towels. Reserve.

4. Add Tomato Concasse, corn, white part of green onions, shallots, and bacon to Lobster Stock and bring to a boil. Add butter and simmer for 2 to 3 minutes, until all ingredients are combined. Add lobster meat and simmer for another 30 seconds, or just until lobster is warm. Sprinkle green part of green onions over all.

To Assemble: Spoon lobster and sauce into 6 large soup plates. Place 1 corn crêpe over each plate. Drizzle ½ tablespoon of Lobster Oil over each crêpe.

Mahimahi Baked on a Plate with Warm Peppered Pineapple and Citrus Vinaigrette

YIELD: 4 SERVINGS

Cook this mahimahi right on dinner plates which I place in the broiler for one minute. I've used fine china for this dish and the plates have never cracked. If you're nervous about putting your dinner plates in a hot oven, you could cook the fish on metal plates that are used for steak.

CITRUS VINAIGRETTE

1 cup olive oil
2 shallots, minced
Juice of 1 grapefruit
Juice of 1 orange
Juice and zest of 1 lemon
2 tablespoons red-wine vinegar
1 teaspoon coarse or kosher salt
2 tablespoons chopped parsley

1. Heat olive oil in a saucepan. Add shallots and cook, stirring, for 1 minute. Add all other ingredients except parsley. Simmer for 4 minutes.

2. Remove from heat and stir in parsley. Reserve.

WARM PEPPERED PINEAPPLE

2 tablespoons olive oil
1 cup cubed fresh pineapple, coated with cracked black pepper
1 grapefruit, peeled and sectioned
1 orange, peeled and sectioned
½ cup cooked green beans, cut into 1-inch pieces

Heat olive oil in a sauté pan. Add pineapple and cook, stirring, for 1 minute. Add all other ingredients and cook only until ingredients are warmed through. Reserve.

MAHIMAHI

1½ pounds fillet of mahimahi, skin and bones removed
Coarse or kosher salt and freshly ground pepper to taste
2 tablespoons olive oil

1. Preheat oven to broil.

2. Slice mahimahi into ¼-inch slices and season with salt and pepper.

3. Paint 4 dinner plates with olive oil and fan fish slices out on each plate to form a pinwheel.

4. Place plates in broiler and cook fish for 1 minute. You might have to do this in 2 or more steps, depending on the size of your broiler.

5. Heat Citrus Vinaigrette and all Peppered Pineapple ingredients. Spoon Citrus Vinaigrette over fish, then strew Peppered Pineapple and citrus sections over and around fish in random manner.

Pan-Roasted Monkfish with Green-Onion Sauce and Ziti and Eggplant Bouquet

YIELD: 4 SERVINGS

*t*he idea of architecture combined with cuisine came to me from José Lampreia at Maison Blanche in Paris. Prepare these miniature ziti towers in your own kitchen to create a dramatic presentation.

GREEN-ONION SAUCE

3 cups chopped green onions (use both green and
    white parts)
3 tablespoons olive oil
½ cup Light Chicken Stock (see page 76) or
    canned chicken broth
2 tablespoons butter
Coarse or kosher salt and freshly ground pepper
    to taste

1. Blanch chopped green onions in boiling salted water for 1 minute. Drain and run under cold water to stop cooking. Drain again.

2. Place blanched green onions in food processor. Add olive oil and Light Chicken Stock or broth, and purée. Spoon into a saucepan, add butter, salt, and pepper, and heat, stirring, until all ingredients are combined. Reserve and keep warm.

ZITI AND EGGPLANT BOUQUET

3 tablespoons olive oil
1 small onion, minced
2 cloves garlic, minced
1 cup diced eggplant
2 teaspoons chopped fresh oregano or ½ teaspoon
    dried oregano
2 teaspoons chopped fresh thyme or ½ teaspoon
    dried thyme
½ cup Tomato Fondue (see page 44)
½ cup ricotta cheese
3 tablespoons grated Parmesan cheese
½ pound ziti cooked al dente, or firm to
    the bite
Coarse or kosher salt and freshly ground pepper
    to taste
3 tablespoons softened butter
4 teaspoons butter
4 teaspoons grated Parmesan cheese
4 sprigs fresh oregano or thyme, or green olive
    slivers

1. Preheat oven to 375°.

2. Heat olive oil in a sauté pan. Add onion, garlic, eggplant, oregano, and thyme. Sauté until eggplant is tender, about 2 minutes. Stir in Tomato Fondue, ricotta cheese, and 3 tablespoons Parmesan cheese. Season to taste.

3. Spoon eggplant mixture into a bowl. Add cooked ziti and stir until combined. Allow to cool.

4. Using 3 tablespoons softened butter, coat inside of 4 1-cup ramekins. When eggplant-ziti mixture is cool enough to handle, take small

handfuls and place in ramekins vertically; ziti should be tightly packed and stand upright at different heights.

5. When ramekins are filled, top each ramekin with 1 teaspoon butter and 1 teaspoon grated Parmesan cheese.

6. Place ramekins on a baking sheet and bake for about 25 to 30 minutes, or until tops are golden brown and ziti-eggplant combination is hot. Prepare fish as ziti is baking.

MONKFISH

4 monkfish steaks, about 6 ounces each
Coarse or kosher salt and freshly ground pepper
    to taste
4 tablespoons olive oil

1. Monkfish is quite moist; therefore, pat each steak with paper towels before cooking. Season fish with salt and pepper.

2. Heat olive oil in an ovenproof sauté pan.

3. Place monkfish in pan and sear over high heat on all sides for 5 minutes.

4. When ziti has been in the oven for 25 minutes, remove from oven and place monkfish in pan in the oven and bake for 5 minutes, turning once.

To Build This Dish

1. Slide ziti carefully out of each ramekin, standing each portion on a dinner plate.

2. Spoon Green-Onion Sauce on half of each plate.

3. Top sauce with monkfish fillet and drizzle pan juices over fish. Place a branch of fresh oregano or thyme or a sliver of green onion in 1 upright ziti on each plate.

Oyster and Horseradish Risotto

YIELD: 4 SERVINGS

2 tablespoons Horseradish Oil (see page 166)

1 shallot, peeled and minced

2 tablespoons freshly grated horseradish, or bottled horseradish with its liquid pressed out

1 cup imported Italian rice, such as Arborio brand

3½ cups Light Chicken Stock (see page 76) or canned chicken broth

16 oysters, shucked, liquid reserved

4 tablespoons butter

4 red radishes, thinly sliced

2 tablespoons chopped chives

Coarse or kosher salt and freshly ground pepper to taste

¼ cup thinly shaved Parmesan cheese (optional)

Sprigs of watercress or arugula

1. Heat Horseradish Oil in a saucepan. Add shallots and horseradish and cook over low heat, stirring, until shallots are translucent.

2. Add the rice and stir until grains of rice are coated with oil.

3. Combine Light Chicken Stock or broth with liquid from oysters. Add 1 cup of mixture to rice. Cook, stirring occasionally, until liquid is absorbed. Add second cup of stock or broth mixture and continue until all liquid has been added and absorbed by rice.

4. Add butter, radishes, and chives, and stir until combined.

5. Fold in oysters and season to taste. Garnish with cheese, if desired, and sprigs of watercress or arugula.

6. Serve in shallow bowls with sourdough toast, if you wish.

Variations: Risotto may also be prepared with shrimp, scallops, chicken, wild mushrooms, or asparagus.

Seared Salmon with Ginger and Cracked Pepper in Burgundy Butter Sauce with Lotus-Root Chips

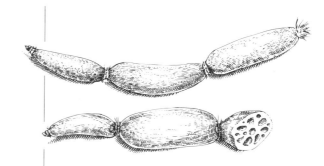

YIELD: 6 SERVINGS

*T*his is my favorite example of what I mean when I say I like to build a dish. Diners are pleasantly surprised by the layers of tastes, textures, and appearance. Seared Salmon combines an Oriental approach with nuances of French cuisine and my own American touch. When you are preparing the salmon, it will be necessary to refer to quite a few other recipes. Be brave and forge ahead; the recipes are not complicated, and this—my signature dish—is worth the time and effort.

BURGUNDY BUTTER SAUCE

2 cups red Burgundy
3 shallots, peeled and minced
½ pound butter, cut into 16 pieces
Coarse or kosher salt and freshly ground pepper
  to taste

1. Combine wine and shallots in a saucepan. Cook until liquid is reduced to ½ cup. Sauce will have a syruplike consistency.

2. Over low heat, add butter piece by piece and whisk until butter is incorporated into sauce. Add salt and pepper. Reserve and keep warm.

SALMON

1 cup Ginger Purée (see page 38)
6 salmon fillets, about 6 ounces each, skin and
  bones removed
6 tablespoons cracked black peppercorns
Coarse or kosher salt to taste
¾ cup Ginger Oil (see page 124) or olive
  oil
2 cups Potato Purée (see page 39)
1 cup Leeks with Snow Peas (see following page)
2 cups Lotus-Root Chips (see page 48)

1. Spread a layer of Ginger Purée over each salmon fillet. Sprinkle fish with cracked peppercorns and season with salt.

2. Heat Ginger Oil or olive oil in a sauté pan, preferably with a nonstick surface. Place salmon fillets, Ginger Purée side down, in pan and cook for about 2 minutes, or until a crust has formed. Turn salmon and cook an additional 3 minutes.

3. Using a slotted spatula, remove salmon from pan and drain on paper towels. Keep warm.

To Build This Dish

1. Using 6 dinner plates, place a serving of Potato Purée on each plate. Top potatoes with Leeks and Snow Peas and place salmon fillets on vegetables.

2. Spoon Burgundy Butter Sauce around perimeter of each plate and garnish with Lotus-Root Chips.

Leeks with Snow Peas

YIELD: ABOUT 2 CUPS

1 large leek
2 tablespoons butter
1 cup snow peas

1. Wash leek thoroughly, making sure to rid vegetable of sand between the leaves.

2. Slice entire leek into ½-inch circles.

3. Heat butter in a skillet. Add leeks and sauté over medium heat for 4 to 5 minutes, or until leeks are tender.

4. Add snow peas and cook, stirring, just until all ingredients are heated through.

Torn Salmon with Shrimp and Ginger Strudel and Pickled-Onion Sauce

YIELD: 6 SERVINGS

*H*ere's another of my favorites. It combines flavors (spicy and sweet); textures (crisp and tender); and colors (scarlet and golden). The dish is intended to look abstract. The salmon is not left in one piece but torn apart, exposing uneven surfaces. Do not cut the salmon fillets evenly in half; a neat line would spoil the intentionally savage look of this dish.

TORN SALMON

6 tablespoons soy sauce
4 teaspoons honey
1 clove garlic, minced
6 fillets salmon, about 4 to 5 ounces each
Olive oil or Clarified Butter (see page 26) for sautéing
Coarse or kosher salt and freshly ground pepper to taste

Combine soy sauce, honey, and garlic in a bowl; mix well. Place salmon fillets on a platter and spoon marinade over fish. Marinate fish for 1 hour, turning fish in marinade every 20 minutes. Do not refrigerate.

SHRIMP AND GINGER STRUDEL

1 pound medium shrimp, peeled and deveined
3 tablespoons Ginger Purée (see page 38)
¼ pound butter, softened almost to liquid
½ cup chopped chives
2 teaspoons lemon juice
1 tablespoon coarse or kosher salt
1 teaspoon freshly ground pepper
6 sheets phyllo dough
½ cup Clarified Butter or olive oil for phyllo dough

1. Place shrimp in food processor and purée until fairly smooth. Add Ginger Purée and butter and purée an additional 2 minutes. Add chives, lemon juice, salt, and pepper and process until ingredients are just combined.

2. Remove 2 sheets of phyllo dough from the package and lay out 1 sheet on a board. Brush with either Clarified Butter or olive oil, cover with second sheet of phyllo, and brush this sheet with butter or oil as well.

3. Cut the sheets of phyllo dough crosswise into 3 sections, and lengthwise across the middle.

4. Divide shrimp mixture into 6 portions. Place 1 portion of mixture along bottom of each section of phyllo dough. Roll once from bottom, fold sides, and continue rolling. Repeat with remaining phyllo dough and shrimp mixture. There will be 6 Shrimp and Ginger Strudels. Reserve.

PICKLED-ONION SAUCE

1½ cups White-Wine Pickling Liquid (see page 183)
½ cup pearl onions, peeled
¼ pound butter, cut into 8 pieces
2 tablespoons chopped parsley

1. Combine Pickling Liquid and pearl onions in a saucepan. Bring to a boil. Reduce by approximately half, until onions are barely covered with liquid.

2. Gradually add butter and whisk until all ingredients are combined. Stir in parsley. Reserve and keep warm.

Final Preparation

1. Preheat oven to 375°.

2. Brush a baking sheet with a small amount of Clarified Butter or olive oil. Place strudels on sheet and bake for 5 minutes.

3. Turn strudels over to bake an additional 5 minutes.

4. While strudels are baking, remove salmon from marinade and pat dry. Heat a small amount of olive oil or Clarified Butter in a sauté pan, preferably with a nonstick surface.

5. Lightly season salmon fillets with salt and pepper and sauté over high heat, turning once. Cook 1½ minutes on first side and an additional 2 to 2½ minutes on second side, depending on thickness of fillets. Remove salmon fillets from pan and drain on paper towels.

To Build This Dish

1. Place each strudel vertically, slightly to one side, on each of 6 dinner plates.

2. Using 2 paper towels, rip each salmon fillet in half.

3. Place half of each fillet on top of a strudel. Place other half of salmon fillet beside strudel in center of plate.

4. The centers of both halves of the fillets should be visible, creating an abstract look. To enjoy the deep-red color and full flavor of the salmon, cook the fish rare to medium-rare.

5. Spoon a small pool of sauce beside the fish. I don't spoon the sauce over the strudel, because it will become soggy. Serve with stir-fried cabbage or cabbage and snow peas, if you wish.

Sea Scallops with Fennel Seed, Pink Pepper, and Curry Oil

YIELD: 4 SERVINGS

*T*his recipe is designed for large sea scallops. If they're not available, sauté the vegetables (see step 2, Scallops, following page), rather than attempt to pierce the scallops with vegetable batons.

CURRY OIL

2 cups olive oil
3 shallots, minced
2 teaspoons toasted fennel seeds*
1 teaspoon pink peppercorns
2 tablespoons curry powder
1 tablespoon coarse or kosher salt

1. Heat 2 tablespoons of oil in saucepan. Add shallots, 1 teaspoon fennel seeds, pink pepper-

corns, and curry powder and cook, stirring, over very low heat for 2 minutes.

2. Add remaining oil and salt and continue cooking for 20 minutes over very low heat.

3. Remove from heat and allow ingredients to settle at bottom. Strain curry oil and reserve.

VEGETABLES

> *1 carrot, cut into batons about 1½ inches long*
> *1 fennel bulb, cut into batons about 1½ inches long*
> *12 French green beans, cut in half lengthwise*
> *1 bunch watercress*
> *2 tablespoons Curry Oil (see above)*
> *1 large baking potato, peeled*
> *Olive oil for sautéing potato*

1. Blanch carrot in salted water for 2 to 3 minutes, or until just tender but still firm.

2. Repeat with fennel bulb and green beans, which should take a minute or two less time than the carrot. Do not overcook. Vegetable batons must be firm. Refrigerate vegetables and chill.

3. Blanch watercress in salted water for 2 minutes. Drain. Place in food processor. Add 2 tablespoons Curry Oil and purée. Spoon into a bowl and reserve.

4. Cut potatoes into thin slices. Heat olive oil in a sauté pan, preferably with a nonstick surface, and fry potatoes into chips. Drain on paper towels and keep warm.

SCALLOPS

> *12 large sea scallops*
> *Coarse or kosher salt and freshly ground pepper to taste*
> *Freshly ground fennel seeds to taste*★
> *½ cup Curry Oil (see above)*

1. Preheat oven to 400°.

2. Pierce scallops with vegetable batons, inserting 2 carrot batons, a fennel baton, and a green bean into each scallop. Vegetable batons will be visible above each scallop.

3. Season scallops with salt, pepper, and ground fennel seeds.

4. Heat remainder of Curry Oil in a sauté pan. Sear scallops over high heat, spooning oil over and around scallops, for 1 minute.

5. Transfer ingredients from sauté pan to a baking pan. Baste with oil from sauté pan. Bake for 3 to 4 minutes, or until scallops are slightly firm.

To Build This Dish

Spoon watercress purée on each of 4 serving plates. Top purée with 3 scallops. Spoon ½ tablespoon Curry Oil over each serving, and garnish with remaining toasted fennel seeds and potato chips.

★This recipe illustrates two uses for fennel seeds. *To toast:* place fennel seeds on a pie plate and heat in a 325° oven for 5 to 6 minutes, or until fennel aroma is released. *To grind:* use a pepper mill filled with fennel seeds.

Layer Cake of Lemon Sole with Ratatouille and Calamari

YIELD: 4 SERVINGS

LEMON SOLE

2 cups Ratatouille (see page 66)
4 fillets lemon sole, about 8 ounces each
3 tablespoons olive oil
Coarse or kosher salt and freshly ground pepper
*   to taste*
¾ cup Red-Pepper Vinaigrette (see page 172)

1. Heat Ratatouille and keep warm.

2. Cut each fillet of lemon sole in half length-wise. Trim off any small tail pieces and discard.

3. Brush a baking sheet with olive oil and place fish fillets on baking sheet. Spoon remainder of olive oil over fish. Season fish with salt and pepper. Reserve.

CALAMARI

4 small calamari, cleaned, and sliced with
*   tentacles into rings*
3 tablespoons olive oil
1 tablespoon lemon juice
2 tablespoons chopped fresh basil
Coarse or kosher salt and freshly ground
*   pepper to taste*
½ teaspoon ground cumin (optional)

Combine all ingredients in a bowl. Mix, and allow calamari to marinate for 15 minutes.

Final Preparation

1. Preheat broiler.

2. As fish fillets are broiled for 2 to 3 minutes, the calamari will cook gently in a saucepan on top of the stove (lemon sole may take an additional 30 to 60 seconds, depending on your oven and thickness of fillet).

To Build This Dish

1. Spoon approximately ¼ cup of Ratatouille in a horizontal line on each of 4 dinner plates. Top with larger fish-fillet halves. Cover with remaining Ratatouille, and top with smaller fish fillets.

2. Scatter calamari rings and sauce from calamari on top of fish and around perimeter of plates.

3. Place drops of Red-Pepper Vinaigrette around perimeter of plates in an abstract fashion. May be served with Noodle Cake (see page 128), Potato Pancakes (see page 65), or White-Bean Purée (see page 53).

Moroccan Barbecued Mako Shark with Shrimp Falafels and Vegetable Ragout

YIELD: 6 SERVINGS

'm often asked how I developed this recipe. I did not visit Morocco. I did not take up residence in a Bedouin tent. I just knew that I wanted to create a dish that covered a spectrum of flavors: from sweet, to sour, to flowery, to spicy hot. I experimented, using various spices, until I finally came upon a combination that pleased me—honey, cinnamon, star anise, coriander, lavender, red-pepper flakes, and ginger—and this is the result. The recipe has many steps, but each step is simple and the final dish is well worth the time spent.

FALAFELS

½ pound cooked chick-peas
1½ tablespoons tahini paste
1½ tablespoons Ginger Purée (see page 38)
½ cup toasted sesame seeds
½ teaspoon cayenne pepper
¼ cup chopped fresh coriander
¼ cup chopped parsley
1 teaspoon sesame oil
1 egg
1 tablespoon coarse or kosher salt
½ pound shrimp, peeled and deveined
1 cup all-purpose flour for dredging Falafels
Clarified Butter or vegetable oil for sautéing

1. Place chick-peas in a food processor and gradually add all other ingredients except flour and Clarified Butter or oil, and process until you have a smooth purée.

2. Place a sheet of parchment paper on a cookie sheet or board and lightly dust paper with flour. Using a small ice-cream scoop or spoon, make 1-inch balls from chick-pea–shrimp mixture. Roll each ball in flour and place on parchment paper.

3. Heat Clarified Butter or vegetable oil in a large sauté pan, preferably with a nonstick surface. Over medium heat, sauté Falafels a few at a time. Do not overcrowd pan. Turn Falafels until they are brown and crisp on all sides and, using a slotted spatula, remove from pan and drain on paper towels. Reserve.

MOROCCAN BARBECUE SAUCE

2½ cups honey
1 cup rice vinegar
1 cup ketchup
½ cup lemon juice
2 cinnamon sticks
5 star anise
3 cloves garlic, minced
1 tablespoon coriander seeds
1 teaspoon red-pepper flakes
1 teaspoon cardamom
1 tablespoon green peppercorns
1 heaping tablespoon dried lavender
1 heaping tablespoon chopped fresh ginger
1 teaspoon whole cloves
1 teaspoon mace
½ cup chopped fresh coriander
1 teaspoon salt

Combine all ingredients in a saucepan. Bring to a boil. Reduce by half. Strain and reserve.

VEGETABLE RAGOUT

3 tablespoons olive oil
½ cup chopped fennel bulb
¼ cup diced cooked green beans
¼ cup cooked corn kernels
¼ cup minced black olives
Zest of 1 lemon
Coarse or kosher salt and freshly ground black
*   pepper to taste*

Heat olive oil in a small saucepan. Add all remaining ingredients. Cook for 2 to 3 minutes, until ingredients are combined and heated through. Reserve.

INGREDIENTS FOR FISH

6 1-inch mako steaks, each about 6 to 7
*   ounces*
6 teaspoons olive oil
Coarse or kosher salt and freshly ground pepper
*   to taste*
Preserved Lemon Rings (see page 32)

1. Brush mako steaks with olive oil on both sides and season with salt and pepper.

2. Fish can be barbecued, broiled, or sautéed. Place mako steaks on a preheated barbecue, or oven broiler, or in a sauté pan, preferably with a nonstick surface. Cook fish approximately 2 to 2½ minutes on each side, until fish is medium-rare.

3. If barbecuing or broiling: baste with Barbecue Sauce while cooking. If sautéing: baste only after fish has been removed from pan.

To Build This Dish

1. While fish is cooking, heat Falafels in a 350° oven for 2 minutes and heat Barbecue Sauce and Vegetable Ragout over low heat for approximately the same time, or until all ingredients are warmed through.

2. Spoon 1 tablespoon of Barbecue Sauce in the center of 6 plates. Form a circle of Falafels, placing them on top of the sauce.

3. Place mako steak on top of this table of Falafels.

4. Spoon Barbecue Sauce over fish and mound Vegetable Ragout in the center of each fish steak. Place Preserved Lemon Rings on top of Vegetable Ragout and spoon remaining Ragout around perimeter of plates.

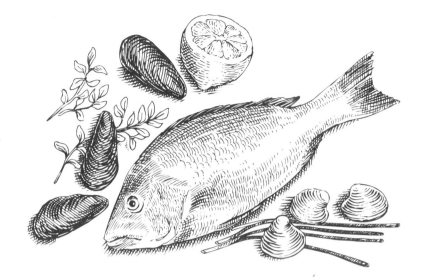

Poached Red Snapper with Saffron Risotto (Paella)

YIELD: 4 SERVINGS

This dish is based on a *paella* I tasted when I was seventeen. My father didn't think much of my idea of becoming a chef, and to discourage me he enrolled me in a cooking class given at our local shopping mall. But I was far from discouraged. One afternoon, an instructor specializing in Spanish cuisine taught a class, and her demonstration included *paella*. I was intrigued—I had never eaten the dish before. I went home and made my own version for my family. Much to my surprise—and theirs—they liked it. At that time, I put everything into the dish—shellfish, chicken, sausages—the works. I've refined my *paella* through the years, and the following is the result.

RISOTTO

> *2 tablespoons olive oil*
> *¼ cup diced onion*
> *1 cup imported Italian rice, such as Arborio brand*
> *4 cups Light Chicken Stock (see page 76) or*
>   *canned chicken broth*
> *1 teaspoon coarse or kosher salt*
> *Freshly ground pepper to taste*
> *1½ teaspoons saffron threads*
> *2 tablespoons butter*

1. Heat olive oil in a saucepan. Add onion and cook, stirring, for 2 minutes. Add rice and cook, stirring, until rice grains are coated with oil.

2. Add Light Chicken Stock or broth gradually, stirring, a cup at a time, until stock is ab-

sorbed by rice. Add salt and pepper. When liquid is almost absorbed, stir in saffron. Remove from heat and stir in butter. Reserve.

RED SNAPPER

2 cups Light Chicken Stock (see page 76) or
canned chicken broth
4 fillets red snapper, about 5 ounces each
Coarse or kosher salt and freshly ground pepper
to taste

1. Preheat oven to 350°.

2. Heat Light Chicken Stock or broth to a simmer.

3. Season fillets and place in a baking dish. Pour stock or broth over fish. Cover, and bake for 7 to 8 minutes, or until fish is slightly firm to the touch. Do not overcook. Reserve.

SAUCE AND GARNISH

8 mussels, scrubbed and bearded
8 littleneck or Manila clams
3 tablespoons olive oil
4 tablespoons Light Chicken Stock (see page 76)
or canned chicken broth
2 tablespoons lemon juice
¼ cup minced yellow bell pepper
¼ cup minced red bell pepper
2 tablespoons chopped black olives
¼ cup cooked green peas
¼ pound cooked chorizo sausage, thinly sliced
2 teaspoons chopped fresh oregano or 1 teaspoon
dried oregano
2 teaspoons chopped chives
Coarse or kosher salt and freshly ground pepper
to taste

1. Place mussels, clams, oil, Light Chicken Stock or broth, and lemon juice in a large saucepan, and bring to a boil.

2. When mussels and clams begin to open, about 3 to 4 minutes, add all remaining ingredients. Stir to combine and adjust seasoning.

To Build This Dish

1. Place ½ cup of Risotto on each of 4 dinner plates. Remove fish from cooking liquid and place fish fillet on top of Risotto (save cooking liquid and use as a fish stock for other dishes).

2. Place 2 mussels and 2 clams on top of fish, and spoon sauce over and around fish and Risotto.

Seared Striped Bass with Lemon Couscous, Bay Scallops, Tomato Oil, and Basil Essence

YIELD: 4 SERVINGS

This dish presents two concentric circles of color: a circle of green spinach outlined by another circle of scarlet Tomato Oil. The oil is accented by the green of the Basil Essence, which creates a reflective image as it floats atop the oil. The inner circle is filled with a mountain of couscous, and there's a contrast of textures: the crisp striped bass against the tender, lemon-scented couscous.

BASIL ESSENCE

2 bunches fresh basil
2 cups olive oil
Coarse or kosher salt and freshly ground pepper
    to taste

1. Blanch basil in salted boiling water for 5 seconds and drain.

2. Roughly chop basil and place it and olive oil in a food processor and purée. Season to taste. Strain purée, pressing out all liquid with the back of a spoon or by hand into a bowl. Reserve liquid only.

LEMON COUSCOUS

½ cup Light Chicken Stock (see page 76) or
    canned chicken broth
1½ cup couscous
2 teaspoons lemon zest
1 small zucchini, minced
Coarse or kosher salt and freshly ground pepper
    to taste
1 tablespoon olive oil

1. Place Light Chicken Stock or broth in a saucepan. Bring to a boil.

2. Stir in couscous and all remaining ingredients, and cook 3 to 4 minutes, or until couscous is tender and all flavors are blended. Reserve.

STRIPED BASS

1 clove garlic, minced
1 tablespoon olive oil
8 ounces cooked and chopped spinach
Coarse or kosher salt and freshly ground pepper
    to taste
4 striped-bass fillets, about 5 ounces each
½ pound bay scallops
Coarse or kosher salt and freshly ground pepper
    to taste
4 tablespoons olive oil
8 tablespoons Tomato Oil (see page 169)

1. Preheat oven to 400°.

2. In a sauté pan, cook garlic in 1 tablespoon olive oil. Add spinach, season, and cook until all ingredients are warm.

3. Season fish and bay scallops with salt and pepper to taste.

4. Heat 4 tablespoons olive oil in an oven-proof sauté pan.

5. Place bass, skin side down, in pan and cook over medium-high heat for 2 minutes. Press fish down with a spatula as it cooks to prevent fillets from curling. Turn fillets over, add bay scallops to pan, place in oven, and bake an additional 2 to 3 minutes.

To Build This Dish

1. Form a hollow ring of spinach in the center of each of 4 dinner plates.

2. Spoon a large mound of couscous into center of each spinach ring (it should resemble a couscous mountain).

3. Spoon a ring of Tomato Oil around each spinach ring.

4. Using a small spoon, drizzle tiny droplets of Basil Essence on Tomato Oil.

5. Place a striped-bass fillet, skin side up, on top of couscous mountain.

6. Tuck a few bay scallops into couscous mountain and place remainder of scallops on top of bass fillets.

Grilled Swordfish with Seared Duck Liver and Wild-Mushroom Polenta

YIELD: 6 SERVINGS

POLENTA

4 tablespoons butter
½ pound assorted wild mushrooms (shiitake, morel, portobello, chanterelle)
1 tablespoon butter
½ onion, minced
1 quart Light Chicken Stock (see page 76), or Mushroom Stock (see variations, page 78), or canned chicken broth
1 cup instant polenta
2 tablespoons chopped fresh tarragon or 2 tablespoons dried tarragon
¼ pound butter, cut into 8 pieces
Coarse or kosher salt and freshly ground pepper to taste
Cornmeal for dredging
4 tablespoons olive oil

1. Heat 4 tablespoons butter in a saucepan. Add mushrooms and sauté over medium heat, stirring occasionally, until very tender. Cook until all mushroom liquid has evaporated. Reserve.

2. Heat 1 tablespoon butter in a large

saucepan. Add onion and cook, stirring, for 2 minutes. Add Light Chicken Stock, Mushroom Stock, or broth. Bring to a boil, and gradually stir in polenta. Cook, stirring, for 4 to 5 minutes, or until liquid is absorbed and polenta is cooked. Stir in tarragon.

3. Add ¼ pound butter, a piece at a time, stirring until butter is absorbed. Season to taste and stir in cooked mushroom mixture.

4. Spoon polenta into a square baking pan and chill until firm, about 1 hour.

5. After polenta has chilled, cut it into squares, approximately 2½ inches by 2½ inches. Dredge each square of polenta in cornmeal.

6. Heat olive oil in a large sauté pan, preferably with a nonstick surface. Sauté polenta, turning each piece from side to side until golden brown. Drain on paper towels and keep warm.

SWORDFISH

6 center-cut swordfish steaks (from the eye only), each about 2 inches thick and about 5 inches in diameter, weighing 5½ to 6 ounces each
¼ cup olive oil
Coarse or kosher salt and freshly ground pepper to taste

1. Preheat grill or broiler.

2. Brush the swordfish steaks with half of the olive oil and season with salt and pepper. Place swordfish steaks on grill or in broiler and cook for 3 to 4 minutes. Turn steaks and cook an additional 3 to 4 minutes. Baste with remaining

olive oil. Swordfish should be medium-rare. Test by piercing with a skewer, which should be warm when removed from fish.

DUCK LIVERS

6 whole duck livers (if not available, substitute 12 chicken livers)
Coarse or kosher salt and freshly ground pepper to taste
2 tablespoons olive oil

1. While swordfish is cooking, trim fat or sinew from livers and season with salt and pepper.

2. Heat olive oil in a sauté pan, preferably with a nonstick surface, and sauté livers for approximately 45 seconds on each side. Remove from pan and drain on paper towels.

To Build This Dish

SAUCE

1½ cups Sherry-Wine-Vinegar and Shallot Sauce (see page 180)

GARNISH

Mushroom Chips (see page 47)

1. Place a polenta square in the center of each of 6 dinner plates.

2. Top each square with a swordfish steak. Place 1 duck liver on top of each fish steak. Spoon sauce over livers, and garnish with Mushroom Chips. Can be served with small bouquets of steamed broccoli florets placed on perimeters of each plate.

Trout and Caviar Sandwiches in Phyllo with Riesling and Chive Sauce

YIELD: 4 SERVINGS

TROUT

8 fillets of trout (from 4 trout), skin and bones
    removed
2 medium sea scallops or shrimp, peeled and
    deveined
2 tablespoons butter, softened until almost
    liquid
½ teaspoon lemon zest
Coarse or kosher salt and freshly ground pepper
    to taste*
2 tablespoons caviar, preferably Osetra, or other
    fish roe, such as American golden whitefish
    caviar or salmon roe
8 sheets phyllo dough
½ cup Clarified Butter (see page 26)
12 asparagus spears, steamed

1. Trim trout, cutting off narrow end pieces.
Reserve trout scraps, which should equal 4 to 6
tablespoons.

2. Combine trout scraps with either sea scallops or shrimp in a food processor. Purée,
adding butter gradually. Add lemon zest, salt,

*As some caviars may be salty, be careful not to oversalt.

and pepper and continue processing until all
ingredients are combined.

3. Spoon trout purée into a bowl and gently
stir in caviar.

4. Spoon purée onto four trout fillets. Spread
evenly with a knife. Top with remaining fillets.
Season with salt and pepper.

5. Remove 2 sheets of phyllo dough from
package. Brush 1 sheet with Clarified Butter.
Cover with second sheet of phyllo dough and
brush with butter.

6. Place a trout sandwich on bottom third of
phyllo sheets. Roll phyllo, tucking sides in.

7. Repeat with remaining sheets of phyllo
and trout. Refrigerate for 30 minutes.

RIESLING AND CHIVE SAUCE

1½ cups Riesling wine
¼ pound butter, cut into 8 pieces
½ cup chives
Coarse or kosher salt and freshly ground pepper
    to taste

1. Place Riesling in a saucepan and bring to a
boil. Reduce by half.

2. Whisk in butter, piece by piece. Add chives
and season to taste.

Final Preparation

1. Preheat oven to 400°.

2. Remove Trout and Caviar Sandwiches in
Phyllo from refrigerator. Brush a baking sheet
with remaining Clarified Butter, about 2 tablespoons. Place sandwiches on baking sheet and
bake for 8 to 10 minutes.

3. While sandwiches are baking, cut each

asparagus spear into 2 long pieces and place in a sauté pan. Add 2 tablespoons of Riesling and Chive Sauce to pan, and heat gently for 1 to 2 minutes.

To Build This Dish

1. Place Trout and Caviar Sandwiches in Phyllo in the center of 4 dinner plates.
2. Spoon sauce around—not on—each sandwich and place asparagus spears beside each sandwich.

Variation: Use Asparagus Butter Sauce (see page 174) in place of Riesling and Chive Sauce.

Carpaccio of Yellowfin Tuna with Asparagus and Mint-Oil Dressing

YIELD: 6 SERVINGS

*T*he yellowfin tuna for this dish must be of the best quality. Look for tuna that's rich in color—either rose or red—and is firm and moist, and has a pleasant aroma. Carpaccio of Tuna is not cooked, and the fish must be fresh.

1 pound yellowfin tuna, cut into 6 thin
    slices
½ cup extra-virgin olive oil
2 tablespoons Mint Oil (see page 167)
Zest of 1 lime
2 teaspoons cracked black pepper
Coarse or kosher salt to taste
18 medium-sized asparagus spears,
    steamed
1 tablespoon toasted sesame seeds
½ cup Lotus-Root Chips (see page 48) or
    Ribbons of Leek (see page 30)
6 sprigs fresh mint

1. Place tuna slices, one at a time, between sheets of waxed paper or Saran Wrap and pound until the slices are as thin as veal scaloppine. Be careful not to make tuna any thinner than that, or there won't be any suggestion of texture. When pounding tuna, use a circular motion. Tuna slices should be as round as possible to cover surface of plates properly. Place 1 tuna slice on each of 6 plates.

2. Cut off and reserve pieces of tuna that extend over plates or that make tuna circles look uneven, and prepare a Tuna Tartar while reserving plates with Carpaccio of Tuna.

TUNA TARTAR

1 shallot, peeled and minced
1 tablespoon olive oil
2 teaspoons chopped capers
½ teaspoon lemon zest
1 teaspoon soy sauce
½ teaspoon ground horseradish
Tuna pieces from Carpaccio

1. Combine shallot and olive oil in a small saucepan, and sauté shallot for 30 seconds. Add capers, lemon zest, soy sauce, and horseradish. Mix until combined. Remove saucepan from heat.

2. Finely chop tuna pieces and add to shallot mixture. Mix thoroughly.

To Build This Dish

1. Combine olive oil, Mint Oil, lime zest, and cracked pepper in a bowl and mix thoroughly. Paint olive-oil mixture on Carpaccio with a pastry brush, or drizzle mixture on tuna and spread with a knife. Sprinkle salt on Carpaccio.

2. Place 3 asparagus spears on each serving of Carpaccio of Tuna and spoon Tuna Tartar onto center of each serving. Sprinkle sesame seeds over all, and add Lotus-Root Chips or Ribbons of Leek. Garnish with fresh mint.

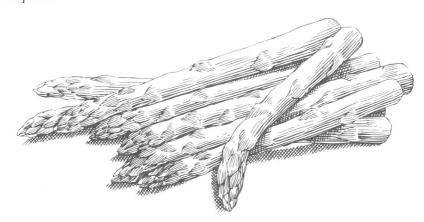

Tuna in Mustard-Seed Crust with Shrimp and Tomato Vinaigrette

YIELD: 4 SERVINGS

SHRIMP AND TOMATO VINAIGRETTE

Shells from 12 medium shrimp (shrimp reserved
for tuna, below)
½ cup tarragon vinegar
1 tablespoon chopped fresh tarragon or 1 teaspoon
dried tarragon
½ cup Tomato Fondue (see page 44)
¾ cup olive oil
Coarse or kosher salt and freshly ground pepper
to taste

1. Combine shrimp shells, vinegar, and chopped tarragon in a saucepan. Bring to a simmer and cook for 3 to 5 minutes, until liquid is reduced by half. Strain and discard shells and tarragon.

2. Return liquid to saucepan. Add Tomato Fondue and gradually whisk in olive oil over low heat. Season to taste. Reserve.

TUNA

1 2-pound tuna steak
Coarse or kosher salt and freshly ground pepper
to taste
2 egg whites, lightly beaten
2 tablespoons Dijon mustard
4 tablespoons mustard seeds
4 tablespoons fresh bread crumbs
½ cup olive oil for sautéing tuna
12 medium shrimp, peeled and deveined
Olive oil or Ginger Oil (see page 124) for
sautéing watercress and corn
2 bunches watercress
½ cup cooked corn kernels
1 tablespoon soy sauce
1 teaspoon chopped ginger
1 tablespoon honey
8 Beer-Batter Fried Onion Rings (see
pages 33–4)
Watercress sprigs

1. Cut steak into 4 portions. Portions will be thick and look like logs. Season steaks.

2. Combine egg whites and Dijon mustard. Mix well. Coat tuna steaks with egg mixture.

3. Combine mustard seeds and bread crumbs. Mix well. Coat tuna steaks with bread-crumb mixture.

4. Heat oil in a sauté pan. Add tuna steaks and cook over medium heat, turning steaks from side to side until golden brown on all sides, approximately 30 seconds on each side, for a total of 2 minutes. Do not over-

cook. Tuna steaks are best rare to medium-rare. Remove tuna steaks from pan and keep warm.

5. Season shrimp with salt and pepper and cook quickly in sauté pan for 1 to 2 minutes, turning, until shrimp are firm. Remove from pan and keep warm.

6. Drain oil from pan and wipe clean with a paper towel. Add olive oil or Ginger Oil to pan. Add watercress and corn. Stir to mix. Add soy sauce, ginger, and honey and cook, stirring, for 30 seconds. Season to taste.

To Build This Dish

1. Place watercress-corn mixture in center of 4 dinner plates.

2. Spoon Tomato Vinaigrette around perimeter of each plate.

3. With a very sharp knife, cut each tuna steak in half, on the bias, and place on plates.

4. Place 3 shrimp on each tuna steak, linking shrimp together.

5. Place 1 or 2 Beer-Batter Fried Onion Rings on shrimp and garnish with watercress sprigs.

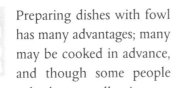

Chapter 6

BUILDING A DISH
WITH FOWL

Preparing dishes with fowl has many advantages; many may be cooked in advance, and though some people won't eat red meat and others are allergic to or don't care for fish, most people will eat poultry—a great plus when giving a dinner party.

Most fowl taste best when their delicate flavor is augmented by sauces and vegetables aromatic with spices and herbs. Contrasting textures are the hallmark of properly cooked poultry: the skin should be crisp, the meat moist and tender. When preparing quail or squab, do not overcook, for they do not contain a great deal of fat, and overcooking results in a dry, uninteresting dish.

Many of the side dishes and garnishes used in my recipes can be enjoyed with roast turkey and broiled or roast chicken, and the noodle cake, polentas, risottos, and hashes go well with fish.

Baked Chicken with Noodle Cake, Vegetable Skewers, Roast-Garlic Sauce, and Candied Garlic

YIELD: 4 SERVINGS

NOODLE CAKE

3 tablespoons olive oil
4 tablespoons Roast-Garlic Purée (see page 28)
3 tablespoons butter, softened
4 tablespoons chopped chives
Coarse or kosher salt and freshly ground pepper
*   to taste*
½ pound linguine
1 teaspoon olive oil (for pie plate)

1. Preheat oven to 400°.

2. Place all ingredients except linguine and 1 teaspoon olive oil in a bowl and mix.

3. Cook linguine *al dente,* and drain.

4. Spoon olive-oil–garlic mixture over linguine and toss until all ingredients are thoroughly combined.

5. Lightly oil an 8-inch pie plate and spoon linguine into plate or 4 8-ounce ramekins. Press down with the back of a spoon. Cover and bake for 30 minutes. Uncover and bake an additional 20 to 25 minutes, baking chicken at the same time.

BAKED CHICKEN

1 tablespoon chopped fresh tarragon or 1 teaspoon
*   dried tarragon*
1 tablespoon chopped fresh thyme or 1 teaspoon
*   dried thyme*
1 tablespoon olive oil
4 chicken breasts, wing bones attached, each about
*   7 to 8 ounces*
Coarse or kosher salt and freshly ground pepper
*   to taste*

1. Combine tarragon, thyme, and olive oil and mix. Season chicken with salt and pepper and spread herb–olive-oil mixture over chicken and beneath skin.

2. Tuck tip of each wing under and place chicken breasts in a shallow baking pan. Fit them closely together. They should nestle one against another, resembling rolls or muffins in a bakery or bread pan.

3. Place chicken in oven when you uncover linguine and roast for 20 to 25 minutes, or until chicken breasts are completely cooked.

4. While linguine and chicken cook, prepare the Vegetable Skewers and sauce.

VEGETABLE SKEWERS

2 tablespoons olive oil
1 zucchini, cut into 4 pieces, each piece
*   quartered*
1 red bell pepper, cut into squares
1 yellow bell pepper, cut into squares
8 mushroom caps
Coarse or kosher salt and freshly ground pepper
*   to taste*

1. Heat olive oil in a sauté pan. Add vegetables and cook, stirring occasionally, until vegetables are just tender. Do not overcook; vegetables should retain their shapes. Season with salt and pepper.

2. Using a slotted spoon, remove vegetables from pan and drain on paper towels. When cool enough to handle, thread vegetables on 8 bamboo skewers. Heat in oven during last 5 minutes of cooking time for chicken and noodles.

ROAST-GARLIC SAUCE

4 tablespoons butter
2 shallots, minced
2 cups white wine
1 tablespoon Roast-Garlic Purée (see page
*   28)*
1 cup Brown Stock (see page 77) or Light
*   Chicken Stock (see page 76) or canned*
*   chicken broth*
4 tablespoons chopped chives
Coarse or kosher salt and freshly ground pepper
*   to taste*
Candied Garlic (see page 29)

1. Heat 2 tablespoons butter in a saucepan. Add shallots and cook, stirring, for 1 minute. Add white wine and cook until liquid is reduced by about half.

2. Stir in Roast-Garlic Purée and add stock or broth. Reduce liquid by half again. Whisk in remaining 2 tablespoons butter and chives and season to taste. Stir in Candied Garlic. Reserve and keep warm.

To Build This Dish

1. Cut baked Noodle Cake in pan into 4 wedges. Place a wedge on each of 4 plates.

2. Place 1 chicken breast on each wedge and pierce each breast with Vegetable Skewer. Spoon Roast-Garlic Sauce around perimeter of plates.

SPECIAL NOTE: I prepare this dish somewhat differently in my restaurant. The noodles are baked in individual molds, as are the chicken breasts. A portion of Noodle Cake is unmolded on each plate, to be covered by a serving of chicken. The noodles and chicken are almost perfectly matched in diameter. This is an attractive look, but the flavor of the dish is not changed by the easier presentation in the above recipe.

Poached Chicken Breasts with Ratatouille Orzo Ragout

YIELD: 4 SERVINGS

1½ cups Light Chicken Stock (see page 76) or canned chicken broth

1½ cups Tomato Coulis (see page 44) or 1 cup canned tomato sauce

4 boneless, skinless chicken breasts, about 6 ounces each

Coarse or kosher salt and freshly ground pepper to taste

1 red bell pepper, diced

1 yellow bell pepper, diced

1 zucchini, diced

1 yellow squash, diced

1 small eggplant, not peeled, outer 1½ inches only, diced

½ small onion, diced

3 cloves garlic, minced

1 cup chopped fresh basil or 2 tablespoons dried basil

2 cups cooked orzo pasta

½ cup mascarpone cheese or grated Parmesan cheese

4 basil leaves or parsley

1. Combine Light Chicken Stock or broth and Tomato Coulis or tomato sauce in a soup pot. Bring to a simmer.

2. Season chicken with salt and pepper and add to pot. Cover and simmer for 5 to 10 minutes, or until chicken is cooked.

3. Add all remaining ingredients except for cheese and basil leaves or parsley, stir, and simmer for an additional 2 minutes. Remove chicken breasts and keep warm.

4. Cook vegetable-pasta mixture until vegetables are tender and orzo is hot. Correct seasoning.

To Build This Dish

1. Spoon Ratatouille Orzo Ragout into 4 large bowls.

2. Cut each chicken breast horizontally into 2 pieces and place over ragout.

3. Top with a tablespoon of mascarpone cheese or grated Parmesan cheese and garnish with a basil leaf or parsley.

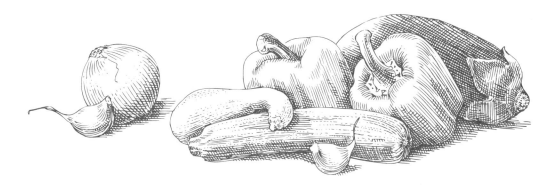

Roast Cornish Hens with Saffron Potatoes and Chorizo Sausages

YIELD: 4 SERVINGS

2 Cornish hens
Coarse or kosher salt and freshly ground pepper
    to taste
2 tablespoons chopped fresh oregano or
    2 teaspoons dried oregano
4 roasted red bell peppers (see page 178), peeled,
    cut into strips
2 bay leaves
5 tablespoons olive oil
2 cups Saffron Potatoes (see variations, page 39)
½ pound cooked chorizo sausages, thinly
    sliced
1 cup cooked green peas

1. Preheat oven to 375°.

2. Season cavities of hens with salt and pepper. Add oregano, pepper strips, and bay leaves. Brush outside of hens with 4 tablespoons olive oil and season with salt and pepper.

3. Place hens in a shallow roasting pan and bake for 25 to 30 minutes.

4. While hens are baking, prepare Saffron Whipped Potatoes. Reserve and keep warm.

5. Remove hens from oven and allow to rest for 10 minutes before carving.

6. Heat remaining tablespoon of olive oil in a sauté pan and sauté chorizos over low heat for 1 minute.

7. Carve each hen into 2 portions, adding all juices and ingredients from the cavities of the hens to chorizos. Stir in green peas and heat all ingredients through.

To Build This Dish

1. Serve family-style: place the Cornish Hens on a large platter and spoon the chorizo–red-pepper sauce over and around the birds.

2. Serve the golden Saffron Whipped Potatoes in a large bowl; pass and serve the hens and potatoes at the table.

3. Accompany with black olives and a vase of Black-Olive Breadsticks (see page 54).

Duck Confit on Barbecued Potatoes

YIELD: 4 SERVINGS

*H*ere's a dish that combines two regional cuisines: southwestern France and the American West. The Duck Confit is based on dishes I prepared when working at La Rapière in Mauvezin, France, and the Barbecued Potatoes are my version of an American favorite.

CONFIT

1 bunch parsley, chopped
1 cup chopped shallots
¼ cup chopped thyme
8 cloves garlic, chopped
6 bay leaves, crushed
4 duck legs, including thighs
Coarse or kosher salt for dredging, about 1 cup
2 to 3 cups rendered duck fat or lard

1. Create a marinade by combining parsley, shallots, thyme, garlic, and bay leaves. Mix well and spread half of mixture in the bottom of a shallow pan.

2. Dredge duck legs in salt, coating heavily on both sides. Place duck legs on top of marinade in pan and top with remainder of marinade. Cover and refrigerate for 4 days.

3. Remove duck legs from marinade and, using a towel, wipe off mixture.

4. Heat duck fat or lard in a heavy pot. Add duck legs. Cover and simmer very slowly for 1½ to 2 hours, or until meat is very tender and almost falls off the bone.

5. Remove legs from the fat and place in a crock or similar container. Strain fat over bird, cover, and refrigerate.

BARBECUED POTATOES

1 cup Coffee Barbecue Sauce (see page 176)
½ cup heavy sweet cream
1 tablespoon butter
5 large potatoes, peeled and thinly sliced
Coarse or kosher salt to taste

1. Preheat oven to 375°.

2. Combine Coffee Barbecue Sauce and cream in a bowl and mix thoroughly.

3. Spread butter over bottom and sides of an ovenproof casserole. Spoon a small amount of Barbecue Sauce–cream mixture into casserole. Top with a layer of sliced potatoes. Salt potatoes. Continue layering sauce, potatoes, and salt until sauce and potatoes are used up.

4. Cover and bake for 45 minutes. Remove foil and bake an additional 15 to 20 minutes, or until potatoes are crisp and brown and sauce is bubbling.

To Build This Dish

1. During the last 10 minutes that the potatoes cook, heat duck legs in oven in a small amount of fat.

2. Place a wedge of Barbecued Potatoes in the center of each of 4 dinner plates. Top with a duck leg. Pass remainder of potatoes.

3. Serve with a crock of cornichon pickles or spoon Pickled-Onion, Cucumber, and Corn Relish (see page 184) around duck.

Roast Quail with Bacon Salsa and Goat-Cheese Fondue

YIELD: 4 SERVINGS

Quail is a great favorite of mine, but if not readily available, this dish may also be prepared with chicken wings.

BACON SALSA

8 slices bacon, diced
2 cups Salsa (see page 179)

1. Cook bacon in a skillet until lightly browned. Remove bacon with a slotted spoon and drain on paper towels.

2. Combine bacon and Salsa in a bowl. Mix, and reserve.

QUAIL

8 to 12 quail (2 to 3 birds per serving)
Coarse or kosher salt and freshly ground pepper
*   to taste*
3 tablespoons olive oil
8 to 12 sprigs watercress

1. Preheat oven to 375°.

2. Season quail with salt and pepper. Heat olive oil in a large sauté pan. Add quail and brown lightly on all sides. (You may have to do

this in 2 or more steps, depending on the size of your pan.) After birds brown, remove to a shallow baking pan.

3. Roast birds for 6 to 8 minutes.

GOAT-CHEESE FONDUE

> *4 ounces soft goat cheese*
> *½ cup heavy sweet cream*
> *2 tablespoons butter*
> *Coarse or kosher salt and freshly ground pepper*
>   *to taste*
> *½ teaspoon freshly ground cumin*
> *2 tablespoons chopped chives*

While birds are roasting, combine cheese and cream in a small saucepan. Bring to a simmer over low heat, whisking to combine. Add butter and whisk together. Season with salt, pepper, and cumin, and stir in chives.

To Build This Dish

1. Create a circle of scarlet by spooning Bacon Salsa on center of each of 4 dinner plates. Do not go to the edge of plates.

2. Place 2 or 3 quail, facing in opposite directions, on top of Bacon Salsa. Place a sprig of watercress into the cavity of each bird.

3. Carefully spoon Goat-Cheese Fondue around the perimeter of each plate. You will have a circle of scarlet banded by a circle of ivory. (The quail can be served over greens with Salsa, if you find the Fondue too rich.)

4. Serve with plenty of bread to sop up the Bacon Salsa and the Goat-Cheese Fondue.

5. Prepare finger bowls.

Barbecued Squab with Cheddar Corn Cakes, Onion and Pistachio Marmalade, and Pistachio Wafers

YIELD: 4 SERVINGS

Squab is a delicious bird, and I consider it the king of all game birds.

CHEDDAR CORN CAKES

> *¼ cup sugar*
> *3 tablespoons butter*
> *1 teaspoon coarse or kosher salt*
> *1 teaspoon freshly ground pepper*
> *1 egg*
> *1 egg white*
> *½ cup milk*
> *6 tablespoons cornmeal*
> *6 tablespoons grated Cheddar cheese*
> *½ cup all-purpose flour*
> *⅓ teaspoon baking powder*
> *2 tablespoons honey*
> *1 tablespoon butter for loaf pan*

1. Preheat oven to 500°.

2. Combine sugar, butter, salt, and pepper in a bowl and cream together, or combine and process in a food processor.

3. Gradually add egg, egg white, and milk to sugar-butter mixture and mix to combine.

4. Add cornmeal, cheese, flour, and baking powder, continuing to mix. When ingredients are combined, add honey and mix again.

5. Butter a loaf pan. Spoon corn-cake mixture into pan and bake 20 to 30 minutes, or until a skewer inserted in center of corn cake comes out clean. Reserve.

BARBECUED SQUAB

4 squabs, about ¾ to 1 pound each
Coarse or kosher salt and freshly ground pepper
* to taste*
1 cup Coffee Barbecue Sauce (see page 176)
1 cup Onion and Pistachio Marmalade (see page
* 177)*
Pistachio Wafers (see variation, page 24)
2 cups corn kernels, sautéed in butter (optional)

1. Preheat grill or broiler.

2. Cut each squab into 4 pieces, separating breast and legs, and trim and discard all visible fat. Season with salt and pepper and brush birds with some of the Coffee Barbecue Sauce. Allow squab to marinate for 30 minutes.

3. Grill or broil squab for 5 minutes on each side, or until birds are brown and slightly crisp. Be careful not to burn squab. Squab are best when they are rare or medium-rare.

To Build This Dish

1. Cut 4 slices, each about 3 inches by 5 inches, from corn cake, and toast lightly.

2. Place a corn cake in the center of each of 4 dinner plates.

3. Place 2 breasts of squab on top of each corn cake and place legs on either side of corn cake.

4. Heat Coffee Barbecue Sauce, spoon over squab, and garnish with Onion and Pistachio Marmalade.

5. Serve with Pistachio Wafers and, if you wish, sautéed corn kernels.

SPECIAL NOTE: There are many additional uses for corn cakes. They can be served with sautéed or roast chicken and with grilled fish. I also prepare corn cakes without cheese for sandwiches by cutting them into small squares and filling them with Chicken Purée. Corn-cake sandwiches are sautéed in butter or baked in a 325° oven for 10 minutes. They make wonderful hors d'oeuvres.

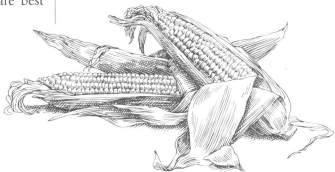

BUILDING A DISH
WITH MEAT

Not too many people today want to eat plain meat and potatoes. Most require more than a perfectly grilled steak or chop. The recipes in this chapter are meant to satisfy the desire for meat dishes prepared with some intricacy. Veal dishes are enhanced by wild mushrooms and shellfish. Lamb is prepared with chestnuts or root vegetables, and though beef and pork demand such traditional elements as potatoes and sauce, these are presented in different guise.

If there is meat left over from any of the dishes offered here, don't let it languish in the refrigerator. Toss the meat with a vinaigrette and serve with a salad of pickled vegetables. You'll find both recipes in Chapter Eight.

Filet of Beef with Bacon and Horseradish Crust in Cabernet Sauce

YIELD: 6 SERVINGS

*C*onsider this dish when giving a party. It's a wonderful showpiece.

BEEF

10 slices bacon

½ cup vegetable oil

2½ pounds filet of beef, trimmed

Coarse or kosher salt and freshly ground pepper
  to taste

3 tablespoons all-purpose flour

3 egg yolks

6 tablespoons freshly ground horseradish,
  or bottled horseradish with liquid
  pressed out

1 cup bread crumbs

6 large Potato Pancakes (see page 65)

12 to 18 Cherry Tomatoes Filled with Duck-Liver
  Mousse (see page 73)

1. Place bacon in saucepan and cover with water. Bring to a boil and blanch for 10 seconds. Remove bacon from saucepan and drain on paper towels. Reserve.

2. Preheat oven to 400°.

3. Heat oil in a large, heavy-bottomed skillet. Season filet generously with salt and pepper. Place filet in a sauté pan and, over medium-high heat, sear meat. Turn meat frequently until all sides are nicely browned. Remove from pan and drain on paper towels.

4. Make a horseradish paste by combining flour, egg yolks, and half the horseradish in a bowl. Mix well. Spread horseradish paste over beef filet, covering all sides and ends of meat.

5. Place a large sheet of aluminum foil on a board or table. Spread bread crumbs and remaining horseradish in center of foil. Place bacon slices on top of breadcrumb–horseradish mixture, overlapping slices slightly.

6. Lay filet in center of bacon strips. Gently pull strips until they wrap around filet. Roll filet in bread-crumb–horseradish mixture. Wrap foil around filet, tucking in ends.

7. Place filet on a baking sheet and roast for 25 minutes. Open foil and bake an additional 10 to 15 minutes.

8. Remove filet from oven and allow meat to rest for 5 to 8 minutes before carving.

CABERNET SAUCE

2 tablespoons butter
1 large onion, diced
2 cups Cabernet Sauvignon
1½ cups Dark Chicken Stock (see page 77)
    or Brown Stock (see page 77) or
    canned beef broth
1 teaspoon coarse or kosher salt
Freshly ground pepper to taste
3 tablespoons butter

1. While beef roasts, heat 2 tablespoons butter in a large saucepan. Add onion and cook, stirring, for 2 minutes. Add wine and reduce liquid by two-thirds. Add stock or broth and reduce by half.

2. Season to taste and whisk in 3 tablespoons butter. Continue cooking for 1 minute and reserve.

To Build This Dish

1. Place 1 large Potato Pancake on each of 6 dinner plates.

2. Slice filet into 12 slices. Place 2 slices of filet on each Potato Pancake, overlapping slightly.

3. Gently heat sauce and spoon around perimeter of plates.

4. Garnish each plate with 2 or 3 Cherry Tomatoes Filled with Duck-Liver Mousse and serve with green beans which have been steamed and tossed in butter.

Building a Dish with Meat   139

Chili with Cheddar Cheese and Apple Crackling

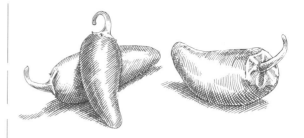

YIELD: 6 SERVINGS

SAUCE

4 tablespoons butter
1 red onion, diced
4 cloves garlic, minced
4 tablespoons dark-brown sugar
3 cups red wine
4 tablespoons red-wine vinegar
4 tablespoons Tomato Fondue (see page 44) or
*   canned tomato sauce*
4 cups Light Chicken Stock (see page 76) or
*   Brown Stock (see page 77) or canned beef*
*   broth*
2 tablespoons Roast-Garlic Purée (see page 28)
1 teaspoon cumin
½ teaspoon cayenne pepper
½ teaspoon chili powder
2 tablespoons freshly chopped coriander
1 teaspoon coarse or kosher salt

1. Heat butter in a large pot. Sauté onion and garlic for 1 minute. Add sugar and cook, stirring, until onion and garlic are slightly caramelized.

2. Add red wine, red-wine vinegar, Tomato Fondue or tomato sauce, stock or broth, and Roast-Garlic Purée, and stir to combine. Add remaining ingredients.

3. Bring sauce to a simmer and cook until liquid is reduced by half. Reserve.

MEAT AND BEANS

4 tablespoons Clarified Butter or vegetable oil
2 pounds diced beef, from rump or chuck, or
*   chicken, preferably leg meat*
Coarse or kosher salt and freshly ground pepper
*   to taste*
2 cups cooked black beans

1. Heat butter or oil in a large sauté pan.

2. Season meat or chicken and sauté, stirring frequently, until meat is brown.

3. Add black beans and stir to combine.

To Assemble: Add mixture of meat or chicken and beans to sauce. Heat to a simmer and cook for about 20 minutes, or until sauce has thickened and all flavors are combined. Adjust seasoning.

1 cup shredded Cheddar cheese

1 cup Apple Crackling (see page 24)

3 apples or pears, or combination, cored and sliced

2 cups sour cream

To Build This Dish

1. Spoon Chili into 6 bowls.

2. Top each bowl of Chili with Cheddar cheese and Apple Crackling.

3. Serve with apples, pears, a bowl of sour cream, and slices of toasted Swiss peasant bread on the side.

Steak Diane with Wild-Mushroom Flan

YIELD: 4 SERVINGS

*D*iana was the mythological Goddess of the Hunt, and this dish is appropriately named for her—with one slight change: Diana has become Diane. This dish is an adaptation of the old favorite, which was originally made with venison.

WILD-MUSHROOM FLAN

2 tablespoons Clarified Butter

½ pound wild mushrooms (chanterelle, shiitake, morel), finely minced

1 cup heavy sweet cream

2 eggs, lightly beaten

1 egg yolk, lightly beaten

Coarse or kosher salt and freshly ground pepper to taste

1 teaspoon chopped truffle (optional)

1 tablespoon chopped foie gras (optional)

1. Preheat oven to 350°.

2. Heat butter in a large saucepan. Add mushrooms and cook, stirring, for 2 minutes. Stir in heavy cream and slowly whip in eggs and egg yolk. Season to taste. Strain.

3. Pour flan mixture into 4 ramekins and add truffle and *foie gras,* if you wish, and place in a *bain-marie.* Cover each ramekin with foil

and bake for 25 minutes, or until flan is set and a skewer piercing side of flan comes out clean.

4. Prepare steaks and sauce while flans bake.

STEAKS

> *4 strip steaks, about 5 to 5½ ounces each*
> *Coarse or kosher salt and freshly ground pepper to taste*
> *4 tablespoons Clarified Butter (see page 26) or olive oil*
> *1 shallot, minced*
> *½ pound chanterelle mushrooms, sliced (white mushrooms may be used)*
> *4 tablespoons red wine*
> *4 tablespoons red-wine vinegar*
> *1 tablespoon cracked peppercorns*
> *1½ cups Brown Stock (see page 77) or Dark Chicken Stock (see page 77) or canned beef broth*
> *1 tablespoon chopped fresh tarragon or 1 teaspoon dried tarragon*
> *4 tablespoons butter*
> *2 tablespoons whole-grain mustard*
> *1 tablespoon Dijon mustard*

1. Season steaks with salt and pepper. Heat Clarified Butter or olive oil in a large sauté pan. Add steaks to pan and sauté for about 3 to 5 minutes on each side, turning, until both sides are nicely browned.

2. Remove steaks from pan and keep warm.

3. Drain all but 1 tablespoon of fat from pan. Add shallot and mushrooms and sauté for 1 minute, stirring.

4. Add red wine, red-wine vinegar, and peppercorns and cook over high heat, stirring, until all but 1 tablespoon of liquid has evaporated.

5. Add Brown Stock, Dark Chicken Stock, or broth and reduce by half. Stir in tarragon, salt, and pepper. Whisk in butter and add both mustards. Continue cooking, over low heat, until sauce has thickened slightly. Remove from heat.

To Build This Dish

1. Carve each steak into thin slices.

2. Turn a Wild-Mushroom Flan into center of each of 4 dinner plates, and fan meat around flan.

3. Spoon sauce over meat.

Variation: This dish may also be prepared with venison loin steaks.

Sirloin Steak with Shiitake-Mushroom Hash and Pickled Vegetables

YIELD: 4 SERVINGS

There are people who love steak above all other foods. I created this dish for them, but, rather than serving a plain, unadorned piece of meat, I added a new touch with my special hash: here's a steak brought up to date.

SHIITAKE-MUSHROOM HASH

¼ pound butter
1 large potato, peeled and diced
1 small onion, finely diced
1 yellow bell pepper, finely diced
1 red bell pepper, finely diced
12 shiitake mushroom caps, diced
1 cup heavy sweet cream
Coarse or kosher salt and freshly ground pepper
*   to taste*

1. Heat butter in a large sauté pan, preferably with a nonstick surface. Add potato and cook for 4 minutes over medium heat, stirring occasionally.

2. Add onion, yellow and red peppers, and mushroom caps and cook an additional 3 to 4 minutes, or until any liquid released by vegetables has evaporated and potatoes are cooked.

3. Add heavy sweet cream and bring to a boil. Continue cooking until mixture becomes very thick. Season to taste. Reserve.

SIRLOIN STEAKS

Clarified Butter (see page 26) for
*   sautéing*
4 sirloin steaks, trimmed, 10 to 12 ounces
*   each*
Coarse or kosher salt and freshly ground pepper
*   to taste*

1. Preheat oven to 375°.

2. Heat butter in a sauté pan. Season steaks and add steaks and cook over high heat until

browned on one side, about 1 minute. Turn and brown on second side. Meat will be seared but not cooked through.

3. Place steaks in a shallow baking pan. Spoon Shiitake-Mushroom Hash over steak. Smooth out with a flat knife. Hash should be contained on top of each steak.

4. Roast between 7 and 11 minutes, depending on how you like your steak: 7 minutes for rare or 11 minutes for medium. Remove from oven.

GARNISH

4 green onions, roughly chopped
Mixed Vegetables in Saffron and Turmeric
Pickling Liquid (see page 137)

To Build This Dish

1. Place a steak on each of 4 dinner plates.
2. Sprinkle two-thirds of chopped green onions over Shiitake-Mushroom Hash.
3. Spoon Vegetables in Pickling Liquid into a large serving bowl. Sprinkle with remaining green onions and serve with steak.

Rack of Lamb in Chestnut Crust with Sweet-Potato and Vanilla Purée with White-Wine Shallot Mint Sauce

YIELD: 4 SERVINGS

ack of lamb is one of my special dishes for the fall. The meat is coated in a crust of Italian chestnut meal or chestnut flour. If you have trouble locating these items, roast fresh chestnuts until tender, peel, and grind in a food processor. Combine ground chestnuts with an equal amount of bread crumbs.

WHITE-WINE SHALLOT MINT SAUCE

2 cups Riesling
4 shallots, minced
1 cup Brown Stock (see page 77) or Dark Chicken
Stock (see page 77) or canned beef broth
2 teaspoons butter
Coarse or kosher salt and freshly ground
pepper
1 teaspoon chopped fresh mint

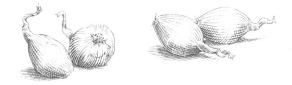

1. Combine wine and shallots in a saucepan. Cook until liquid is reduced by half.

2. Add stock or broth and continue cooking until liquid is reduced by half once again. Whisk in butter and season to taste. Remove from heat and stir in fresh mint. Reserve.

RACK OF LAMB

2 racks of lamb, about 1 to 1½ pounds per rack, each with 8 chops, chine bone and all visible fat removed
Coarse or kosher salt to taste
2 egg whites, lightly beaten
2 tablespoons freshly ground pepper
1 cup chestnut meal or chestnut flour
4 tablespoons Clarified Butter

1. Preheat oven to 350°.

2. Season racks of lamb with salt and brush meat with beaten egg whites.

3. Combine pepper with chestnut meal or chestnut flour and spoon into a shallow dish. Place rack of lamb in dish and coat with chestnut-pepper combination, pressing coating into both sides of each rack with hands.

4. Heat butter in a large sauté pan, preferably with a nonstick surface. Brown racks of lamb, one at a time, in pan, turning over until both sides are nicely browned.

5. Place racks of lamb in a shallow baking dish and roast for 25 to 30 minutes. Lamb is best served rare to medium-rare. Cook an additional 5 minutes for medium.

6. Remove lamb racks from oven and allow to rest for 5 minutes before carving each rack into double chops.

7. While lamb is roasting, prepare the Sweet-Potato and Vanilla Purée.

SWEET-POTATO AND VANILLA PURÉE

6 medium sweet potatoes, peeled and cubed
¼ pound butter, cut into 8 pieces
2 vanilla beans, split and scraped
Coarse or kosher salt and freshly ground pepper to taste

1. Place sweet potatoes in a saucepan with water to cover and cook until tender, about 20 minutes. Drain potatoes and return to saucepan.

2. Over low heat, mash potatoes until puréed, adding butter, vanilla, salt, and pepper. Remove from heat and reserve.

To Build This Dish

1. Using a pastry bag, pipe a platform of Sweet-Potato Purée onto the center of each of 4 dinner plates. (Potatoes may also be mounded onto plates with a large spoon.)

2. Arch double chops over Sweet-Potato Purée so that lamb bones intertwine above potatoes.

3. Spoon a small amount of White-Wine Shallot Mint Sauce over meat and spoon the rest around the perimeter of each plate.

4. As side dishes, serve sautéed spinach, mushrooms, or cauliflower.

Braised Lamb Shanks with Honey-Baked Turnips and Bacon

YIELD: 6 SERVINGS

Lamb shanks are wonderful in late fall or winter, and I serve them with baked turnips—a neglected root vegetable—which I bake much as you would a potato.

LAMB SHANKS

½ cup vegetable oil
6 lamb shanks
Coarse or kosher salt and freshly ground pepper
    to taste
1 head garlic, split into 2 pieces
3 stalks celery, chopped
1 carrot, chopped
1 onion, chopped
2 tablespoons Tomato Coulis (see page 44) or
    canned tomato sauce
2 quarts Light Chicken Stock (see page 76) or
    canned chicken broth

1. Heat oil in a large pot or Dutch oven. Add lamb shanks and sear, turning from side to side until lamb is browned on all sides. Season lamb.

2. Drain all fat except 1 tablespoon from pot. Add garlic and vegetables and brown lightly, stirring occasionally.

3. Add Tomato Coulis or sauce and stock or broth. Stir and cover pot. Simmer for about 2 hours, or until lamb is tender. Skim and discard fat or foam that rises as lamb cooks.

4. While lamb cooks, prepare turnips.

HONEY-BAKED TURNIPS

6 large white turnips
6 slices bacon
2 tablespoons butter
½ onion, sliced
Coarse or kosher salt and freshly ground pepper
    to taste
2 tablespoons honey
1 tablespoon chopped fresh rosemary or 1 teaspoon
    dried rosemary

1. Preheat oven to 375°.

2. Place turnips on a baking sheet and bake for about 1½ hours or until turnips are tender. Peel baked turnips and cut into ¼-inch slices.

3. While turnips are baking, sauté bacon. Drain on paper towels and dice. Reserve 2 tablespoons of bacon fat.

4. Heat butter and reserved bacon fat in a sauté pan. Add onion and turnip slices and sauté for 6 minutes, stirring occasionally. Season with salt and pepper.

5. Add bacon, honey, and rosemary to onion-turnip mixture and cook, stirring, for 2 minutes. Reserve.

To Build This Dish

1. After lamb shanks are tender, remove from sauce and keep warm.

2. Strain sauce, return liquid to pot, and reduce to approximately 1½ cups of liquid.

3. Spoon onion-turnip mixture on 6 dinner plates and top with lamb shanks. Spoon sauce over meat and around perimeter of plates. Serve with sautéed French string beans.

Grilled Lamb Chops with Black-Olive Couscous, Almond Wafers, and Curry Oil

YIELD: 4 SERVINGS

I want to present meals with a variety of colors as well as counterpoints of flavor. This is one of my most colorful lamb dishes: the grilled brown lamb contrasts with the ivory-and-black couscous. The Almond Wafers are tender beige, and the Curry Oil rich gold. There is a lot going on in tastes, textures, and visual appeal, and the appetite is piqued before the first bite of food is taken.

BLACK-OLIVE COUSCOUS

*1 cup Light Chicken Stock (see page 76) or
    canned chicken broth*
¾ cup couscous
1 tablespoon minced carrot
1 tablespoon minced celery
3 tablespoons Black-Olive Purée (see page 35)
1 tablespoon minced chives
*1 tablespoon minced fresh coriander or 1 teaspoon
    dried coriander*
Ground cumin to taste
*Coarse or kosher salt and freshly ground
    pepper to taste*

1. Bring stock or broth to a boil in a saucepan.

2. Add couscous, carrot, and celery and cook for 1 to 1½ minutes, or until couscous is tender.

3. Stir in Black-Olive Purée and chives. Add all remaining ingredients and stir to combine.

4. Lightly oil the inside of 4 6- to 8-ounce glasses, cups, or ramekins. These will be molds

for the couscous. Spoon couscous mixture into these molds, packing down with the back of a spoon, and reserve.

CORIANDER GARNISH

2 tablespoons vegetable oil
¼ cup fresh coriander leaves*

1. Heat vegetable oil in a small sauté pan and fry coriander leaves over high heat.
2. Remove leaves from pan with a slotted spoon and drain on paper towels. Reserve.

LAMB CHOPS

¼ cup olive oil
1 tablespoon chopped fresh thyme or 1 teaspoon dried thyme
1 tablespoon cracked pepper
Coarse or kosher salt to taste
8 double rib lamb chops, all visible fat removed
8 Almond Wafers (see page 24)
½ cup Curry Oil (see page 121)

*Mint may be used in place of coriander leaves.

1. Preheat grill or broiler.
2. Combine olive oil, thyme, cracked pepper, and salt. Mix well, and brush on both sides of lamb chops.
3. Place lamb chops on grill or in broiler and cook for approximately 3 to 4 minutes on each side for rare. Cook an additional 1 or 2 minutes for medium-rare or medium. Cooking time will depend on thickness of chops.

To Build This Dish

1. While lamb is cooking, unmold couscous onto center of each of 4 dinner plates. Garnish with fried coriander leaves.
2. When lamb is cooked, rest 2 pairs of double rib chops against each couscous column. Rib bones should be touching across the couscous.
3. Place one Almond Wafer against each couscous column and place a second wafer beside the lamb.
4. Drizzle Curry Oil over lamb and, with a small spoon, add droplets of oil to perimeter of each plate.

Rabbit, Fennel, and Mustard Pot Pie

YIELD: 2 SERVINGS

call this dish a pot pie, though it's not topped with the traditional pastry crust. I use a thin Potato Pancake instead, and my pot pie needs very little cooking time, whereas some can take hours. This recipe calls for rabbit meat, but you can use chicken—preferably meat cut from chicken legs.

½ pound cubed rabbit meat (preferably from the leg) or cubed chicken (use 2 whole chicken legs)

1 tablespoon coarse or kosher salt

½ teaspoon freshly ground pepper

2 tablespoons olive oil

1½ cups Light Chicken Stock (see page 76) or canned chicken broth

½ cup diced fennel bulb

1 cup sliced chanterelle mushrooms (white mushrooms may be substituted)

½ cup diced carrot

½ cup pearl onions

½ tablespoon chopped fresh thyme or ¼ teaspoon dried thyme

1 tablespoon Dijon mustard

1 tablespoon butter

2 thin Potato Pancakes (see page 65)

1. Season meat with salt and pepper.

2. Heat oil in a large sauté pan and sear meat over medium-high heat, stirring, until all sides are lightly browned.

3. Add all remaining ingredients except mustard, butter, and Potato Pancakes. Stir, bring to a simmer, and cover. Cook for 5 to 6 minutes, or until meat is cooked and tender.

4. Add mustard and butter, stir, and cook for an additional 2 minutes.

5. Spoon into 2 large bowls* and cover each serving with a Potato Pancake. (Diameter of pancake will depend on size of bowl.)

6. Serve with large chunks of crusty black bread or pumpernickel and a crock of cornichon pickles.

*This is a perfect quick supper for 2 people, with the addition of a good bottle of hearty red wine, or it can be served in smaller bowls as a first course for 4.

Roast Pork Loin with Boneless-Sparerib Homefries and Honey Mustard Sauce

YIELD: 4 TO 5 SERVINGS

A whole new way of cooking homefries is to prepare them with boned spareribs in combination with potato and onion. In the following recipe, these spareribs are served with roast pork, but they can also be presented at a barbecue or a picnic, spooned onto hamburger buns or hot-dog rolls. They're also great served in place of corned-beef hash and topped with an egg. Sparerib Homefries and eggs in any form is one of my favorite ways to start a weekend breakfast or brunch.

HONEY MUSTARD SAUCE

4 tablespoons butter
3 shallots, minced
2 tablespoons honey
2 cups white wine
1½ cups Brown Stock (see page 77) or Dark Chicken Stock (see page 77) or canned beef broth
2½ tablespoons Dijon mustard
½ teaspoon salt

1. Heat 2 tablespoons butter in a large saucepan. Sauté shallots, stirring, for 3 minutes. Add honey and cook, stirring, for an additional 5 minutes.

2. Add white wine and continue cooking until liquid is reduced to approximately ½ cup. Add stock or broth and cook until liquid is reduced by half.

3. Stir in mustard and remainder of butter, and add salt. Cook 1 minute and reserve.

SPARERIB HOMEFRIES

1½ pounds spareribs
4 tablespoons butter
1 large potato, peeled and diced
1 small onion, diced
4 tablespoons Coffee Barbecue Sauce (see page 176)
½ cup cooked corn kernels
1 tablespoon caraway seeds
½ cup chopped chives
Coarse or kosher salt and freshly ground pepper to taste

1. Cover spareribs with salted water and bring to a boil. Cook spareribs for 1½ hours, drain, and allow spareribs to cool until they can be easily handled.

2. Bone spareribs and trim all visible fat. Discard bones and fat. Cut remaining meat into ½-inch cubes and reserve.

3. Heat butter in a large sauté pan, preferably with a nonstick surface. Add potato and onion and cook until potato is tender.

4. Add meat and Coffee Barbecue Sauce and cook until all ingredients are heated through. Stir in corn, caraway seeds, and chives, and correct seasoning. Reserve.

ROAST PORK LOIN

1½ pounds boned and trimmed pork
loin
Coarse or kosher salt and freshly ground pepper
to taste
2 tablespoons olive oil
Honey Mustard Sauce
1 cup chopped parsley

1. Preheat oven to 350°.

2. Season pork with salt and pepper and place in a shallow baking pan. Spoon olive oil over pork.

3. Roast pork for approximately 35 to 45 minutes, or until pork is completely cooked. Turn pork after 15 minutes and baste with 4 tablespoons Honey Mustard Sauce. Reserve remainder of sauce.

4. Remove pork loin from oven and allow it to rest for 10 minutes before carving into thin slices.

To Build This Dish

1. Spoon a mound of Sparerib Homefries into the center of each of 4 or 5 dinner plates.

2. Fan slices of pork around Sparerib Homefries.

3. Spoon Honey Mustard Sauce over meat and garnish with chopped parsley.

4. Serve with Cheddar Corn Cakes (see page 134), Pickled-Onion, Cucumber, and Corn Relish (see page 184), and remaining Honey Mustard Sauce.

Calves' Liver with Mustard Seeds and Sorrel Sauce

YIELD: 4 SERVINGS

4 ½-inch-thick slices calves' liver, about 6 ounces
    each
¼ cup all-purpose flour
2 eggs, lightly beaten
6 tablespoons whole-grain mustard
4 tablespoons mustard seeds
4 tablespoons fresh bread crumbs
4 tablespoons butter
1 shallot, minced
4 tablespoons Dark Chicken Stock (see page 77)
    or canned beef broth
1 bunch fresh sorrel, chopped, or 1 cup chopped
    chives
Coarse or kosher salt and freshly ground pepper
    to taste
¼ cup Clarified Butter (see page 26) for
    sautéing

1. Rinse liver and pat dry with paper towels.

2. Coat liver slices with flour. Combine eggs and whole-grain mustard. Mix well. Coat liver with egg mixture.

3. Combine mustard seeds and bread crumbs. Mix well. Coat liver with mustard-seed mixture. Reserve.

4. Heat 1 tablespoon butter in saucepan. Add shallot and cook for 1 minute, stirring. Add stock or broth and remainder of butter and sim-mer, stirring, until ingredients are combined. Stir in sorrel and simmer for an additional minute.

5. Season to taste. Keep sauce warm.

6. Heat Clarified Butter in a sauté pan, preferably with a nonstick surface.

7. Sauté liver slices, turning, until both sides are lightly browned. Liver will be medium-rare in 2 to 3 minutes. Cook 1 or 2 minutes longer for medium, but don't overcook.

8. Place cooked liver on a serving platter or on 4 individual plates. Spoon sauce over liver and serve with Wild-Mushroom Flan (see page 141).

Veal and Shrimp Stew with Chanterelles and Asparagus

YIELD: 4 SERVINGS

4 tablespoons butter
1 pound veal, cubed (preferably from the leg)
Coarse or kosher salt and freshly ground pepper
    to taste
1 medium onion, diced
3 cups Light Chicken Stock (see page 76) or
    canned chicken broth
16 chanterelle-mushroom caps
8 asparagus stalks, peeled and steamed, cut into
    2-inch lengths

Sautéed Veal Chops with Wild-Mushroom Risotto and Watercress Sauce

YIELD: 4 SERVINGS

8 large shrimp, peeled and deveined
½ cup cooked corn kernels
2 tablespoons butter
½ cup chopped chives

1. Heat butter in a large sauté pan. Season veal with salt and pepper and sauté for 1 minute, turning so that meat sears.

2. Add onion and sauté for another minute. Add stock or broth and simmer for 6 to 8 minutes. Add chanterelles and cook for an additional 5 minutes.

3. Add asparagus, shrimp, and corn and continue simmering until shrimp are cooked, approximately 5 minutes.

4. Transfer liquid from sauté pan into a small saucepan and cook over high heat until liquid is reduced by approximately half.

5. While sauce is cooking, spoon stew into 4 soup plates.

6. When sauce is reduced to about 1½ cups, whisk in butter and chives. Correct seasoning and top stew with sauce.

WATERCRESS SAUCE

2 bunches watercress

1. Blanch watercress in boiling salted water for 2 minutes. Drain and place watercress in food processor.

2. Purée and reserve.

WILD-MUSHROOM RISOTTO

4 tablespoons butter
½ pound assorted wild mushrooms (chanterelles, morels, shiitakes, etc.), quartered
2 tablespoons olive oil
¼ cup minced onion
1 cup imported Italian rice, such as Arborio brand
4 cups Light Chicken Stock (see page 76) or canned chicken broth
1 teaspoon coarse or kosher salt
Freshly ground pepper to taste

1. Heat butter in a small saucepan. Add mushrooms and cook, stirring occasionally, for 2 minutes. Reserve.

2. Heat olive oil in another saucepan. Add onion and cook, stirring, for 30 seconds. Add

rice and continue cooking for another 30 seconds, or until rice grains are coated with oil.

3. Gradually add stock or broth, adding more liquid as it is absorbed by rice, and stirring frequently.

4. Continue cooking until all liquid is absorbed and rice is tender, about 20 to 25 minutes. Fold in mushrooms and season.

VEAL CHOPS

> 4 tablespoons Clarified Butter or olive oil
> Coarse or kosher salt and freshly ground pepper
>   to taste
> 4 veal chops, center-cut rib, 1 to 1½ inches thick,
>   about 10 ounces each
> 1 cup Light Chicken Stock (see page 76) or
>   canned chicken broth
> Juice of 1 lemon
> 4 tablespoons butter
> ½ cup minced carrots
> Mushroom Chips (see page 47)

1. Preheat oven to 400°.

2. Heat butter in a large sauté pan, preferably with a nonstick surface. Season chops and sauté

over medium-high heat for about 3 minutes on each side, or until chops are lightly browned.

3. Place chops on a baking sheet and transfer to oven. Cook an additional 6 to 8 minutes.

4. While chops roast, drain fat from sauté pan. Add stock or broth and lemon juice and reduce by half.

5. Add watercress purée and 2 tablespoons butter and cook an additional minute, stirring to combine. Correct seasoning.

6. Heat remaining 2 tablespoons butter in a small saucepan. Add carrots and cook, stirring, for 1 to 2 minutes or until carrots are tender. Season to taste. Reserve.

To Build This Dish

1. Spoon Wild-Mushroom Risotto into the center of each of 4 dinner plates. Flatten with the back of a spoon.

2. Place 1 chop on top of each serving of risotto. Spoon Watercress Sauce around the perimeter of each plate.

3. Mound carrots on top of each chop. Garnish with Mushroom Chips.

Medallions of Veal with Calvados Sauce

YIELD: 6 SERVINGS

CALVADOS SAUCE

2 tablespoons butter

2 shallots, minced

2 Granny Smith or similar apples, peeled and chopped

½ cup plus 1 tablespoon Calvados (applejack may be substituted)

2 cups Brown Stock (see page 77) or Dark Chicken Stock (see page 76) or canned beef broth

2 tablespoons butter

Coarse or kosher salt and freshly ground pepper to taste

1. Heat butter in a saucepan. Add shallots and cook, stirring, for 30 seconds. Add apples and continue cooking for 2 minutes.

2. Add ½ cup Calvados and reduce by approximately half.

3. Add stock or broth and reduce liquid by half again. Whisk in butter and add remaining tablespoon Calvados. Season to taste. Reserve.

INGREDIENTS FOR VEAL

1 celery root, peeled and quartered

1 large carrot, cut in half crosswise

1 tablespoon olive oil

½ cup Clarified Butter (see page 26) or olive oil

6 medallions of veal, about 6 ounces each, lightly pounded

Coarse or kosher salt and freshly ground pepper to taste

6 large Potato Pancakes (see page 65)

2 to 3 Granny Smith or similar apples, cut into total of 12 round slices

1. Place celery root in salted water. Bring to a boil and blanch for about 10 minutes, or until celery-root pieces can be pierced by a fork. (Celery root is a dense vegetable and needs a longer blanching time to reach a semi-tender stage. Blanching also eliminates much of this vegetable's bitterness.) Drain. When celery root has cooled enough so that it can be easily handled, cut each quarter into slices, and then cut slices into matchsticks and reserve.

2. Place carrot in salted water. Bring to a boil and blanch for about 2 minutes, or until carrot

halves can be pierced by a fork. Drain. When carrot has cooled enough so that it can be easily handled, cut each half into matchsticks and reserve.

3. Heat Clarified Butter or olive oil in a sauté pan. Season veal medallions with salt and pepper and sauté veal over medium-high heat for about 2 minutes on each side, or until veal is lightly browned.

4. Remove veal from sauté pan and keep warm. Drain all but 1 tablespoon of fat from pan. Add celery root and carrots and cook, stirring, for 1 minute.

To Build This Dish

1. Place a Potato Pancake in the center of each of 6 dinner plates.

2. Top each pancake with 2 slices of apple.

3. Place a veal medallion on top of the apple slices and top the veal with celery root and carrots.

4. Spoon Calvados Sauce around the perimeter of each plate.

Variation: When building this dish, place a slice of Sweetbread and Raisin Terrine (see page 72) between the apple and the veal medallions.

Osso Buco with Pasta and Preserved Lemon Rings

YIELD: 4 SERVINGS

OSSO BUCO

4 veal shanks, about 12 ounces each
Coarse or kosher salt and freshly ground pepper to taste
1 tablespoon olive oil
1 carrot, minced
1 stalk celery, minced
1 small onion, minced
4 sprigs fresh rosemary or ½ teaspoon dried and crushed rosemary
2 quarts Brown Stock (see page 77) or canned beef broth

1. Preheat oven to 350°.

2. Season veal shanks with salt and pepper. Heat oil in an ovenproof casserole or Dutch oven. Sauté veal shanks, turning once or twice, until they are lightly browned.

3. Add carrot, celery, and onion to veal. Stir, and allow meat and vegetables to brown for an additional 5 minutes. Stir in rosemary.

4. Add stock or broth. Cover and bring sauce to a simmer.

5. Place veal in oven and braise for 1½ to 2 hours, or until veal is tender.

6. Remove veal shanks from pot and keep warm. Strain the sauce and reduce to approximately 1½ cups.

2 tablespoons butter

¼ cup diced yellow squash

¼ cup diced zucchini

1 small carrot, blanched and diced

Coarse or kosher salt and freshly ground pepper
 to taste

1 cup orecchiette pasta, or small pasta shells,
 cooked al dente

1. Heat butter in a large sauté pan. Add squash, zucchini, and carrot, and sauté for 2 minutes. Season to taste.

2. Add pasta and toss to combine. Reserve.

GARNISH

(The Lemon Rings must be prepared a day in
 advance, but the remaining ingredients can be
 readied while the veal is braising.)

2 lemons, each cut into 6 sections

8 Preserved Lemon Rings (see page 33)

4 sprigs fresh rosemary or fresh parsley

1 tablespoon lemon zest

To Build This Dish

1. Create a pool of sauce in the center of each of 4 dinner plates. Spoon vegetable-pasta mixture into the middle of the sauce and set a veal shank on top.

2. Place 3 lemon sections beside each chop. Top veal with Lemon Rings and rosemary and scatter lemon zest around the plates.

Chapter 8

FLAVORED OILS, VINAIGRETTES, AND SAUCES

Here are the recipes for the extras, the glosses that can make a simple dish very special. The vinaigrettes and some of the sauces use flavored oils as a base. These infused oils are a recent invention of New American Cuisine. They add a bright flavor and, when offered in glass containers at dinner, add sparkle to a table.

My sauces—in this chapter and throughout the book—are not heavy. Sauces dependent on a fat-flour mixture, the old-fashioned *roux,* are definitely less in use today. Now cooking calls for light sauces that point up rather than disguise the flavor of a main ingredient. Most of the recipes can be simply and quickly prepared. Experiment with them. This chapter can be a playground for your creativity.

A Bouquet of
Flavored Oils

I started experimenting with flavored—or infused—oils a few years ago. I was looking for something new to brighten sauces and marinades, and I wanted to work less with creams and butters. The dazzling variety of available herbs and spices inspired me to develop a bouquet of flavored oils. As I combined ingredients, I realized that it wasn't enough to add a clove of garlic or a spoonful of curry powder to an oil at the last minute. If you are truly to marry flavors, an herb, a spice, or some other ingredient has to develop a relationship with an oil.

I prepare flavored oils using three methods:

I cook a vegetable such as celery in oil to release the flavor, and then I purée the celery with the oil. The result is a purée-oil, which I use to decorate a plate or to garnish fish or meat.

The second method is to steep a spice, an herb, or a citrus fruit in an oil that is barely warm. These oils are put away unstrained and continue steeping while refrigerated. I then strain the oil when I need it.

The third method calls for cooking ingredients such as lobster shells, shrimp shells, crab shells—things you would normally discard—in oil and straining before using. Garlic skins—those thin, papery skins—can be used to make Roast-Garlic Oil. Horseradish peel steeped in oil will make a wonderful Horseradish Oil. Ginger peelings can be used the same way. The result is an oil that glows with a new color and contains a serious essence of flavor. These clear oils are the prettiest of all—when they catch the light, they look like jewels.

Flavored oils have to be prepared in advance—they need a little time to come to full strength. Once made, they last for about two weeks when refrigerated or kept in a cool place. The exceptions are fish oils and shellfish oils, which last about one week.

For the most part, I use regular olive oil for flavored oils, because virgin or extra-virgin oils are so strong that they tend to overpower other ingredients. However, I do use an oil with more body when I know I'll be using droplets of oil to create a pattern on a plate. It's important then to use a thicker oil that won't run. Other exceptions are tomatoes and caviar, which marry well with full-bodied virgin olive oils. I use grapeseed oil when preparing a dessert oil, and vegetable oil where a thinner consistency is needed.

You can cook with flavored oils, using them in marinades and vinaigrettes, and you can also offer dinner guests a variety of oils. Collect a batch of small glass beakers or tiny crystal pitchers and fill them with an assortment of variously colored oils. Let your guests decide whether they want Curry Oil or Cumin Oil on their Carpaccio of Tuna, and offer them Horseradish Oil or Roast-Garlic Oil to go with a baked potato—a healthy and interesting substitute for the usual cliché of butter and sour cream.

AN IMPORTANT COOKING NOTE: Flavored oils need a gentle touch. You have to be careful not to let herbs or spices burn—they mustn't even toast! You want the flavors to be released—to flower—and this has to be done without a hint of scorching. The same is true when you're preparing an oil with a vegetable such as celery. The celery must not fry—let it mellow and soften in a slow, meditative manner.

Celery Oil

YIELD: ABOUT 2 CUPS

½ cup chopped celery
1½ cups olive oil
Coarse or kosher salt and freshly ground pepper
  to taste

1. Combine all ingredients in a saucepan. Simmer over very low heat until celery is tender. Celery should not fry; it should poach in oil.
2. Spoon celery-oil combination into a food processor and purée.

Uses for Celery Oil: Oil can replace a cream sauce for poultry, veal, or fish, or can be spooned over pasta or used to garnish or decorate a plate.

Variations: Use the same method to prepare an oil with carrots or red, yellow, or green bell peppers.

Clove Oil

YIELD: 1½ CUPS

3 tablespoons cloves
1½ cups vegetable oil or grapeseed oil
Coarse or kosher salt and freshly ground pepper
  to taste

1. Combine all ingredients in a saucepan and mix. Warm through.
2. Allow oil to steep in a warm place for 30 minutes. Store without straining, and strain oil as needed.

Uses for Clove Oil: In pickling liquid; to baste hams, ducks, chicken; and for marinating shrimp.

Cranberry Oil

YIELD: ABOUT 1½ CUPS

½ cup Cranberry Sauce (see page 176)
1 cup vegetable oil
Coarse or kosher salt and freshly ground pepper
*   to taste*

Combine ingredients in a saucepan and bring to a simmer over low heat, stirring. Remove from heat, spoon into a food processor, and purée.

Uses for Cranberry Oil: Serve with *pâtés,* sliced breast of smoked turkey. Serve on the side with game stews and duck salad.

Cumin Oil

YIELD: ABOUT 1½ CUPS

4 tablespoons cumin seeds
1½ cups olive oil
Coarse or kosher salt and freshly ground pepper
*   to taste*

1. Combine all ingredients in a saucepan and mix. Warm through.

2. Allow oil to steep in a warm place for 30 minutes. Store without straining, and strain oil as needed.

Uses for Cumin Oil: Add to couscous, use in a marinade for fish or lamb, spoon over grilled or roasted lamb, use in a vinaigrette.

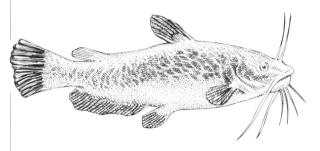

Curry Oil

YIELD: 2 CUPS

2 cups olive oil
1½ tablespoons curry powder
1 shallot or ½ small onion, minced
1 teaspoon fennel seeds
1 teaspoon pink peppercorns
Coarse or kosher salt and freshly ground pepper
*   to taste*

1. Heat 4 tablespoons of oil in a heavy saucepan. Add all other ingredients. Sauté, stirring, over very low heat for 2 minutes. This allows curry flavor to open.

2. Add remaining oil and simmer an additional 10 minutes over very low heat. (This gentle simmer is referred to as a "smile" in cooking language.)

3. Allow ingredients to settle to bottom of pan. Strain oil, leaving sediment in saucepan, and store.

Uses for Curry Oil: Serve with grilled fish, lamb, or chicken. Excellent with falafels. Stir into rice in place of butter. Sauté chicken cutlets or fish or stir-fry vegetables in Curry Oil. Drizzle drops of oil on surface of Roast-Eggplant and Roast-Garlic Soup (see page 82).

Citrus Oils

YIELD: ABOUT 2 CUPS

Zest and juice of 6 oranges (or 3 grapefruits, 6 limes, or 6 lemons)
2 cups grapeseed or olive oil
Coarse or kosher salt and freshly ground pepper to taste

Combine all ingredients in a saucepan. Cook slowly, over low heat, until juice has evaporated, about 20 minutes. Store.

Uses for Citrus Oils: Serve with fresh fruit compotes and in duck salads. Add to mayonnaise for fish. Use as a dipping sauce for such hors d'oeuvres as fried shrimp or oysters. Baste chicken with Orange Oil.

Roast-Garlic Oil

YIELD: 1½ CUPS

1 head roasted garlic, with skin (see page 28)
1½ cups olive oil
Coarse or kosher salt to taste

1. Combine all ingredients in a saucepan and mix. Warm through.
2. Allow oil to steep in a warm place for 30 minutes. Store without straining, and strain oil as needed.

Uses for Roast-Garlic Oil: Spoon over baked chicken, baked potatoes, beef dishes, pastas.

Cinnamon Oil

YIELD: 1½ CUPS

2 cinnamon sticks, cracked
1½ cups vegetable oil or grapeseed oil
Coarse or kosher salt and freshly ground pepper to taste

1. Combine all ingredients in a saucepan and mix. Warm through.
2. Allow oil to steep in a warm place for 30 minutes. Store without straining, and strain oil as needed.

Uses for Cinnamon Oil: Spoon over stir-fried fruits, baked apples, baked bananas.

Chili Oil

YIELD: ABOUT 1½ CUPS

1 shallot, minced
2 cloves garlic, minced
1 teaspoon cayenne pepper
1 teaspoon paprika
1 teaspoon chili powder
1 teaspoon red-pepper flakes
1½ teaspoons ground cumin
1 tablespoon fresh oregano or 1 teaspoon dried oregano
½ teaspoon coarse or kosher salt
1½ cups olive oil

1. Combine all ingredients in a heavy saucepan. Simmer over very low heat for about 10 minutes, or until flavors are extracted from ingredients. Be careful not to let spices burn. The chili flavor will be enjoyed as a subtle taste suspended in the oil.

2. Store without straining, and strain as needed.

Uses for Chili Oil: Serve with steak, beef carpaccio, and *pâtés*. Toss a handful of croutons in Chili Oil and add to soups. Sauté quesadillas in Chili Oil. Add it to whipped potatoes, scrambled eggs.

Ginger Oil

YIELD: 1½ CUPS

Ginger Oil can be prepared in two ways: with grapeseed oil if you are planning to use it for dessert, or with olive oil if it is to be used for other courses.

½ cup chopped fresh ginger
1½ cups grapeseed oil or olive oil
*Coarse or kosher salt and freshly ground pepper
to taste*

1. Combine ingredients in a saucepan and simmer over low heat for 5 minutes.
2. Allow oil to cool. Strain and store.

Uses for Ginger Oil: If it is prepared with grapeseed oil, spoon oil over fruit salad, baked apples, baked pears. If it is prepared with olive oil, use it with fish, seafood, Smoked-Fish Falafel, Shrimp and Ginger Wontons.

Herb Oil

YIELD: 1½ CUPS

3 tablespoons mixed or chopped fresh herbs: any
    combination of tarragon, thyme, basil, sage,
    chives, rosemary
1½ cups olive oil
Coarse or kosher salt and freshly ground pepper
    to taste

1. Combine all ingredients and mix. Place in
a turned-off oven or other warm place, or heat
very gently, for 30 seconds.

2. Allow oil to steep for 30 minutes. Store
without straining and strain oil as needed.

Uses for Herb Oil: In a vinaigrette, basting
broiled or roast chicken, spooned over puréed
potatoes.

Horseradish Oil

YIELD: 2 CUPS

½ cup chopped fresh horseradish or horseradish
    peel
1½ cups olive oil
Coarse or kosher salt and freshly ground pepper
    to taste

1. Combine ingredients in a saucepan and
simmer over low heat for 5 minutes.

2. Allow oil to cool. Strain and store.

Uses for Horseradish Oil: Serve with boiled beef,
oysters, shrimp. Spoon over baked potatoes.

Variation: Use the same method to prepare oils
with lemongrass and fresh fennel bulb.

Lavender Oil

YIELD: 1½ CUPS

2 tablespoons dried lavender
1½ cups grapeseed oil or vegetable oil
Coarse or kosher salt and freshly ground pepper
  to taste

1. Combine all ingredients and mix. Place in a turned-off oven or other warm place, or heat very gently, for 30 seconds.
2. Allow oil to steep for 30 minutes. Store without straining and strain oil as needed.

Uses for Lavender Oil: Whip into Orange Lavender Sabayon (see page 207), add to sautéed pineapples and fresh fruit.

Licorice Oil

YIELD: ABOUT 1½ CUPS

½ cup thinly sliced black or red licorice
1 cup grapeseed oil

1. Combine licorice and oil in a saucepan. Cook over low heat until licorice is tender.
2. Store and use without straining.

Uses for Licorice Oil: Spoon over fruit salad; add to syrup for poached oranges and to pickled fruit rinds.

Mint Oil

YIELD: 1½ CUPS

2 tablespoons chopped fresh mint
1½ cups grapeseed oil or vegetable oil
Coarse or kosher salt to taste

1. Combine all ingredients and mix. Place in a turned-off oven or other warm place, or heat very gently, for 30 seconds.
2. Allow oil to steep for 30 minutes. Store without straining and strain oil as needed.

Uses for Mint Oil: Spoon over Carpaccio of Tuna, grilled salmon, lamb carpaccio. Prepare stir-fried dishes with Mint Oil. Float on top of fruit soups.

Lobster Oil

YIELD: ABOUT 1½ CUPS

Shells from two lobsters (cooked or uncooked),
*   broken into large pieces*
½ onion, minced
½ cup olive oil
6 tablespoons Tomato Fondue (see page 44)
Coarse or kosher salt and freshly ground pepper
*   to taste*

1. Combine all ingredients in a saucepan. Simmer gently until lobster and tomato flavors have been absorbed by the oil and the liquid has evaporated, about 15 to 20 minutes.

2. Strain and store. Lobster Oil will keep about 1 week, refrigerated.

Uses for Lobster Oil: Combine with equal amounts of Curry Oil and serve with sea scallops. Add to a marinade, vinaigrette, or mayonnaise that is to be used with fish or shellfish. Serve with broiled lobster in place of drawn butter.

Variation: Use 2 cups shrimp shells, preferably from uncooked shrimp, and follow same technique to prepare Shrimp Oil.

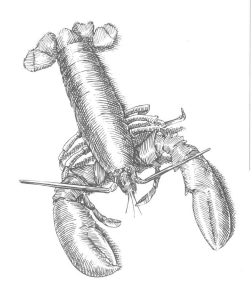

Riesling and Chive Oil

YIELD: ABOUT ¾ CUP

1½ cups Riesling
½ cup virgin olive oil
½ cup chopped chives
Coarse or kosher salt and freshly ground pepper
*   to taste*

1. Heat wine in a saucepan until it is reduced to a syrup.

2. Whisk in olive oil. Add chives, salt, and pepper and mix. Store.

Uses for Riesling and Chive Oil: Use in salad dressing. Spoon over poached salmon, baked bass, sautéed fillets of sole. Use in any dish that needs a sweet-and-sour flavor.

Saffron Fish Oil

YIELD: ABOUT 1½ CUPS

½ pound fish bones and trimmings
½ small onion, minced
1 teaspoon saffron threads
4 tablespoons white wine
1½ cups olive oil
Coarse or kosher salt and freshly ground pepper
    to taste

1. Combine all ingredients in a saucepan. Simmer until white wine has evaporated.
2. Strain and serve.

Uses for Saffron Fish Oil: Pour oil over baked fish and fish carpaccio. Incorporate in a *rouille.* Spoon over warm oysters.

Tomato Oil

YIELD: ABOUT 1 CUP

½ cup Tomato Fondue (see page 44)
1 cup virgin olive oil
Coarse or kosher salt to taste

1. Combine all ingredients in a saucepan. Simmer over very low heat for 30 minutes.
2. Strain and store.

Uses for Tomato Oil: Serve with steamed lobster, poached fish. Spoon over shrimp salad, sautéed calamari, angel-hair pasta.

Watercress Oil

YIELD: ABOUT 1½ CUPS

½ cup Watercress Sauce (see page 153)
1 cup olive oil
Coarse or kosher salt and freshly ground pepper
 to taste

Combine all ingredients in a food processor and purée until ingredients are thoroughly combined. Store.

Uses for Watercress Oil: Serve with grilled scallops, grilled chicken, poached fish.

Basic Vinaigrette

YIELD: ABOUT 2¼ CUPS

I use both extra-virgin olive oil and regular olive oil in this vinaigrette. Extra-virgin olive oil has a very strong flavor, and by itself I think it would overpower most salads; hence the combination of these oils.

1 cup olive oil
¾ cup extra-virgin olive oil
1 tablespoon mustard oil
¼ cup tarragon vinegar
¼ cup sherry-wine vinegar
1 teaspoon freshly ground pepper
Coarse or kosher salt to taste

Combine oils and vinegars in a bowl and mix thoroughly. Add seasonings and mix again.

Uses for Basic Vinaigrette: This is the vinaigrette to have on hand for mixed green salads or salads composed of a variety of vegetables. It's also an excellent dip for raw vegetables.

Bacon Vinaigrette

YIELD: ABOUT I CUP

3 slices bacon
4 tablespoons Light Chicken Stock (see page 76)
 or canned chicken broth
2 tablespoons mustard oil
4 tablespoons olive oil
2 tablespoons sherry-wine vinegar
2 teaspoons Dijon mustard
2 tablespoons crumbled blue cheese
Coarse or kosher salt and freshly ground pepper
 to taste

1. Sauté bacon. Remove from pan and crumble.

2. Add stock or broth, mustard oil, olive oil, and vinegar to sauté pan. Heat, stirring. Add mustard and stir until all ingredients are combined. Remove vinaigrette from heat.

3. Stir in crumbled bacon and whisk in blue cheese. Season to taste and use immediately.

Uses for Bacon Vinaigrette: Spoon over baked chicken or spinach salad, and serve with French fried potatoes, Duck Confit, or steamed asparagus and artichokes.

Balsamic Vinaigrette

YIELD: ABOUT 1½ CUPS

There's balsamic vinegar—and then there's balsamic vinegar. The more expensive variety is smooth, with just a touch of a tang, and has very little bite. In Italy, they serve this balsamic over strawberries and combined with soda water for a refreshing drink. I'm not suggesting you buy the most expensive balsamic vinegar for a vinaigrette. All balsamics have a slight touch of sweetness, which adds a subtle flavor to a salad.

½ cup olive oil
1 clove garlic, minced
1 shallot, minced
1 teaspoon minced fresh oregano
1 teaspoon minced fresh thyme
1 teaspoon minced fresh tarragon
½ cup extra-virgin olive oil
6 tablespoons balsamic vinegar
Coarse or kosher salt and freshly ground pepper
    to taste

1. Heat ¼ cup of olive oil in a saucepan. Add garlic, shallot, oregano, thyme, and tarragon and sauté over low heat, stirring, for 2 minutes.

2. Remove from heat and stir in remaining olive oil, extra-virgin olive oil, and vinegar. Mix thoroughly, and season to taste.

Uses for Balsamic Vinaigrette: This vinaigrette can be used with any salad. It will add special interest to a chicken salad, *salade niçoise,* shrimp salad.

Citrus Vinaigrette

YIELD: ABOUT 2 CUPS

¼ cup lime juice
¼ cup rice-wine vinegar
1½ cups olive oil
2 shallots, minced
2 tablespoons chopped parsley
Coarse or kosher salt and freshly ground pepper
    to taste

Combine lime juice, vinegar, and olive oil in a bowl and mix. Stir in remaining ingredients and continue mixing until all ingredients are thoroughly combined.

Uses for Citrus Vinaigrette: On mixed green salads, spooned over green beans, and served with fish carpaccio and oysters.

Red-Pepper Vinaigrette

YIELD: ABOUT ¾ CUP

6 tablespoons Red-Pepper Purée (see page
    178)
6 tablespoons olive oil
2 tablespoons red-wine vinegar
Coarse or kosher salt and freshly ground pepper
    to taste

Combine all ingredients in a bowl and mix until thoroughly combined.

Uses for Red-Pepper Vinaigrette: With grilled fish or chicken, and with Layer Cake of Lemon Sole with Ratatouille and Calamari (see page 113).

Ginger Vinaigrette

YIELD: ABOUT ½ CUP

¼ cup Ginger Oil (see page 165)
1 tablespoon rice-wine vinegar
1 tablespoon soy sauce
1 tablespoon thinly sliced green onions
Coarse or kosher salt and freshly ground pepper
    to taste

Combine all ingredients in a bowl and mix thoroughly.

Uses for Ginger Vinaigrette: Preparing stir-fried duck, chicken and mixed vegetables (snow peas, water chestnuts, bamboo shoots).

Thick Walnut-Oil Vinaigrette

YIELD: ABOUT 2 CUPS

1 egg yolk
1½ cups walnut oil
2 tablespoons tarragon vinegar
1 teaspoon coarse or kosher salt
Freshly ground pepper to taste

1. Place egg yolk in a food processor. Gradually add oil and vinegar and process until mixture is thick. Add salt and pepper.
2. Chill before using.

Uses for Thick Walnut-Oil Vinaigrette: Dot vinaigrette on mushroom cap in Shiitake-Mushroom Caps on Mousse Stems (see page 60), and add to lettuce used to garnish mousse or *pâté*. Serve with steamed artichokes or asparagus.

Uses for Asparagus Butter Sauce: Adds flavor and color to pasta primavera, Baked Cod with Roast-Shallot Crust (see page 98), and other fish and shellfish dishes.

Asparagus Butter Sauce

YIELD: ABOUT 2 CUPS

12 large asparagus spears
¾ cup Light Chicken Stock (see page 76) or
*   canned chicken broth*
½ pound butter, cut into 16 pieces
3 tablespoons chopped parsley
1 teaspoon coarse or kosher salt
Freshly ground pepper to taste

1. Peel each asparagus spear. Cut off 2 inches from the bottom of spear and reserve with peel. Save remainder of asparagus for another dish.

2. Roughly chop reserved asparagus peel and spears.

3. Combine chopped asparagus and stock or broth in a saucepan. Bring to a boil, lower to barely a simmer, and gradually add butter, piece by piece, stirring, until sauce is completely combined. Add parsley, salt, and pepper, stir, and allow sauce to steep for 10 minutes, off heat.

4. Strain sauce, pressing all liquid from vegetables, and return to saucepan. Heat gently before serving.

Beurre Blanc

YIELD: ABOUT 1¼ CUPS

6 tablespoons white wine
2 tablespoons white-wine vinegar or tarragon
*   vinegar*
1 shallot, minced
½ pound butter
Coarse or kosher salt and freshly ground pepper
*   to taste*

1. Heat wine, vinegar, and shallot in a saucepan and bring to a boil over very high heat. Reduce liquid by half.

2. Add ¼ pound butter. When butter is almost melted, add remaining ¼ pound butter. When this butter is almost melted, remove from heat and whisk until butter is incorporated and sauce cools slightly, 1 to 2 minutes. Season and serve immediately.

Uses for Beurre Blanc: This basic butter sauce can be seasoned with spices or herbs and combined with vegetable purées. Serve with veal, fish, shellfish, and vegetables. If the amount of butter is a concern, serve Beurre Blanc in small quantities.

Caramelized-Bell-Pepper and Shellfish Sauce

YIELD: ABOUT 1½ CUPS

¾ cup chopped red bell pepper
¼ cup honey
2 cups Shellfish-Flavored Stock (see page 79)
¼ cup red-wine vinegar
2 tablespoons Tomato Fondue (see page 44)
2 tablespoons red pepper flakes
¼ teaspoon fennel seeds
1 clove garlic, minced
Coarse or kosher salt and freshly ground pepper to taste
¼ cup olive oil

1. Combine red bell pepper and honey in a small saucepan. Cook, stirring, over low heat until pepper is glazed and caramelized.

2. Add all other ingredients except olive oil. Cook for 10 minutes, until peppers are very soft. Reduce by almost half.

3. Pour sauce into a food processor and purée. Strain and return to saucepan. Stir in olive oil.

4. Adjust seasoning and heat before serving.

Uses for Caramelized-Bell-Pepper and Shellfish Sauce: Serve with fish, shrimp, scallops, and lobster.

Chili Mayonnaise

YIELD: ABOUT 2 CUPS

2 egg yolks
1½ cups Chili Oil (see page 164)
4 tablespoons red-wine vinegar
Coarse or kosher salt and freshly ground pepper to taste

1. Whip egg yolks in a food processor.

2. Add Chili Oil gradually and continue processing. Add vinegar, salt, and pepper and process until all ingredients are combined into a thick mayonnaise.

Uses for Chili Mayonnaise: Spread on roast beef, ham sandwiches, Swiss-cheese sandwiches. Use with croques, pork chops, and turkey, and as a dip for raw vegetables.

Variations: Use the same method to prepare a mayonnaise with Horseradish Oil, Curry Oil, Fennel Oil, Roast-Garlic Oil.

Coffee Barbecue Sauce

YIELD: ABOUT 1½ CUPS

*T*he following sauce is simple to prepare, but because the list of ingredients is long, I've divided them into three sections to make the recipe easier to follow.

¼ cup vegetable oil
½ onion, chopped
½ cup chopped garlic
¼ cup chopped fresh coriander
1 Serrano or small green chili pepper
1 teaspoon ground cumin
1 teaspoon chili powder
1 teaspoon red pepper flakes
Zest of 1 lemon
¾ cup coffee beans

1. Heat oil in a large saucepan. Add all the above ingredients and cook, stirring, for 2 minutes.
2. Then add:

¼ cup dark-brown sugar
¾ cup red-wine vinegar
Juice of 1 lemon
1 cup ketchup

3. Stir all the above ingredients into saucepan. Cook, stirring occasionally, until liquid is reduced by approximately half.
4. Then add:

2 tablespoons coarse or kosher salt
2 tablespoons freshly ground pepper
2 cups Tomato Fondue (see page 44)

5. Stir all the above ingredients into the saucepan. Cover and simmer over low heat for 2 to 3 hours, stirring occasionally.
6. Strain and adjust seasoning.

Cranberry Sauce

YIELD: ABOUT 2½ CUPS

½ cup white wine
¾ cup sugar, or to taste
1 lime with peel, seeded and chopped
1 orange with peel, seeded and chopped
12 ounces raw cranberries
Freshly ground black pepper to
taste

1. Combine wine and sugar in a large saucepan and cook, stirring occasionally, until liquid is syrup.
2. Add lime and orange to syrup and cook another 2 minutes, stirring. Add cranberries. Cover and cook for 15 to 20 minutes, or until thickened.
3. Add pepper, and more sugar if necessary.

Onion and Pistachio Marmalade

YIELD: ABOUT 1 CUP

I like pistachios, and after I had prepared a batch of Pistachio Wafers (see variations, page 24), I thought about other dishes I could prepare with pistachios. I concocted this marmalade as a relish—and I serve it with all manner of barbecued or roast fowl. It's especially fine with roast duck and adds a sweet-sour note to roast pork.

4 tablespoons olive oil
1 large onion, diced
3 tablespoons sugar
3 tablespoons red wine
6 tablespoons red-wine vinegar
½ teaspoon coarse or kosher salt
¼ teaspoon cracked black pepper
½ cup shelled pistachio nuts
½ teaspoon cayenne pepper
2 teaspoons dark molasses or honey

1. Heat olive oil in a saucepan. Add onion and sauté, stirring, for 2 minutes, or until onion is translucent. Add sugar and continue cooking over low heat, stirring occasionally, until onion is glazed.

2. Add wine, vinegar, salt, and pepper to saucepan and continue cooking until mixture is reduced and thick. Reserve.

3. Preheat oven to 350°.

4. In a small bowl, combine pistachios, cayenne, and molasses or honey. Stir to mix, and spoon into a pie plate or other small, shallow baking dish. Bake for 10 to 15 minutes, or until pistachio mixture is crisp and dry.

5. Add pistachio mix to sauce and stir. Serve warm or at room temperature.

Honey Mustard Sabayon

YIELD: ABOUT 1 CUP

1 egg
1 egg yolk
2 tablespoons honey
2 tablespoons white-wine vinegar or White-Wine Pickling Liquid (see page 183)
1 teaspoon coarse or kosher salt
Freshly ground pepper to taste
2 teaspoons Dijon mustard
2 tablespoons mustard oil or olive oil

Combine egg, egg yolk, honey, vinegar, salt, and pepper in a double boiler. Whisk together over low heat. After mixture has thickened, fold in mustard and whisk in mustard oil until all ingredients are combined.

Uses for Honey Mustard Sabayon: Keep Sabayon warm and serve with grilled fish, roast pork, and baked Virginia or fresh ham.

Roasted Red Bell Peppers

4 large, red bell peppers

1. Preheat broiler to high.
2. Wash peppers and place on broiling tray or baking sheet.
3. Broil peppers, turning from side to side until skin is blackened and charred.
4. Remove peppers from broiler and place in paper bag. Close bag tightly, allowing peppers to steam.
5. When peppers are cool enough to handle, remove from bag and peel off charred skin using a sharp knife. This is easiest done under cold, running water.

Red-Pepper Purée

4 peppers, roasted (see previous recipe)
1 tablespoon olive oil

Peel and seed roasted peppers. Place in food processor with olive oil and purée until fine.

Red-Pepper Butter

There are two ways to prepare Red-Pepper Butter: with Beurre Blanc and with softened butter. Either can be used on grilled fish or steamed vegetables, with shellfish, and with quesadillas. Prepared with Beurre Blanc, it can be used as a dip; made with softened butter, it can be spread on canapés.

RED-PEPPER BUTTER WITH BEURRE BLANC

6 tablespoons Red-Pepper Purée (see previous recipe)
6 tablespoons Beurre Blanc (see page 174)
Coarse or kosher salt and freshly ground pepper to taste

Combine all ingredients in a small saucepan. Whisk to combine and heat gently.

RED-PEPPER BUTTER WITH SOFTENED BUTTER

> 6 tablespoons Red-Pepper Purée (see previous recipe)
> 12 tablespoons softened butter
> Coarse or kosher salt and freshly ground pepper to taste

1. Combine all ingredients in a food processor and process until combined.
2. Roll butter into a cylinder. Wrap in foil or Saran Wrap and use as needed.

Salsa

*T*his hot sauce is excellent with fish carpaccio or a quesadilla, and I like to top Black-Bean Soup (see page 80) with a tablespoon of Salsa. It also adds a spicy touch to oysters on the half-shell and can be used as the basis of a vinaigrette with the addition of olive oil. Try Salsa spooned over a baked potato when you're serving steak.

> Tomato Concasse, made with 3 tomatoes (see page 43)
> ½ small cucumber, peeled and chopped
> 2 jalapeño or Serrano peppers, minced, or 2 teaspoons cayenne pepper
> ½ cup chopped onion
> 2 tablespoons chopped coriander
> 2 tablespoons chopped chives
> 2 tablespoons red-wine vinegar
> Juice of 2 limes
> Coarse or kosher salt and freshly ground pepper to taste

Combine all ingredients in a bowl. Mix well and allow to marinate in refrigerator for 3 to 4 hours.

Sherry-Wine-Vinegar and Shallot Sauce

YIELD: ABOUT 1½ CUPS

3 tablespoons butter
6 shallots, minced
1 cup sherry-wine vinegar
1 cup red wine
2 cups Dark Chicken Stock (see page 77) or
    Brown Stock (see page 77) or canned beef
    broth
2 tablespoons butter
Coarse or kosher salt and freshly ground pepper
    to taste

1. Heat 3 tablespoons butter in a saucepan. Add shallots and sauté, stirring, for 1 minute.

2. Add sherry-wine vinegar and red wine and reduce liquid by three-quarters. Stir in stock or broth and reduce liquid by half.

3. Whisk in 2 tablespoons butter. Season to taste, and simmer for 1 minute, or until all ingredients are blended and sauce has thickened slightly.

PICKLING

Many people are put off by the idea of pickling, because they think of it primarily as a method used to preserve food. But the pickling that I do is meant to add flavor—sweet, sour, or spicy—to vegetables, which are then used in combination with other foods, adding an unusual fillip to many dishes.

All kinds of vegetables can be pickled—carrots, onions, leeks, broccoli, garlic, ginger—and they add color as well as flavor to a dish. Let me give an example: An escalope of salmon is a lovely, light pink. To create contrast to both the flavor and the color of the fish, I'll serve it with carrot slices pickled in saffron-flavored liquid. The golden carrot slices will enhance the delicate flavor and color of the salmon.

Pickled vegetables can replace a cocktail sauce, substitute for a mignonette with oysters, and are an excellent garnish for fish, meat, and fowl. Pickles are also a great *digestif*. Automatically served with hamburgers and sandwiches, pickles have a sharpness that makes fat-containing meat easier to digest.

I use a variety of vinegars rather than a salt

brine when I pickle vegetables, and the flavor of the vinegar depends on how I plan to use the pickle. Onions pickled in red-wine vinegar are served with smoked fish, and garlic pickled in clove-oil vinegar is served with duck.

Pickled vegetables can be prepared at the last minute and served immediately, or they can be kept refrigerated for about two weeks.

After you've pickled vegetables, the remaining liquid can be used to pickle other foods. Poached salmon in a Red-Wine Pickling Liquid, for example, will have a much more interesting flavor than the same fish poached in a court bouillon. All pickling liquids can be reduced and used in vinaigrettes and sauces that call for vinegar.

Clove-Oil Pickling Liquid

YIELD: ABOUT I PINT

use this pickling liquid for vegetables that have a strong flavor, such as cabbage and garlic.

1 cup Clove Oil (see page 161)
1 cup rice-wine vinegar
6 tablespoons sugar
2 tablespoons cayenne pepper
2 tablespoons coarse salt

Combine all ingredients in a nonreactive saucepan and bring to a boil. Reduce heat to a simmer and cook for 3 minutes.

Mustard Pickling Liquid

YIELD: ABOUT 1 QUART

I like this strong mustard flavor for pickling grapefruit, orange, or watermelon rind. Mustard-pickled fruits are a successful match with strongly flavored fish, such as mackerel, bluefish, or sturgeon, and can also be served with roast duck.

1 pint white-wine vinegar
1 pint water
2 bay leaves
8 to 10 whole peppercorns
1 teaspoon cinnamon
6 tablespoons dry mustard powder
2 tablespoons mustard oil
½ cup sugar

1. Combine all ingredients in a nonreactive saucepan and bring to a boil. Cook for 10 minutes.

2. Chill. Mustard Pickling Liquid will keep, refrigerated, for about 2 months.

Red-Wine Pickling Liquid

YIELD: ABOUT 1 CUP

*U*se Red-Wine Pickling Liquid for ginger baby onions, cauliflower florets, salsify, and beets, and to marinate fish—salmon, swordfish, shrimp, or tuna steak are flavorful when prepared with Red-Wine Pickling Liquid. You can also replace vinegar with Red-Wine Pickling Liquid when preparing a vinaigrette.

½ cup red wine, preferably Burgundy
½ cup red-wine vinegar
½ cup sugar
2 tablespoons black peppercorns
1 teaspoon cayenne pepper (optional)
2 tablespoons coarse or kosher salt

1. Combine all ingredients in a nonreactive saucepan and bring to a boil. Reduce to a simmer and cook for 5 minutes.

2. Allow to cool and strain into a glass jar. Will keep for 3 or more months in refrigerator.

Wild Mushroom Flan baked in egg shell with shrimp garnish

Parfait of Salmon and Tuna Tartars with Crème Fraîche and caviar

Poached Red Snapper with Saffron Risotto (Paella) with mussels, clams, and chorizo sausage

Poached Chicken Breasts with Ratatouille Orzo Ragout and Black Olive Purée

Harlequin (Black-Bean and White-Bean) Soup with Shrimp and Jalapeño Jack Cheese Strudels

Braised Lobster with Corn Crêpes and Bacon

Orange and Strawberry Tart with Candied-Bell-Pepper Caramel and Lemon Ice Cream

CHOCOLATE DESSERTS: *whiskey torte, sorbet, meringue sticks, and truffles on antique toy stove*

Saffron and Turmeric Pickling Liquid

YIELD: ABOUT 1 PINT

Use this pickling liquid for vegetables or fish. The vegetables will keep in the liquid for about two weeks, or, if the vegetables are eaten immediately, the liquid can be used again.

2 cups water
1 tablespoon coarse or kosher salt
½ cup white-wine vinegar
1 teaspoon cayenne pepper
1 tablespoon coriander seeds
1 tablespoon turmeric
1 pinch saffron threads
5 peeled shallots

Combine all ingredients in a nonreactive saucepan and bring to a boil. Reduce heat to a simmer and cook for 3 minutes.

White-Wine Pickling Liquid

YIELD: ABOUT 1 CUP

Use White-Wine Pickling Liquid to pickle mushrooms, cabbage, and carrots. Reduced, the liquid can be a basis for the Honey Mustard Sabayon, which I serve with fish, roast pork, and baked ham. The liquid can deglaze stir-fried vegetables and glaze roast ham or roast duck.

½ cup white wine, preferably Burgundy
½ cup white-wine vinegar
½ cup sugar
1 tablespoon whole peppercorns
1 teaspoon coarse or kosher salt

1. Combine all ingredients in a nonreactive saucepan and bring to a boil. Reduce to a simmer and cook for 5 minutes.
2. Allow to cool and strain into a glass jar. Will keep for 3 or more months in refrigerator.

Mixed Vegetables in Saffron and Turmeric Pickling Liquid

YIELD: ABOUT 2 CUPS

*U*se these pickles with roast duck, pork, or lamb, and with sandwiches. They add a real surprise to lobster salad and poached fish.

> *2 pints Saffron and Turmeric Pickling Liquid*
> *(see page 183)*
> *3 leeks, white part only, cut into thin strips*
> *2 carrots, cut into thin strips*
> *4 stalks celery, cut into thin strips*

1. Bring pickling liquid to a boil in a nonreactive saucepan. Add all vegetables and allow liquid to return to a boil.

2. Remove from heat and allow vegetables to steep in liquid for 20 minutes.

3. Serve pickled vegetables immediately, or store in pickling liquid for later use. Vegetables will keep, refrigerated, for 2 weeks.

Pickled-Onion, Cucumber, and Corn Relish

YIELD: ABOUT 1½ CUPS

> *½ cup pearl onions*
> *½ cup Red-Wine Pickling Liquid (see page 182)*
> *½ cup cooked corn kernels*
> *½ cup peeled, seeded, and diced cucumbers*
> *Coarse or kosher salt and freshly ground pepper to taste*

Combine all ingredients in a bowl and mix well. Refrigerate for 30 minutes before serving.

Fruit Rinds in Mustard Pickling Liquid

YIELD: ABOUT 2 CUPS

F ruit rinds can be combined or used singly. When working with watermelon, peel off the outer green skin before cutting the rind into strips.

1 quart Mustard Pickling Liquid (see page 182)

Peel from 3 grapefruit, cut into ¼-inch strips

Peel from 3 oranges, cut into ¼-inch strips

2 cups watermelon rind, cut into ½-inch strips

1. Place pickling liquid in a nonreactive saucepan. Add rind and bring to a boil. Reduce heat to a simmer and cook for 30 minutes.

2. Allow rind to cool in liquid and reserve until ready to use.

Chapter 9

DESERTS

My idea of the perfect dessert is a lavish spread, a presentation of at least three dishes that will create a feeling of opulence at the end of a meal. I believe in serving cake or cookies with ice cream, and my ice-cream desserts are usually embellished with special sauces.

Many of my desserts call for chocolate, because that ingredient is the favorite of so many people. I have included light fruit desserts as well, and I recommend that they be served with ice cream or cookies. Combine the recipes that follow to fulfill your own personal dream of the perfect dessert.

Crispy Chocolate-Meringue Sticks

YIELD: ABOUT 20 STICKS

4 egg whites
½ cup white sugar
½ cup confectioners' sugar
1½ tablespoons cocoa powder, unsweetened

1. Preheat oven to 275°.
2. Begin whipping egg whites in an electric mixer and gradually add white sugar. When sugar is absorbed, slowly add confectioners' sugar. Gradually add cocoa powder and continue whipping until stiff peaks are formed.
3. Place meringue into a pastry bag with a straight-sided Number 3 or Number 4 tip and pipe meringue into narrow lines down the length of a nonstick baking pan. Leave an inch between the lines of meringue (you may need 2 pans).
4. Bake for 1 hour. Turn heat off and allow meringues to remain in oven for an additional hour, or overnight. Meringues should be very dry.

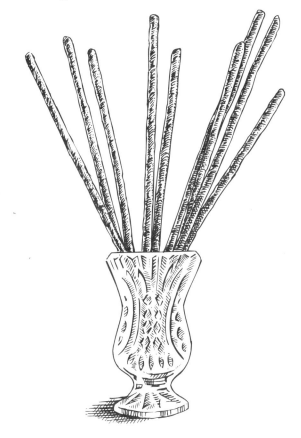

Chocolate Whiskey Torte with Chocolate Sauce and Caramel Ice Cream

YIELD: 8 SERVINGS

Butter and flour for cake pan
4 tablespoons butter
½ cup cornstarch
1 cup all-purpose flour
½ cup unsweetened cocoa powder
5 egg yolks
3 eggs
1 pound sugar
Cocoa powder for dusting cake

1. Preheat oven to 375°.
2. Prepare an 8-inch cake pan by coating with butter and flour. Reserve.
3. Melt butter and allow to cool.
4. Sift together cornstarch, flour, and cocoa powder.
5. Combine egg yolks, eggs, and sugar in a double boiler and heat, stirring continuously, until mixture is just warm. Beat with an electric mixer until this batter has tripled in volume.
6. With a spatula, fold cornstarch-flour mixture into batter and mix together slowly. Add melted butter gradually and mix until all ingredients are just combined.
7. Spoon batter into prepared cake pan and bake for about 30 minutes, or until cake begins to pull away from sides of pan.

8. Remove pan from oven, invert over a wire rack, and unmold. Allow cake to cool.
9. After cake has cooled, carefully cut it into 3 equal layers. Reserve. Prepare the following syrup.

SYRUP

4 tablespoons sugar
4 tablespoons water
Whiskey to taste

Combine sugar and water in a saucepan and bring to a boil. Add whiskey to taste, stir, and allow to cool slightly. Reserve. Prepare filling.

CHOCOLATE WHISKEY FILLING

½ pound bittersweet chocolate
½ pound butter
2 ounces whiskey
½ cup plus 1 tablespoon heavy sweet
 cream
2 teaspoons cinnamon

1. Combine chocolate and butter in a double boiler.
2. Cook over simmering water, with low heat, stirring, until chocolate is melted.
3. Add all remaining ingredients and continue stirring until thoroughly combined.
4. At this point, the filling is thin and pourable; it should be used at once.

To Assemble

1. Place 1 layer of cake in the bottom of a springform pan and brush with syrup. Spoon a

third of Chocolate Whiskey Filling over cake. Add second layer of cake, brush with syrup, and spoon a third of filling over cake. Top with third layer of cake, brush with syrup, and finish with remaining filling. (If filling has hardened, heat until consistency is right and pour over top layer.) Refrigerate.

2. Remove cake from refrigerator 1 hour before serving. Cake should be served at room temperature for maximum flavor and softer texture.

3. Remove sides of springform pan and dust top and sides of cake heavily with cocoa powder.

To Serve: Spoon Chocolate Sauce (see page 197) onto eight dessert plates. Place a slice of cake in the center of the pool of sauce. Top with a scoop of Caramel Ice Cream (see page 202) and garnish with Caramel Sticks (see page 192).

Variations: Chocolate Whiskey Filling can also be used as a cold terrine or formed into truffles.

Stir-Fried Fruits with Ginger Ice Cream and Jasmine Caramel

YIELD: 4 TO 6 SERVINGS

2 tablespoons grapeseed oil
½ cup diced melon (except watermelon)
½ cup diced pineapple
1 apple (Granny Smith or similar), cut into
    wedges
1 cup strawberries, hulled
1 cup raspberries
1 cup blueberries
4 tablespoons orange juice or Grand Marnier
½ cup Jasmine Caramel (see page 193)
Ginger Ice Cream (see page 200)

1. Preheat a wok or large sauté pan and add oil. Add melon, pineapple, and apple and cook, stirring, for 1 minute.

2. Add remainder of fruit and orange juice or Grand Marnier. Remove from heat and add Jasmine Caramel to pan. Stir to combine.

3. A nice way to present this dish is to spoon the fruit into 4 to 6 Oriental-style bowls, top with Ginger Ice Cream, and serve with porcelain spoons.

Orange Tuile Cookies

YIELD: ABOUT 60 COOKIES

½ pound confectioners' sugar
¼ pound butter
1 cup all-purpose flour
1 cup chopped almonds
Zest and juice of 1 orange
1 tablespoon Grand Marnier or
*   Cointreau*

1. Preheat oven to 350°.

2. Cream sugar and butter together in an electric mixer, or mix in a bowl by hand. Gradually add flour and continue mixing for 2 to 3 minutes, until ingredients are thoroughly combined.

3. Add remaining ingredients and mix until just blended.

4. Drop tablespoonfuls of cookie mixture onto a baking sheet with a nonstick surface. Dip your fingers in water and pat down gently. Bake until golden brown and crispy, about 5 to 8 minutes.

5. If you want the cookies to have the authentic *tuile*—or roof-tile—shape, drape them while warm over a rolling pin or glass. (What I sometimes do is cut a small wedge out of each cookie and pinch the cookie together to form a cone, which I then fill with berries.) Store in an airtight container.

Variation: These cookies can also be used as part of small napoleons. Do not shape the cookies, but allow them to remain flat and build layers: a cookie, a layer of whipped cream, second cookie, layer of berries, all topped by a third cookie.

Caramel Sticks or Discs

YIELD: ABOUT 20 STICKS
OR 1 DISC

⅓ cup corn syrup
½ pound sugar
⅔ cup water

Combine all ingredients in a heavy saucepan and bring to a boil, brushing inside of pan with water from time to time to prevent crystallization. Test with a candy thermometer, which should register 350°. Check the color, which should be a deep amber. Mixture should harden immediately when a teaspoonful is placed on a plate.

To Form Caramel Sticks

1. You will need a special surface to form these. Use a board covered with a sheet of parchment, or lightly oil a stainless-steel platter or marble board.

2. Once the surface is prepared, dip a spoon into the caramel and allow the caramel to drip from the spoon onto the prepared surface. To make sticks, drip the caramel in long thin lines. You can create parallel lines by dripping the caramel from the tines of a fork.

To Form Other Designs

Other designs can be made with the caramel: circles, abstract shapes, initials. Or take three pastry bags, put one inside the other, and pipe the caramel through the bag or cone. Make sure you are wearing gloves if you use this method.

To Form Caramel Discs

To create a large disc, place bottomless spring-form pan on an oiled surface. Pour caramel onto the surface, which is now enclosed. When the caramel hardens, you have a clear caramel disc which can be used as a plate to serve chocolate truffles or cookies. The disc can be used again, broken into pieces and eaten along with the truffles, or pulverized in a food processor and sprinkled over ice cream or other desserts.

Jasmine Caramel

YIELD: ABOUT 2 CUPS

*T*his caramel is an excellent addition to Stir-Fried Fruits (see page 190), baked pears, or pineapple skewers that are prepared like Banana Beignets (see page 206).

1 cup water
4 jasmine tea bags
Juice of 1 lemon
1½ tablespoons honey
2 cups sugar
½ cup water

1. Prepare a jasmine tea by bringing 1 cup water to a boil and adding tea bags, lemon, and honey. Allow tea to steep for 1 hour. Squeeze liquid from tea bags and discard.

2. Prepare a caramel by combining sugar and ½ cup water. Bring to a boil over high heat and cook until caramelized, about 5 minutes.

3. Pour tea slowly into caramel. Return to a boil and cook for 3 to 4 minutes, or until liquid has the consistency of a thick syrup.

Maple Crisps

YIELD: ABOUT 50 COOKIES

4 tablespoons butter
½ cup confectioners' sugar
2 egg whites
2 tablespoons maple syrup
1 cup plus 2 tablespoons all-purpose flour, sifted

1. Cream butter and sugar together in an electric mixer, or mix in a bowl by hand. Add egg whites and maple syrup gradually. Gradually add flour, and continue mixing until ingredients are just combined.

2. Chill cookie mixture in refrigerator for 2 hours before using.

3. Preheat oven to 350°.

4. Using a small spatula or palette knife, spread a thin layer of cookie mixture on a baking sheet with a nonstick surface. If you wish, cookie dough can be formed by pressing into molds or stencils before baking. Bake until brown and crisp, about 5 to 8 minutes.

5. While sheet of cookies is warm, cut into desired shapes—squares, rectangles, or an abstract design—or, when it is chilled, break into pieces.

Three-Layered Mousse Parfait

YIELD: 10 TO 12 SERVINGS

BANANA MOUSSE

¾ pound milk chocolate

5 tablespoons heavy sweet cream

1 cup banana purée (about 1½ bananas)

1. Melt chocolate in a double boiler.
2. Heat cream in another saucepan and bring to a boil. Add cream to chocolate and stir. Off heat, add banana to mixture and stir to combine.
3. Spoon Banana Mousse into an 8-inch-by-2-inch cake pan and smooth top with a spatula. Chill.

BITTERSWEET-CHOCOLATE MOUSSE

¾ pound bittersweet chocolate

3 egg yolks

4 tablespoons sugar

1 cup heavy sweet cream, whipped

1. Melt chocolate in a double boiler.
2. Combine egg yolks and sugar in another double boiler and heat, stirring, until egg yolks are pale and form a light ribbon.
3. Off heat, combine yolk mixture with melted chocolate. Allow to cool slightly.
4. Fold in whipped cream.

5. Spread Bittersweet-Chocolate Mousse over Banana Mousse. Smooth top with a spatula. Chill.

PRALINE MOUSSE

6 tablespoons creamy peanut butter

6 ounces semi-sweet chocolate

3 ounces butter

2 egg yolks

4 tablespoons sugar

3 egg whites

1 cup heavy sweet cream, whipped

1. Heat peanut butter, chocolate, and butter in a double boiler. Mix to combine.
2. Combine egg yolks and half the sugar in another double boiler. Beat until yolks are pale and form a light ribbon. Off heat, fold egg-yolk mixture into chocolate mixture.
3. Whip egg whites with remaining sugar until soft peaks are formed. Fold a third of egg whites into chocolate mixture. Fold in remaining egg whites and whipped cream.
4. Spread Praline Mousse over Bittersweet-Chocolate Mousse and smooth top with a spatula. Chill.

To Serve: Cut the mousse into squares and place each square on a dessert plate. Decorate with fresh raspberries or a mixture of raspberries and blackberries, and Chocolate Sauce (see page 197).

Pastry Cream

YIELD: ABOUT 2 CUPS

4 egg yolks
1½ tablespoons cornstarch
5 tablespoons sugar
2 cups milk
1½ vanilla beans, split
Confectioners' sugar

1. Combine yolks, cornstarch, and sugar in a bowl. Beat until ingredients are pale and form a light ribbon.

2. Combine milk and vanilla beans in a saucepan and bring to a boil. Add a third of the milk mixture to egg-yolk mixture and stir to combine. Return egg-yolk mixture to milk and bring to a boil, beating. Continue cooking until mixture thickens. Remove from heat and remove vanilla bean and reserve for another use.

3. Dust top of cream lightly with confectioners' sugar to prevent formation of a skin, and keep warm.

Butterscotch Sauce

YIELD: ABOUT 1 CUP

To prepare this sauce, you'll need a candy thermometer. Sauce can be served over ice cream, Banana Beignets (see page 206), and cakes.

½ cup dark-brown sugar
4 tablespoons water
2 tablespoons corn syrup
2 tablespoons butter
½ cup heavy sweet cream

1. Combine sugar, water, and corn syrup in a heavy saucepan and bring to a boil. Remove from heat when a candy thermometer registers 320°, or when sauce starts to smoke.

2. Add butter and stir until dissolved. Add cream and return to heat for 1 minute, stirring to combine.

3. Remove from heat, strain, and keep warm.

Crème Anglaise

YIELD: ABOUT 3 CUPS

This basic Crème Anglaise contains the same ingredients as the mixture for ice cream except that it is made with less sugar. If you have Crème Anglaise left at any time, you can convert it to ice cream by adding sugar and processing in an ice-cream maker.

1½ cups milk
½ cup heavy sweet cream
½ vanilla bean
6 tablespoons sugar
6 egg yolks

1. Combine milk and cream in a saucepan. Split the vanilla bean, scrape seeds, and add seeds and bean to saucepan. Add 3 tablespoons sugar. Stir and bring to a boil. Remove from heat and allow vanilla bean to steep for 10 minutes.

2. Remove bean but do not discard. It can be used again.

3. Combine remaining sugar and egg yolks. Beat for about 2 minutes, or until ingredients are thoroughly combined.

4. Gradually add milk mixture to egg-yolk mixture. Stir to combine and return to saucepan. Cook over low heat, stirring constantly, until mixture coats the back of a spoon. Be careful not to allow mixture to boil. Chill before using.

Variations

Coffee Anglaise: Substitute 2 tablespoons finely ground coffee for vanilla. Strain before chilling.

Cinnamon Anglaise: Substitute 2 sticks cinnamon, each stick broken into 2 pieces, for vanilla. Strain before chilling.

Mint and Honey Anglaise: Substitute 2 tablespoons chopped fresh mint and 3 tablespoons honey for vanilla. Strain before chilling.

Lavender Anglaise: Substitute 2 teaspoons dried lavender for vanilla. Strain before chilling.

Coconut Anglaise: Substitute ½ cup shredded coconut for vanilla.

Rum Anglaise (or other liquor): Omit vanilla and add rum or other liquor to Anglaise before chilling.

Rum Raisin Anglaise: Omit vanilla and combine ¾ cup raisins with 3 tablespoons rum. Toss, and add to Anglaise before chilling.

Chocolate Sauce

YIELD: ABOUT 3 CUPS

Served warm, this sauce can be poured over ice cream or cake. Slightly chilled, chocolate sauce can be used to paint or decorate with an abstract design plates to be used for cake, pastry, or ice cream.

¼ pound bittersweet chocolate, finely chopped
¼ pound semi-sweet chocolate, finely chopped
¾ cup sugar
¾ cup water
½ cup heavy sweet cream

1. Combine chocolate, sugar, and water in a heavy saucepan. Bring to a boil, stirring occasionally. Remove from heat.
2. Bring cream to a boil and add to chocolate mixture. Stir to combine.

Variation: Combine Chocolate Sauce with Butterscotch Sauce (see page 195) and use over ice cream or cake.

Applejack Caramel

YIELD: ABOUT 2 CUPS

2 cups sugar
½ cup apple cider
3 tablespoons water
3 tablespoons applejack brandy
2 tablespoons butter
2 apples, peeled and cut into small balls with a melon-ball cutter

1. Combine sugar and cider in a heavy saucepan and cook until caramelized.
2. Add water, brandy, and butter and cook until ingredients are combined. Stir in apples.

Berry Coulis

YIELD: ABOUT 2 CUPS

Serve this quick fruit sauce with vanilla or fruit-flavored ice creams, or over plain cakes that are not filled or iced.

½ pint blueberries
½ pint strawberries
½ pint raspberries
½ cup sugar

Wash and hull berries. Combine with sugar. Place in food processor and purée.

Variation: Prepare a Kiwi Coulis by peeling and puréeing 6 kiwis with 3 teaspoons sugar. Pulse machine on and off quickly. Do not let Kiwi Coulis become too fine or you will pulverize the seeds.

Tahitian-Vanilla Ice Cream

YIELD: ABOUT I QUART

I love the flavor of vanilla. As I experimented with ice cream, I added more and more vanilla, which is why this ice cream contains five or six times more vanilla than is found in other ice creams—it's positively perfumed with vanilla. The wonderful flavor will last long after you have finished eating the ice cream—you'll experience not just a little teasing touch, but the essence of the Tahitian bean, which I believe is the best vanilla in the world. Another advantage to using a great deal of vanilla is that it enables you to cut down on sugar. This is true in all my recipes that call for vanilla.

1½ cups milk
½ cup heavy sweet cream
4 Tahitian vanilla beans
¾ cup sugar
6 egg yolks

1. Combine milk and cream in a saucepan. Split the vanilla beans, scrape the seeds, and add vanilla beans and seeds to saucepan. Add half the sugar. Stir and bring to a boil.

2. Remove from heat and allow vanilla beans to steep for 10 minutes.

3. Remove beans but do not discard; they can be used again.

4. Combine remaining sugar and egg yolks.

Beat for about 2 minutes, or until thoroughly combined.

5. Gradually add milk mixture to egg-yolk mixture. Stir to combine and return to saucepan. Cook over low heat, stirring continuously, until mixture coats the back of a spoon. Be careful not to allow mixture to boil.

6. Cool and pour into an ice-cream machine. Follow manufacturer's directions.

Licorice Ice Cream

YIELD: ABOUT 1 QUART

1½ cups milk
½ cup heavy sweet cream
½ to ¾ cup minced black licorice
¾ cup sugar
6 egg yolks

1. Combine milk and cream in a saucepan. Add the licorice and half the sugar. Stir and bring to a boil. Remove from heat and allow licorice to steep for 10 minutes.

2. Combine remaining sugar and egg yolks. Beat for about 2 minutes, or until ingredients are thoroughly combined.

3. Gradually add milk mixture to egg-yolk mixture. Stir to combine and return to saucepan. Cook over low heat, stirring constantly, until mixture coats the back of a spoon. Be careful not to allow mixture to boil.

4. Cool and pour into an ice-cream machine. Follow manufacturer's directions.

Spice Ice Cream

YIELD: ABOUT 1 QUART

1½ cups milk
½ cup heavy sweet cream
1 teaspoon ground cinnamon
1 teaspoon ground ginger
½ teaspoon ground cloves
½ teaspoon ground nutmeg
¾ cup sugar
6 egg yolks

1. Combine milk and cream in a saucepan. Add spices and half the sugar. Stir and bring to a boil. Remove from heat.

2. Combine remaining sugar and egg yolks. Beat for about 2 minutes, or until thoroughly combined.

3. Gradually add milk mixture to egg-yolk mixture. Stir to combine and return to saucepan. Cook over low heat, stirring constantly, until mixture coats the back of a spoon. Be careful not to let mixture boil.

4. Cool and pour into an ice-cream machine. Follow manufacturer's directions.

Ginger Ice Cream

YIELD: ABOUT 1 QUART

1½ cups milk
½ cup heavy sweet cream
3 tablespoons minced fresh ginger
¾ cup sugar
6 egg yolks

1. Combine milk and cream in a saucepan. Add ginger and half the sugar. Stir and bring to a boil. Remove from heat and strain.

2. Combine remaining sugar and egg yolks. Beat for about 2 minutes, or until ingredients are thoroughly combined.

3. Gradually add milk mixture to egg-yolk mixture. Stir to combine and return to saucepan. Cook over low heat, stirring constantly, until mixture coats the back of a spoon. Be careful not to allow mixture to boil.

4. Cool and pour into an ice-cream machine. Follow manufacturer's directions.

Cinnamon Ice Cream

YIELD: ABOUT 1½ QUARTS

1½ cups milk
½ cup heavy sweet cream
4 sticks cinnamon, each stick broken into 2 or 3 pieces
¾ cup sugar
6 egg yolks

1. Combine milk and cream in a saucepan. Add cinnamon sticks and half the sugar. Stir and bring to a boil. Remove from heat and allow cinnamon sticks to steep for 10 minutes. Remove sticks and discard.

2. Combine remaining sugar and egg yolks. Beat for about 2 minutes, or until ingredients are thoroughly combined.

3. Gradually add milk mixture to egg-yolk mixture. Stir to combine and return to saucepan. Cook over low heat, stirring constantly, until mixture coats the back of a spoon. Be careful not to allow mixture to boil.

4. Cool and pour into an ice-cream machine. Follow manufacturer's directions.

Lemon Ice Cream

YIELD: ABOUT 1 QUART
AND 1 CUP

Zest of 2 lemons
1 tablespoon Superfine or other finely milled
    sugar
¼ cup lemon juice
4 egg yolks
1 tablespoon corn syrup
1 cup milk
1 cup heavy sweet cream
1 vanilla bean
½ cup sugar
5 egg yolks

1. Prepare the lemon flavoring by combining lemon zest and sugar in a bowl and mixing until ingredients develop a pastelike consistency. Add lemon juice, egg yolks, and corn syrup, mix, and spoon into a double boiler. Heat, stirring, until all ingredients are warmed through.

2. Transfer lemon mixture to an electric mixer and beat until mixture doubles in volume. Reserve.

3. Prepare the ice cream by combining milk and cream in a saucepan. Split the vanilla bean, scrape seeds, and add seeds and bean to saucepan. Add half the sugar. Stir and bring to a boil. Remove from heat and remove vanilla bean. Do not discard the bean; it can be used again.

4. Combine remaining sugar and egg yolks. Beat for about 2 minutes, or until thoroughly combined.

5. Gradually add milk mixture to egg-yolk mixture. Stir to combine and return to saucepan. Cook over low heat, stirring continuously, until mixture coats the back of a spoon. Be careful not to allow mixture to boil. Cool and add lemon mixture, stirring until blended.

6. Pour into ice-cream machine. Follow manufacturer's directions.

Caramel Ice Cream

YIELD: ABOUT 1½ QUARTS

¾ cup sugar
½ cup milk
5 egg yolks, lightly beaten
½ cup heavy sweet cream
2 cups milk

1. Prepare the caramel by combining sugar and ½ cup milk in a heavy saucepan. Cook over very high heat, stirring occasionally, until mixture caramelizes. Caramel should be an amber color, not dark brown. You can check the color by placing a teaspoonful of mixture on a white plate. If caramel becomes too dark it will have a bitter flavor.

2. While preparing the caramel, combine egg yolks and heavy cream in a bowl and whisk together.

3. When sugar and milk are caramelized, slowly stir in remaining 2 cups of milk and bring to a boil. Remove from heat and allow to cool.

4. Slowly add caramel-milk mixture to egg mixture, whisking continuously. When all ingredients are combined, return to saucepan and cook over low heat until mixture has thickened enough to coat the back of a spoon.

5. Allow mixture to cool and pour into ice cream machine. Follow manufacturer's directions.

Champagne Sorbet

YIELD: ABOUT 1 PINT

1 bottle champagne (750 ml)
¾ cup sugar

1. Combine champagne and sugar in a saucepan and reduce to about 2½ cups.

2. Allow to cool and pour into ice-cream machine. Follow manufacturer's directions.

Red-Berry Sorbet

YIELD: ABOUT 1½ PINTS

¾ cup sugar
¾ cup water
1 pint raspberries
1 pint strawberries
Lemon juice (optional)

1. Combine sugar and water in a saucepan. Bring to a boil and cook for 2 minutes.

2. While syrup is cooking, place fruit in a food processor and purée until smooth.

3. Allow syrup to cool slightly. Add fruit purée and mix to combine. Taste; add sugar or lemon juice as necessary. Pour into ice-cream machine and follow manufacturer's directions.

Chocolate Sorbet

YIELD: ABOUT 1 PINT

This is one of the simplest sorbets to prepare—and one of the most delicious. People are often surprised that there is a Chocolate Sorbet; they are accustomed to fruit sorbets and chocolate ice cream, and this presents an interesting surprise. You can serve this sorbet by itself, with a dollop of whipped cream, or as part of other dessert dishes, such as Chocolate Crêpes (see page 218).

2 cups water
¾ cup sugar
3 tablespoons corn syrup
5 tablespoons unsweetened cocoa powder

1. Combine all ingredients in a saucepan. Stir to combine and cook over medium heat for 10 to 15 minutes, or until cocoa has bloomed and released its aroma.

2. Chill and pour into ice-cream machine. Follow manufacturer's directions.

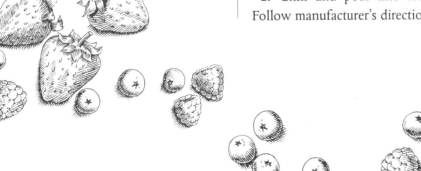

Crème Brûlée

YIELD: 12 SERVINGS

2 cups milk
2 cups heavy sweet cream
1 vanilla bean, split
1½ cinnamon sticks
10 tablespoons sugar
8 egg yolks
6 tablespoons white sugar
6 tablespoons brown sugar

1. Preheat oven to 300°.

2. Combine milk, cream, vanilla bean, cinnamon sticks, and 5 tablespoons sugar in a heavy saucepan. Bring to a boil, stirring occasionally. Remove from heat just after mixture has come to a boil and allow to cool. Remove vanilla bean and cinnamon sticks; dry them and store for another use.

3. While mixture is cooling, combine 5 tablespoons sugar with egg yolks and beat until egg yolks are pale and a ribbon is formed. Pour a third of milk mixture into egg-yolk mixture and beat to combine. Return ingredients to saucepan and cook over very low heat, stirring, just until mixture is thick enough to coat the back of a spoon. Be careful not to let mixture come to a simmer.

4. Beat the sauce for 1 minute, off heat, to cool, and strain through a fine sieve.

5. Pour custard mixture into 12 4-ounce ramekins or custard cups.

6. Place in a *bain-marie* and bake for 30 minutes, or until custard has set.

7. Remove ramekins from *bain-marie* and allow to cool.

8. Preheat broiler.

9. Combine white sugar and brown sugar and mix. Spoon sugar mixture over custards. Place ramekins on a baking sheet and broil custards until sugar has caramelized. Check broiler after 2 minutes, and turn ramekins around if sugar appears to be browning only in 1 spot.

Pumpkin Brûlée

YIELD: 6 SERVINGS

In the fall, I like to use miniature pumpkins as very special serving dishes for soups and desserts. Pumpkin Brûlée calls for pumpkin purée and creates quite a stir when it's presented at the table in individual pumpkin shells.

6 miniature pumpkins, each about ½ pound
¾ cup milk
¾ cup heavy sweet cream
4 tablespoons sugar
1 teaspoon ground cinnamon
½ teaspoon ground nutmeg
1 vanilla bean, split
3 egg yolks
3 tablespoons white sugar
3 tablespoons dark-brown sugar
Spice Ice Cream (see page 199)
Pumpkin Chips (see page 48)

1. Preheat oven to 300°.

2. Remove stems from pumpkins and cut off tops. Hollow out pumpkins, discarding seeds, reserving pulp, and leaving ¼-inch perimeter of pulp in shells.

3. Cut pumpkin pulp into cubes and place in a saucepan. Cover with water and bring to a boil. Cook until pumpkin is tender, about 20 to 30 minutes. Drain pumpkin and place in a food processor. Purée until very fine, and strain. Reserve ¾ cup pumpkin pulp for this recipe and refrigerate remainder of pulp for another use.

4. Combine milk, cream, 2 tablespoons sugar, cinnamon, nutmeg, and vanilla bean in a saucepan. Bring to a boil, stirring occasionally. Remove from heat just after mixture has come to a boil. Remove vanilla bean and add pumpkin purée. Stir until ingredients are combined and allow mixture to cool.

5. Combine 2 tablespoons sugar and egg yolks and beat until eggs are pale and form a light ribbon. Add a third of milk-pumpkin mixture to egg-yolk mixture and beat to combine. Return ingredients to saucepan and cook over very low heat, stirring, for 2 minutes. Be careful not to let mixture come to a simmer.

6. Beat the sauce for 1 minute, off heat, to cool, and strain through a fine sieve.

7. Spoon custard mixture into pumpkin shells. Place shells on a baking sheet and bake for 45 minutes to 1 hour, or until custard has set. Remove from oven and allow to cool on baking sheet.

8. Preheat broiler.

9. Combine white sugar and brown sugar and mix. Spoon sugar mixture over custards. Place pumpkin shells under broiler and broil until sugar has caramelized. Check broiler after 2 minutes and turn pumpkin shells if sugar appears to be browning only in one spot.

To Serve: Place pumpkin shells on six dessert plates. Place a scoop of Spice Ice Cream on top of each pumpkin. Garnish with Pumpkin Chips.

Banana Beignets with Butterscotch Sauce

YIELD: 4 SERVINGS

This recipe is based on a treat that my father made for our family when I was a kid. My dad didn't do any real cooking, but he liked the idea of dessert fondues, and on Saturday nights he'd melt chocolate in the fondue pot and kids came from all over the neighborhood to dip pieces of fruit into the hot chocolate sauce. These Banana Beignets are my version of fondue cooking.

1 cup seltzer or club soda
1 cup all-purpose flour
1 egg
4 bananas, peeled, each cut into 4 or 5
*   pieces*
Oil for frying
Confectioners' sugar
Butterscotch Sauce (see page 195)

1. Combine seltzer, flour, and egg in a bowl. Mix very lightly with a fork. Do not overbeat, mixture will be lumpy.

2. Dip banana pieces in batter and coat on all sides.

3. Heat oil in a deep fryer and fry bananas until golden brown. Remove bananas from fryer and drain. Dust with confectioners' sugar and place each banana piece on a bamboo skewer.

I LIKE to place these Banana Beignets upright in a straw basket into which I've placed a narrow, deep dish filled with warm butterscotch sauce. Use any serving dish that you feel will enhance the Beignets, and serve with a bowl of Butterscotch Sauce on the side.

Gratin of Berries with Orange Lavender Sabayon and Berry Coulis

YIELD: 4 TO 6 SERVINGS

2 pints assorted berries, hulled and
    washed
2 eggs
2 egg yolks
6 tablespoons sugar
4 tablespoons Grand Marnier
4 tablespoons Lavender Oil (see page 167),
    or to taste
¼ cup heavy sweet cream, whipped
Berry Coulis (see page 198)

1. Divide berries among 4 to 6 6- to 8-ounce ramekins or ovenproof bowls.

2. Combine eggs, egg yolks, sugar, and Grand Marnier in a double boiler. Warm until just heated through, stirring constantly. Transfer to an electric mixer and beat until mixture is thick.

3. Add Lavender Oil gradually and continue beating just until ingredients are combined. Remove bowl from machine and fold in whipped cream.

4. Preheat broiler.

5. Spoon Sabayon mixture over berries in prepared ramekins and broil until Sabayon is lightly browned, about 1 minute. Place each ramekin on a dessert plate and spoon Berry Coulis around the perimeter of Sabayon.

Apple Tart with Cinnamon Ice Cream and Applejack Caramel

YIELD: 4 TO 6 SERVINGS

This is a very special apple tart. Prepared with puff pastry and presented upside down, it's similar to a tart Tatin. I serve it with an Applejack Caramel sauce that accentuates the apple flavor, and I add Cinnamon Ice Cream as a perfect partner.

1 10-inch sheet puff pastry
8 tablespoons white sugar
8 tablespoons dark-brown sugar
2 tablespoons cinnamon
4 apples (Granny Smith or similar type)
4 tablespoons lemon juice
4 tablespoons melted butter
Applejack Caramel (see page 197)
Cinnamon Ice Cream (see page 200)

1. Roll out puff pastry until about ⅛ inch thick. Place pastry sheet in refrigerator for 30 minutes.

2. While pastry is resting, combine white sugar, brown sugar, and cinnamon in a bowl. Mix and reserve.

3. Peel and core the apples, and cut into thin slices. Add lemon juice and toss.

4. Remove pastry from refrigerator and place on a board. Invert a 10-inch plate over pastry

and, with a pastry cutter or sharp knife, cut around the edge of the plate. Remove plate and carefully place circle of pastry dough on a baking sheet with a nonstick surface. Using point of a sharp knife, prick holes in a circular pattern over entire sheet of pastry and return to refrigerator for 10 minutes.

To Assemble Tart

1. Preheat oven to 400°.

2. Remove pastry from refrigerator and, starting from the center, layer apple slices on pastry, forming a circular pattern. Apple slices should overlap.

3. Brush the apple slices with melted butter and top with half the sugar-cinnamon mixture.

4. Bake tart until apples begin to brown slightly, about 10 to 15 minutes.

5. Remove tart from oven and, using a spatula, slide tart onto a plate. Invert plate over baking pan. Pastry will now be on top. Sprinkle pastry with remaining sugar-cinnamon mixture and return to oven. Bake an additional 10 to 15 minutes, or until pastry is golden.

6. Allow tart to rest for 5 minutes, and cut into 4 to 6 servings. Place each serving on a dessert plate. Spoon Applejack Caramel around tart and place a scoop of Cinnamon Ice Cream beside each portion of tart.

Orange and Strawberry Tart with Candied-Bell-Pepper Caramel and Lemon Ice Cream

YIELD: 4 TO 6 SERVINGS

*T*his is a fruit tart that comes with a major surprise: the Candied-Bell-Pepper Caramel that is used as a sauce. I tasted something similar in Denmark, and when I returned to the States I worked out my own version. I like the idea of turning things about and using a vegetable to create a dessert sauce. Prepare the caramel before you start making the tart.

CANDIED-BELL-PEPPER CARAMEL

1½ cups minced bell peppers (use a combination of red and yellow peppers)
1 cup sugar
1 cup apple cider
1 to 2 tablespoons Grand Marnier
3 tablespoons butter

1. Combine peppers, sugar, and cider in a heavy saucepan and cook, stirring occasionally, until sauce has caramelized.

2. Remove from heat and whisk in Grand Marnier and butter. Reserve.

ORANGE AND STRAWBERRY TART

1 10-inch sheet puff pastry
2 tablespoons white sugar
2 tablespoons dark-brown sugar
1 teaspoon cinnamon
2 pints strawberries
4 oranges
1 cup whipped cream
Mint sprigs
Lemon Ice Cream (see page 201)

1. Roll out puff pastry until about ⅛ inch thick. Place pastry sheet in refrigerator for 30 minutes.

2. While pastry is resting, combine white sugar, brown sugar, and cinnamon. Mix in a bowl and reserve.

3. Wash and hull strawberries and reserve.

4. Zest the oranges before peeling and separating into sections. Remove membrane and seeds, toss orange sections with zest, and reserve.

5. Remove pastry from refrigerator and place on a board. Invert a 10-inch plate over pastry and, with a pastry cutter or sharp knife, cut around the edge of the plate. Remove plate and carefully place circle of pastry dough on a baking sheet with a nonstick surface. Using point of a sharp knife, prick holes in a circular pattern over entire surface of pastry and return to refrigerator for 10 minutes.

6. Remove pastry from refrigerator. Dust pastry with half of reserved sugar mixture and bake for about 10 minutes, or until pastry is a golden brown. Remove pastry from oven and, using a spatula, slide pastry onto a plate. Invert plate over baking pan and return pan to oven. Dust with remaining sugar mixture. Pastry will now bake on second side for about 5 to 7 minutes, or until golden brown.

7. Remove from oven and allow pastry to rest for 5 minutes. Carefully slide onto a cake platter.

To Assemble Tart

1. Preheat oven to 400°.

2. Spread whipped cream over pastry. Arrange strawberries, points up, in 2 rows around the perimeter of the pastry.

3. Place orange sections in a heap in the center of the pastry. (The casual look of the oranges are in contrast to the neat rows of strawberries.) Any remaining strawberries can be sliced and added to the oranges.

4. Heat Candied-Bell-Pepper Caramel and pour over oranges and strawberries. Garnish with mint and serve with Lemon Ice Cream.

Warm Cinnamon Plum Cake with Champagne Sorbet and Berry Coulis

YIELD: 6 TO 8 SERVINGS

¼ pound butter
9 tablespoons confectioners' sugar
4 tablespoons all-purpose flour
4 tablespoons finely ground almonds
1½ teaspoons lemon zest
½ teaspoon cinnamon
4 egg whites
Butter and flour for baking dish
4 large fresh plums (any variety), pitted and
    thinly sliced
1 tablespoon dark-brown sugar
1 tablespoon white sugar
Champagne Sorbet (see page 202)
Berry Coulis (see page 198)

1. Preheat oven to 375°.

2. Melt ¼ pound butter in a saucepan. Heat until butter is a light brown and releases a nutty aroma. Reserve.

3. Sift confectioners' sugar, flour, and almonds together. Stir in lemon zest and cinnamon, mix to combine, and spoon into an electric mixer.

4. With the machine turned on, add egg whites gradually and blend. Continue mixing until all ingredients are combined.

5. Coat an 8-inch baking dish with butter and flour. Pour cake batter into the dish. Place plum slices on top of cake batter in a circular pattern.

6. Combine brown sugar and white sugar, mix well, and spoon over plums.

7. Bake cake for about 25 minutes, or until cake is firm when touched and a knife comes out clean when inserted near center of cake.

8. Slice cake and place slices on 6 to 8 dessert dishes. Garnish with Champagne Sorbet and spoon Berry Coulis over all.

Warm Fruit and Almond Cake with Mint and Honey Anglaise

YIELD: 10 SERVINGS

¼ pound sugar
¼ pound almond paste or marzipan paste
¼ pound butter
Seeds from 1 scraped vanilla bean
3 eggs
1 cup all-purpose flour
2 cups assorted berries, hulled and washed
Butter for ramekins
Mint and Honey Anglaise (see variations, page 196)

1. Preheat oven to 350°.

2. Cream sugar, almond paste, butter, and vanilla seeds in an electric mixer. Add eggs, 1 at a time, and gradually add flour. Continue mixing until all ingredients are combined.

3. Fold berries into cake mixture.

4. Butter 10 4-ounce ramekins. Spoon cake mixture into ramekins.

5. Bake until cakes have risen slightly and are firm to the touch, about 30 to 40 minutes.

6. Cakes may be presented in ramekins or unmolded. Serve warm with Mint and Honey Anglaise.

Cheesecake Beignets with Red-Berry Sorbet

The following dessert can be served in a variety of ways. I prefer to take baked Cheesecake and convert it into warm Cheesecake Beignets, which I then serve with Red-Berry Sorbet. Or you can serve the Cheesecake alone.

CHEESECAKE

½ pound cream cheese
5 tablespoons sugar
Zest of ½ lemon
⅛ teaspoon coarse or kosher salt
6 tablespoons sour cream
3 eggs
4 tablespoons milk
4 tablespoons heavy sweet cream
Butter and flour for cake pan

1. Preheat oven to 325°.

2. Combine cream cheese and sugar in an electric mixer and cream together, or place ingredients in a bowl and cream together by hand. Add zest, salt, and sour cream and continue mixing.

3. Add the eggs, 1 at a time, and mix until blended.

4. Add milk and cream and mix until all ingredients are just combined. Do not overmix.

5. Butter and flour an 8-inch cake pan and spoon mixture into pan. Place pan in a *bain-marie*. Bake for 1 hour. Reduce heat to 300° and

bake for an additional 30 minutes, or until a skewer or knife comes out clean when inserted in the middle. (Cheesecake mixture can also be baked in 6 to 8 individual ramekins, with cooking time reduced to about 30 minutes.)

YIELD: 1 CHEESECAKE,
SERVING 6 TO 8

CHEESECAKE BEIGNETS

1 cup confectioners' sugar
1 cup cornstarch
4 eggs, lightly beaten
2½ cups grated coconut
1 baked Cheesecake
Vegetable oil or peanut oil for deep-frying
Powdered sugar
Red-Berry Sorbet (see page 203)
Sprigs of fresh mint
2 pints fresh berries (raspberries or
strawberries)

1. Combine sugar and cornstarch in a bowl and mix well.

2. Ready beaten eggs in a second bowl and grated coconut in a third bowl.

3. Using a small ice-cream scoop, form cheesecake into balls. Coat balls with sugar-cornstarch mixture, dip in beaten egg, and roll in grated coconut.

4. Heat oil in a deep fryer and fry Beignets until golden brown. Drain Beignets on paper towels and dust with powdered sugar.

YIELD: 8 TO 10 SERVINGS

To Assemble

1. Using 8 to 10 shallow bowls, place 3 Beignets in each bowl.

2. Top with Red-Berry Sorbet, garnish with mint leaves, and surround with fresh berries.

Carrot Cake with Cream-Cheese Soufflé and Cream-Cheese Caramel

YIELD: 6 SERVINGS

The idea for this recipe came to me when I was flying home from Atlanta and was served a carrot cake as a snack. I don't usually eat on planes, but I was hungry and the cake was good. I began to think of how to make a carrot cake something special, and this is the result.

These carrot cakes are baked in individual tart molds. After they're baked, a slightly smaller flan ring is placed on top of each cake and filled with a soufflé mixture. The cake and soufflé are then baked. If you prefer, bake the carrot cake in a loaf pan and the soufflé in a soufflé dish. Serve the cake with the soufflé on the side. In either case, prepare the sauce first.

CREAM-CHEESE CARAMEL

½ cup sugar

¼ cup water

¼ pound cream cheese, cut into small pieces

¼ cup orange juice

¾ cup carrot juice

1. Combine sugar and water in a saucepan and cook, stirring, for 1 to 2 minutes or until ingredients are caramelized.

2. Add cream cheese and continue cooking for 1 minute, stirring. Add juices gradually and bring to a boil, stirring, until all ingredients are thoroughly combined.

3. Remove from heat and keep warm.

CARROT CAKE

¼ pound butter

¼ pound sugar

2 eggs

½ cup all-purpose flour

⅛ teaspoon baking powder

¼ teaspoon ground cloves

2 teaspoons cinnamon

1 cup grated carrots

¼ cup toasted walnuts, coarsely chopped

1. Preheat oven to 375°.

2. Lightly grease 6 4-inch tartlet tins with loose bottoms, 4-inch ramekins, or 1 loaf pan.

3. Using an electric mixer or by hand, cream butter and sugar together. Add eggs, 1 at a time, scraping the bottom of the bowl after the addition of each egg.

4. Add flour, baking powder, cloves, cinnamon, carrots, and walnuts gradually and con-

tinue mixing until all ingredients are incorporated.

5. Spoon carrot mixture into tartlet tins, ramekins, or loaf pan. Bake 20 to 25 minutes if using tartlet tins or ramekins, about 45 minutes if using a loaf pan. Test by piercing with a toothpick or skewer (which should come out clean) and by tapping gently with finger (cake should be firm to the touch).

6. Remove cakes from oven and allow to cool. Turn tartlet tins or ramekins upside down and tap to loosen cakes from tins.

7. While cakes are cooling, prepare Cream-Cheese Soufflé.

CREAM-CHEESE SOUFFLÉ

2 tablespoons butter

2 tablespoons sugar

½ pound cream cheese

½ pound Pastry Cream (see page 195)

3 egg yolks

½ cup sugar

2 tablespoons cornstarch

6 egg whites

1. Preheat oven to 375°.

2. Lightly coat the inside of 6 3½-inch flan rings with butter and sugar.

3. Using an electric mixer or by hand, whip cream cheese and Pastry Cream together until smooth. Add egg yolks and continue to mix.

4. Sift together sugar and cornstarch.

5. Using another bowl, whip egg whites until frothy. Slowly add sugar-cornstarch mixture and continue whipping until egg whites form soft peaks.

6. Using a spatula, fold a third of egg-white

mixture into cream-cheese mixture. Add remaining egg-white mixture and fold until incorporated.

7. Place flan rings on top of carrot cakes. Spoon cream-cheese mixture into flan rings and fill to the top.

8. Bake for 10 to 12 minutes, or until soufflé is golden brown and set.

9. Remove cakes from oven and run a knife with a thin, sharp blade around inside of flan ring and underneath bottom of ring. Carefully lift rings off soufflés.

10. Place a carrot cake in the center of each of 6 dessert plates and spoon Cream-Cheese Caramel around the perimeter of each plate.

Chocolate Marquise

YIELD: 8 SERVINGS

*T*his is the richest, most chocolate dessert of them all. I serve it with nothing more than a large bowl of whipped cream on the side and with fanciful chocolate decorations.

3 ounces butter
1 pound semi-sweet chocolate
4 eggs, room temperature
4 tablespoons sugar
½ pint heavy sweet cream, whipped with
*   1 tablespoon sugar*

1. Preheat oven to 300°.

2. Place butter and chocolate in a double boiler and heat until ingredients are melted and combined.

3. Combine eggs and sugar in an electric mixer and beat until doubled in volume.

4. Gradually add egg mixture to chocolate mixture and beat until thoroughly blended.

5. Spoon mixture into 8 4- to 6-ounce ramekins and place ramekins in a *bain-marie*. Bake for 45 minutes to 1 hour. The Chocolate Marquise will rise very slightly and will be soft when removed from the oven. It will harden as it cools and may be served at room temperature or chilled.

6. Serve with whipped cream on the side.

Bittersweet-Chocolate Pudding with Tahitian-Vanilla Ice Cream and Orange Tuile Cookies

YIELD: 6 TO 8 SERVINGS

This chocolate pudding resembles a soufflé, and makes a fine dessert by itself, but is even better when served with Tahitian-Vanilla Ice Cream and Orange Tuile Cookies.

Butter and sugar to coat ramekins or molds
½ pound bittersweet chocolate
4 egg whites
6 tablespoons sugar
1 cup Pastry Cream (see page 195)
12 tablespoons shaved bittersweet chocolate
Tahitian-Vanilla Ice Cream (see page 198), optional
Orange Tuile Cookies (see page 191), optional

1. Preheat oven to 400°.

2. Lightly butter 6 to 8 4-ounce ramekins or molds and coat with sugar. Refrigerate and reserve.

3. Heat chocolate in the top of a double boiler and keep warm.

4. Beat egg whites in an electric mixer or by hand. Add sugar gradually and continue beating until mixture is stiff but not dry.

5. Add Pastry Cream to chocolate and mix to blend. Add a third of beaten egg whites to chocolate mixture and gently blend. Fold in remaining egg whites until just combined.

6. Spoon pudding mixture into prepared ramekins and bake for 10 to 12 minutes, or until puddings rise like miniature soufflés.

7. Sprinkle puddings with shaved bittersweet chocolate and top with Tahitian-Vanilla Ice Cream. Add a touch of crispness by tucking an Orange Tuile Cookie into ice cream and serve additional cookies on the side.

Chocolate Soufflé with Coffee Anglaise and Licorice Ice Cream

YIELD: 8 SERVINGS

*t*he secret of this, or any other, soufflé is not to overwhip the egg whites. Egg whites have the capacity to expand in volume eight times. But if you beat egg whites until they have expanded as much as they possibly can, they will not be able to rise when baked in a soufflé.

It's best, therefore, to beat egg whites only until their volume has increased fourfold—the egg whites will not be dry but will look like soft clouds. There will be no peaks. At this point, you should be able to pour, not spoon, the soufflé mixture into a baking dish. Prepared this way, the soufflé will rise as it bakes and you will have a lovely, tender soufflé with great volume.

Butter and sugar for individual soufflé dishes

12 ounces bittersweet chocolate

7 egg yolks

4 tablespoons water

½ cup white sugar

4 egg whites

6 tablespoons confectioners' sugar

Licorice Ice Cream (see page 199)

Coffee Anglaise (see variations, page 196)

1. Preheat oven to 400°.

2. Lightly butter 8 individual soufflé dishes and coat with sugar. Make sure that the rim of each dish is especially well buttered, so that soufflés will rise evenly. Refrigerate and reserve.

3. Melt chocolate in the top of a double boiler.

4. Place egg yolks in bowl of an electric mixer.

5. Combine water and white sugar and bring to a boil. Slowly add water-sugar mixture to egg yolks and beat until mixture triples in volume.

6. In another bowl, beat egg whites until frothy. Add confectioners' sugar and continue beating until soft clouds are formed.

7. Add egg-yolk mixture to chocolate and mix until blended. Add a third of beaten egg whites and blend. Fold in remaining egg whites until just combined.

8. Spoon mixture into soufflé dishes and place dishes on a baking sheet. Bake for 12 to 15 minutes, or until soufflés have risen.

To Assemble

1. Before the soufflés are baked, scoop Licorice Ice Cream into balls and place in a serving dish. Store in freezer until ready to use.

2. Place a soufflé in the center of each of 8 dessert dishes.

3. Spoon Coffee Anglaise in and over soufflés.

4. Offer Licorice Ice Cream, licorice sticks, and chocolate cigarettes when you serve the soufflés. (The licorice sticks and chocolate cigarettes look especially effective when presented at the table in a small vase.)

Milk-Chocolate Banana Terrine with Banana Caramel Sauce and Maple Crisps

YIELD: 10 SERVINGS

BANANA TERRINE

1 pound milk chocolate
½ cup plus 2 tablespoons heavy sweet
    cream
3 very ripe bananas, puréed
Cocoa powder
Maple Crisps (see page 193)

1. Heat chocolate in a double boiler.

2. Heat cream in a heavy saucepan and bring to a boil. Add chocolate and stir. Add banana purée and stir until all ingredients are thoroughly combined.

3. Pour chocolate-banana mixture into a terrine or loaf pan and refrigerate overnight.

BANANA CARAMEL SAUCE

½ cup sugar
2 tablespoons water
1 banana, minced
½ cup heavy sweet cream
1 teaspoon lemon zest

1. Combine sugar and water in a saucepan and cook until caramelized. Stir in banana. Cook until banana is combined with caramel.

2. Slowly add cream and lemon zest, stirring. Bring to a boil and strain. Sauce will be very thick. If you prefer a thinner consistency, stir in ¼ cup milk. Keep warm.

YIELD: ABOUT 1½ CUPS

To Assemble

1. Remove terrine from refrigerator and dip bottom of dish into hot water for a few seconds.

2. Carefully run a knife around sides of terrine.

3. Invert dish and unmold onto a large serving platter.

4. Dust top and sides of terrine with cocoa powder and decorate with Maple Crisps.

5. Present terrine to your guests before cutting into individual slices.

6. Using 10 dessert plates, place a slice of terrine in the center of each plate.

7. Spoon Banana Caramel Sauce over and around terrine and serve with additional Maple Crisps.

Variation: Banana Terrine can be served with two sauces—create a harlequin presentation by spooning Banana Caramel Sauce on one side of each slice of terrine and Chocolate Sauce (see page 197) on the other.

Chocolate Crêpes with Rum Raisin Anglaise and Chocolate Sorbet

YIELD: 8 SERVINGS

1 cup plus 1 tablespoon all-purpose
*   flour*
2 tablespoons unsweetened cocoa
*   powder*
4 eggs
¼ teaspoon coarse or kosher salt
3 tablespoons sugar
4 tablespoons melted butter
¾ cup milk
Butter for cooking crêpes
Powdered sugar
Chocolate Sorbet (see page 203)
Rum Raisin Anglaise (see variations, page 196)

1. Place flour, cocoa, eggs, salt, sugar, and butter in a food processor. Start blending, and add milk gradually. Continue processing until batter has the consistency of light cream. Pour crêpe batter into a container and refrigerate for 2 hours before using.

2. Lightly butter a 6-inch skillet or omelette pan with a nonstick surface. Using a small ladle, spoon enough batter into pan to coat bottom. Tilt pan so that crêpe batter spreads evenly. Cook until lightly browned on one side; turn and lightly brown on second side. Remove crêpe to a plate and continue until all batter is used.

3. Fold each crêpe into quarters and place on a shallow baking sheet. Dust crêpes with powdered sugar.

4. Before serving, heat in a 350° oven for about 3 minutes or until crêpes are warm.

To Assemble

1. Using 8 dessert plates, place 3 crêpes on each plate, with points angled toward center of plate.

2. Place a scoop of Chocolate Sorbet in the center of each plate and spoon Rum Raisin Anglaise over sorbet and crêpes.

CHOCOLATE TRUFFLES

Chocolate Truffles are well named. They're rich, dark, slightly uneven in shape, and they taste of a luxurious life—much the same as black truffles. Truffles can be flavored in a variety of ways, and the truffle mixture can also be used as a filling to layer between cakes or cookies.

3. Add butter gradually and continue beating.

4. Chill mixture and form into cherry-sized balls—the truffles should look uneven, similar to black truffles. Roll truffles in cocoa and place in paper candy cups or into a parchment- or waxed-paper-lined box.

Spice Truffles

YIELD: ABOUT 60 TRUFFLES

1½ cups heavy sweet cream
2 tablespoons minced fresh ginger
1 cinnamon stick
1 clove
1 vanilla bean, split
1 pound milk chocolate, finely chopped
6 ounces butter, slightly softened
Unsweetened cocoa powder

1. Combine cream, ginger, cinnamon, clove, and vanilla bean in a saucepan. Bring to a boil. Remove from heat, allow to steep for 30 minutes, and strain. Bring to a second boil.

2. Place chocolate in a bowl, add hot cream mixture to chocolate, and beat until chocolate has melted and all ingredients are combined.

Coconut Truffles

YIELD: ABOUT 60 TRUFFLES

2 cups heavy sweet cream
¾ cup grated coconut
1½ pounds white chocolate, finely chopped
4 ounces butter, slightly softened
1 pound bittersweet chocolate, melted

1. Combine cream and coconut in a saucepan and bring to a boil. Allow to steep for 30 minutes and strain. Bring to a second boil.

2. Place white chocolate in bowl and add hot cream mixture to chocolate. Beat until chocolate has melted and all ingredients are combined.

3. Add butter gradually and continue beating.

4. Chill mixture and form into cherry-sized balls. Dip each ball into melted chocolate. Place truffles in paper candy cups or into a parchment- or waxed-paper-lined box.

Chocolate Truffles with Coffee Flavor

YIELD: ABOUT 30 TRUFFLES

2 cups heavy sweet cream
4 tablespoons finely ground coffee (not instant)
½ pound bittersweet chocolate, finely chopped
4 tablespoons butter, slightly softened
Unsweetened cocoa powder

1. Combine cream and coffee in a saucepan and bring to a boil. Allow to steep for 30 minutes and bring to a second boil.

2. Place chocolate in a bowl, add hot cream mixture to chocolate. Beat until chocolate has melted and all ingredients are combined.

3. Add butter gradually and continue beating.

4. Chill mixture and form into balls. Roll truffles in cocoa and place in paper candy cups or into a parchment- or waxed-paper-lined box.

Chapter 10

PRESENTATIONS

When I was living in France, an artist friend took me to the Beaubourg Museum at the Pompidou Center in Paris. There was an exhibition which demonstrated the technique of *trompe l'oeil,* art that fools the eye. A view through a window was a painted scene; a floor that seemed to rise step by step was really flat; a three-drawer cabinet was part of the wallpaper. A change in perspective changed everything for the viewer.

I was impressed by those eye-fooling paintings and objects, and their accomplishment stayed with me. I could see adapting *trompe l'oeil* to food and the way food was presented.

I enjoy surprising people with unusual food combinations. Every home and kitchen contains glasses, cups, and boxes that can be used to create special presentations; the only trick is to learn to look at objects in a different way. Consider new uses for familiar objects, as I have done in the following presentations.

BRANDY SNIFTERS: A brandy snifter can be used for more than brandy. I often start a meal by serving two or three tablespoons of warm consommé or bouillon in a snifter. Consommé presented that way, rather than in a familiar soup cup, establishes a wonderful mood. It is different, unusual, and it sets an exciting tone at the beginning of a meal.

DEMITASSE CUPS: If you don't own brandy snifters, serve the consommé in demitasse cups.

AQUAVIT GLASSES: If it's summer, serve the consommé or bouillon cold and in an aquavit glass. The glass holds just enough liquid to whet the appetite for the rest of dinner.

EGG CUPS: Attractive egg cups—and they can be fine porcelain or pottery—can make wonderful holders for foods other than eggs. Spoon in bean purée or *crème fraîche* and top with Mushroom Chips, smoked salmon, diced shrimp, or, if you want to splurge, caviar.

Egg cups can also be used for eggs—but not plain boiled eggs. Spoon scrambled eggs into egg cups and top with a dice of smoked salmon or bacon. One of my favorite ways to use egg cups is to cut off the top third of uncooked eggs with a pair of egg scissors. I scoop out the eggs and use the larger shell halves as containers in which I bake a flavored flan. After the flan

is baked, I place the eggs in the egg cups, and serve with a demitasse spoon.

Egg cups do not have to match. A variety of egg cups—or plates—can make a table look interesting. It isn't mandatory always to use matching plates.

A VARIETY OF BOXES: I have found uses for boxes of all shapes and sizes. I fill a highly lacquered box from Japan with warm peppercorns, top the peppercorns with warmed oysters on the half-shell, cover the box, and bring it to a table. It looks like a very special present. The cover is raised, and there is the aroma of peppercorns and the sight of oysters—a visual, edible treat.

Look around your house—not only in the kitchen but in other rooms as well. A silver jewelry box is a fine container for chocolate truffles; a wooden box such as I've described can hold peppercorns with shrimp. Or layer a box with cinnamon sticks and strew cloves and star anise over them. Top the sticks with chocolates, Maple Crisps, or an assortment of cookies.

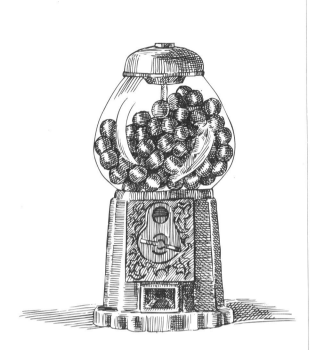

I kept it on a table for a while, and then filled the back of the truck with chocolates. You can do the same thing with other crystal or glass ornaments: a crystal piano might hold chocolate truffles, and Black-Olive Crackers look especially dramatic in crystal boxes.

GLASS BRICKS: I love the glass bricks that were considered the height of modernity in the thirties. I fill them with flowers—they make great vases—or lay them down for use as a tray for candies or hors d'oeuvres.

VASES: Small vases, preferably glass or crystal, make fine holders for Black-Olive Breadsticks or Caramel Sticks.

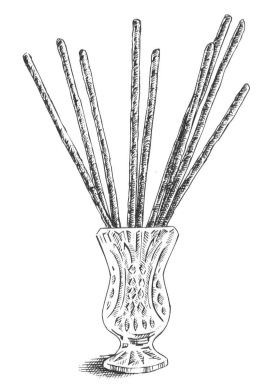

TOYS, ANTIQUE OR NEW: Place a railroad car from a toy train set in the center of a dinner table and fill it with flowers or small pastries. Use a toy milk wagon or circus cart to hold a cache of candies or cookies. (The next time you tell your kids to pick up their toys, tell them to bring the toys into the kitchen or dining room and see how they can be used.)

I found an antique gumball machine at a country fair, and cleaned it up and filled it with chocolate truffles and small pralines. I presented it to guests with a supply of polished copper pennies, and everyone had a fine time.

CRYSTAL ORNAMENTS: I was given a fine piece of crystal cut in the shape of a dump truck.

MARBLE BOARDS OR SLABS: If you have a marble cheese board, it can be used for more than cheese. Parfait of Salmon and Tuna Tartars with *crème fraîche* looks especially splendid when presented on marble, and a larger slab of marble can hold an assortment of desserts or hors d'oeuvres.

SKEWERS: Keep a package of bamboo skewers in the kitchen. I like to place one or two shrimps or scallops on a skewer, and then place the skewer across a bowl of soup. Skewers can also be used for Candied Garlic and Banana Beignets.

BASKETS: Save all small and medium-sized baskets that come your way. I have collected a number of small baskets that have a rustic look. I use them to hold skewers of Banana Beignets. I stand the skewered fruit upright in the baskets and place a narrow glass container filled with Butterscotch Sauce in the center of each basket. The basket looks like a country well, and as the Beignets are dipped into the sauce the image is fulfilled.

case is closed and deposited carefully on a table. It is then opened slowly—no one knows what to expect—and there are oohs and aahs of pleasure at this surprising way of presenting a dessert.

A SMALL WICKER SUITCASE: I came upon a small wicker suitcase—and I mean small—that had been used to house doll clothes. I now use it to serve dessert. I place a layer of cinnamon sticks in the suitcase and top the sticks with rows of petits fours and chocolates. The suit-

FLAVORED OILS: I have written about this in Chapter Eight, and would like to draw your attention to the idea once again: prepare a variety of flavored oils and transfer small amounts to attractive glass bottles (the bottles don't have to match). An assortment of oils on your dinner table will gleam like jewels, and guests will be able to season salads and other dishes with their favorite flavors.

Use droplets of flavored oils to circle a plate of salad or fish, and with a never-before-used eyedropper add drops of oil to the surface of a sauce, creating a colorful reflection.

Acknowledgments

WE WANT to thank our editor, Jonathan Segal, for approaching us with his idea for this book. Were it not for his initiative, the project never would have happened and we wouldn't be the friends we are now.

To my parents, and to all the teachers and mentors I've had in my life, I'd like to extend a special thank you, starting with the faculty at the Culinary Institute of America. Thanks to Waldy Malouf, for my first *sous-chef* position at La Crémaillière; Daniel Boulud, for the opportunity to work with him at the Hotel Plaza Athénée; and Charlie Palmer, for leading the way at The River Café. In between were all the chefs in France who let me observe and work in their kitchens: the Troisgros brothers in Roanne; Marc Meneau at L'Espérance; Georges Blanc in Vonnas; José Lampreia at Maison Blanche; Pierre Hermé at Fauchon; Basil Kamir at Moulin de la Vierge; and Gaston Lenôtre at École Lenôtre.

Michael "Buzzy" O'Keefe and Alan Stillman have allowed me the forum of their restaurants in which to experiment and grow. This freedom has been invaluable.

And, since no chef works alone, I would like to thank all the cooks who have worked with me who are now chefs—David Amorelli, Dan Budd, Richard "Whitey" Calton, Diane Forley, Eric Gouteyron, Gerry Hayden, Rick Laakkonen, John Loughran, Stanley Novak, Brad Steelman, and Paul Zweben—and thanks, too, to all the cooks from around the country and the world who have spent time in my kitchens.

I would like to thank my collaborator, Carmel Berman Reingold, for her patience and hard work, and Chef Carolyn Giacolomo for testing recipes.

And thanks to Wendy Gertler for her friendship, ideas, and honest opinions.

Most important, I would like to thank my sons, Connor and Dillon, for inspiring me and giving me the greatest pleasure in life next to cuisine, and Kim for being such a good mother.

DAVID BURKE

Index

A NOTE ABOUT THE AUTHORS

In April 1988 at the International Cooking Festival, David Burke became the first American to be honored by the prestigious Meilleurs Ouvriers de France Association with a medal and diploma. He won the Nippon Award of Excellence that same year in Tokyo, and was voted Chef of the Year by his American peers in 1991. Burke studied at the Culinary Institute of America and worked in France with the Troisgros brothers, Marc Meneau, and Gaston Lenôtre, before becoming executive chef at The River Café in Brooklyn. He is now executive chef and co-owner of the Park Avenue Cafe in New York City, where he lives.

Carmel Berman Reingold has written nine cookbooks, among them *California Cuisine* and the prizewinning *Cuisinart Food Processor Cookbook*. A contributor to national magazines on food history and food trends, she studied cooking in Paris with renowned chef and restaurateur Gabriel Gros. She lives in New York City.

A NOTE ON THE TYPE

The text of this book was set in Monotype Columbus, a contemporary face designed specifically for digital typesetting by Patricia Saunders. Named for Christopher Columbus, and released on the quincentenary of his 1492 voyage from Spain to the Americas, Monotype Columbus has a distinctly Spanish flavor to its letterforms. Saunders did, in fact, draw inspiration from fonts created by Jorge Coci in sixteenth-century Spain, as well as by the brilliant typographer, Robert Granjon, to create this lively and highly readable new face.

Line illustrations by Karin Kretschmann

Composed by North Market Street Graphics,
Lancaster, Pennsylvania

Printed and bound by Arcata Graphics / Martinsburg,
Martinsburg, West Virginia

Designed by Cassandra J. Pappas